DRAW IN
THE DUNES

ALSO BY NEIL SAGEBIEL

The Longest Shot: Jack Fleck, Ben Hogan, and Pro Golf's
Greatest Upset at the 1955 U.S. Open

DRAW IN THE DUNES

*The 1969 Ryder Cup and the Finish
That Shocked the World*

NEIL SAGEBIEL

THOMAS DUNNE BOOKS
ST. MARTIN'S PRESS
NEW YORK

THOMAS DUNNE BOOKS.
An imprint of St. Martin's Press.

DRAW IN THE DUNES. Copyright © 2014 by Neil Sagebiel. Foreword copyright
© 2014 by Jack Nicklaus and Tony Jacklin. All rights reserved. Printed in the United
States of America. For information, address St. Martin's Press, 175 Fifth Avenue,
New York, N.Y. 10010.

www.thomasdunnebooks.com
www.stmartins.com

Designed by Omar Chapa

The Library of Congress Cataloging-in-Publication Data is available upon request.

ISBN 978-1-250-01595-2 (hardcover)
ISBN 978-1-250-02116-8 (e-book)

St. Martin's Press books may be purchased for educational, business, or promotional
use. For information on bulk purchases, please contact Macmillan Corporate
and Premium Sales Department at 1-800-221-7945, extension 5442, or write
specialmarkets@macmillan.com.

First Edition: September 2014

10 9 8 7 6 5 4 3 2 1

For Sally

CONTENTS

CONTENTS

AUTHOR'S NOTE

In search of a follow-up to *The Longest Shot,* my first book, I rediscovered the 1969 Ryder Cup and the famous moment in which Jack Nicklaus picked up Tony Jacklin's ball mark on the final green in the final match. That brief clip had flashed across my screen during golf telecasts on more than a few occasions. It was a dramatic and unusual moment in golf—a conceded 2-foot putt that resulted in a 16–16 tie, the first deadlock in the history of the Ryder Cup.

Ties are uncommon and mostly unwanted in sports, and yet many people would come to agree that Jack Nicklaus's concession to Tony Jacklin was a fitting and inspiring result for the Ryder Cup during an era when the event was struggling to survive. That first tie, assured by a climactic display of sportsmanship, reignited hopes for competitive matches in the future, although the Ryder Cup would continue to wobble along until the British side was expanded to become a European team. As I delved into the 1969 Ryder Cup and the two captains and twenty-four players on the Great Britain and U.S. teams, I uncovered the compelling circumstances and the external and internal human conflicts that made a 2-foot putt matter so much. I also rediscovered the history and significance of the Ryder Cup, and how it progressed to being the huge international sports event it is today.

I had good material at my disposal to tell the story: the official program, course descriptions, player profiles, draw sheets, hole-by-hole scores of the thirty-two matches, newspaper and magazine coverage, player interviews, and several Ryder Cup books, most notably Paul Trevillion's *Dead Heat*. The autobiographies of Tony Jacklin, Jack Nicklaus, and Peter Alliss were also invaluable. My biggest surprise and disappointment were that only about three minutes of the many hours of BBC-TV coverage were archived by rights-holder IMG. I wasn't able to watch much of the 1969 Ryder Cup, but I did see a lot through the eyes of others. I've attempted to present a factual account, without fictionalization or embellishment, based on the material and sources available to me.

The idea that "the Concession" is golf's greatest gesture and one of the greatest acts of sportsmanship in any sport is not my own. It has been chronicled and listed in recent years in many articles, including by ESPN (U.K.), *The Independent*, Golf Channel, Yahoo! (U.K. and Ireland), *Golf Digest*, and *The London Evening Standard*. Bernard Gallacher, a rookie on the 1969 Great Britain Ryder Cup team, may have said it best in 2013. "It was a great Ryder Cup and I saw a great sporting gesture that has endured to this time. And wherever the Ryder Cup is being played, they still talk about Jack's concession."

FOREWORD

By Jack Nicklaus and Tony Jacklin

The 1969 Ryder Cup at Royal Birkdale Golf Club in Southport, England, was the first of many times as players and later as captains that we faced each other in Ryder Cup competition. We were considered by most to be the leading players of our respective 1969 teams and were good friends yet competitive rivals. Our friendship began long before we arrived at Royal Birkdale that week, and we would become even closer friends in the years that followed.

This particular Ryder Cup unfolded during an era when the United States dominated the biennial matches. Since the official beginning of the Ryder Cup in 1927, America had competed against a team composed of players from Great Britain and Ireland. This was the case until the ruling bodies made the decision, prior to the 1979 matches, to include all of Continental Europe. The United States had won fourteen of seventeen Ryder Cups, and most onlookers on both sides of the Atlantic expected another U.S. victory in September 1969.

We were both young men, but we were very seasoned golfers by the summer of 1969.

Tony: Playing in my second Ryder Cup, I was twenty-five and near the top of my game. That July I won the British Open at Royal Lytham & St. Annes, the first Brit to capture the Claret Jug since Max Faulkner in 1951. I would go on to win the U.S. Open at Hazeltine in Minnesota the following year, becoming the first player to simultaneously hold both Open titles since Ben Hogan in 1953. It would be more than four decades until another Englishman—Justin Rose—would in the U.S. Open.

Jack: I was twenty-nine and playing in my first Ryder Cup. During that time, a pro had to be a PGA of America member to be eligible to play on the U.S. Ryder Cup team. The process of becoming an official "Class A" PGA member took between four and five years, and I received my membership in the fall of 1966. I just missed making the 1967 squad, having only nine months to accumulate enough points. By the summer of 1969, I had twenty-eight Tour wins and seven professional major championship titles. Although I would go on to win another eleven, I was in the midst of a three-year period without a victory in a major. But that did not matter, as I was excited to play in my first Ryder Cup.

We first met and played against each other in 1966 at the Canada Cup (now the World Cup) in Tokyo, Japan. After Tony qualified to play on the PGA Tour in late 1967 (which was very uncommon and difficult for a British player in those days), we played practice rounds together, we fished together, and we always enjoyed each other's company, on and off the golf course.

At Royal Birkdale, our friendship and mutual respect as players was an important aspect of our head-to-head competition in a fourball match (with Great Britain's Neil Coles and the United States' Dan Sikes as our respective partners) won by the Brits on Friday and two singles matches on Saturday, the final day. In the end, it would be far more important than we could have foreseen. While neither of us could have predicted or scripted what happened late on that Saturday afternoon, our relationship, competitiveness, and feelings about the Ryder Cup no doubt had a bearing on the outcome of our final singles match and the entire 1969 Ryder Cup.

Our anchor singles match, the last of the week's thirty-two matches, ended in a tie when Jack conceded a 2-foot putt on the 18th green. Moreover, as a result of Jack's concession, all the matches ended in the first draw in the forty-two year history of the Ryder Cup. Unbeknownst to us at the time, that concession would leave an indelible mark on the Ryder Cup and the sport.

Our 1969 teammates also deeply cared about the Ryder Cup. Like us, they were extremely proud to represent their countries. Fifteen of the twenty-four players on our two teams were Ryder Cup rookies. Under the intense pressure that's unique to the Ryder Cup, our teammates boldly played the exciting, tight matches that led to the surprising finish.

For Great Britain, those teammates were Peter Alliss, Brian Barnes, Maurice Bembridge, Peter Butler, Alex Caygill, Neil Coles, Bernard Gallacher, Brian Huggett, Bernard Hunt, Christy O'Connor, and Peter Townsend. For the United States, they were Tommy Aaron, Miller Barber, Frank Beard, Billy Casper, Dale Douglass, Raymond Floyd, Dave Hill, Gene Littler, Dan Sikes, Ken Still, and Lee Trevino.

Our captains, Great Britain's Eric Brown and the United States's Sam Snead, were battle-hardened competitors who never gave an inch. The two of us shared our captains' competitive spirit and will to win, although our demeanor and tactics sometimes differed from their approach.

The closeness and sheer drama of the 1969 Ryder Cup helped keep the matches alive at a time when interest was waning. In the following years, we both welcomed roles in ushering in a new Ryder Cup era that saw the establishment and rise of the European team. We served as Ryder Cup captains (Jack twice, Tony four times), facing each other in 1983, a U.S. victory, and in 1987, a European win—the first on American soil. In more recent years, together we designed a top-ranked golf course in Florida dedicated to our historic moment at Royal Birkdale in September 1969—the Concession Golf Club.

Through all these years, our friendship has been a constant. Another constant is our deep affection and respect for the game that led to our friendship and to countless other experiences and opportunities, such as representing our countries in the Ryder Cup. We are permanently and happily indebted to the game of golf.

DRAW IN
THE DUNES

PROLOGUE

Tony Jacklin sat upright in his bed. It was the dead of night in Bradenton, Florida, located on the coast of the Gulf of Mexico. The Jacklin home bordered a golf course, and something had awakened Tony from a deep sleep. His wife, Astrid, was undisturbed, though, sleeping peacefully beside him.

The Englishman could recall other long nights. He had stared into the darkness when in contention to win major golf championships. He had marveled at others who slept soundly prior to those big moments, when the wait for a Sunday afternoon tee time seemed like an eternity, when the world watched intently to see if the Claret Jug, or the U.S. Open trophy, or the Ryder Cup, would rest comfortably in your hands or tragically slip from your grasp.

"Me? Sure, I could sleep—until a bird farted outside, up a tree, down the street," Jacklin once quipped.

This graying middle-aged man had also suffered through the sleepless nights and wide-awake nightmare that followed the tragic death of his first wife, Vivien, a vibrant forty-four-year-old woman who suffered a cerebral hemorrhage and was gone in an instant. "Everything that I was

was over and done with," Jacklin said about the sudden loss of his wife of twenty-two years.

Despite the curse of sleeplessness or with the benefit of good rest, this man had achieved much in his fifty-eight years. Born and raised in the industrial town of Scunthorpe in northern England, Anthony Jacklin was the son of a truck driver and a strong-willed mother with unfulfilled singing ambitions. Tony started playing golf before his tenth birthday, and the game took possession of him. When he was thirteen, he and his father traveled sixty miles north to the Lindrick Golf Club in Yorkshire for the Ryder Cup, where Great Britain defeated the United States to break a victory drought that had stretched to twenty-four years. "I was enthralled," he later said about seeing golf's greatest players in the flesh for the first time in his life. To be one of those heroic men walking inside the gallery ropes became his life ambition.

At sixteen, Tony won the Lincolnshire Open, which "lit a fuse" under the teenager anxious to prove that he could be great. At seventeen, he turned professional and went to work as an assistant to a hard man named Bill Shankland at Potters Bar Golf Club. Victories in the professional ranks soon followed, first in Great Britain and later in the United States, where twenty-three-year-old Jacklin became the first British pro to win an important tournament on American soil since Ted Ray captured the U.S. Open in 1920. As both a player and a captain, Jacklin went on to win golf's three most coveted trophies, achieving the greatness he had imagined as a boy growing up in postwar England. The truck driver's son was a national hero and an international golf superstar. He also was a recipient of the Order of the British Empire, personally awarded by Her Majesty the Queen. Tony Jacklin had come such a long way from such humble beginnings.

On this particular Florida night in 2002, a bird, farting or otherwise, hadn't awakened Jacklin, nor had any other noise outside or inside his comfortable Bradenton home. It certainly wasn't the fitful sleep of a keyed-up player leading a golf tournament that had caused him to bolt upright in his bed. He had competed on the U.S. Senior Tour since turning fifty, winning twice, but was now, for all practical purposes, retired from tournament golf.

No, this awakening stemmed from something entirely different, "a vision," as he called it. "The idea was in my head," Jacklin said about that memorable night. "It was almost fully formed," he added.

The next day Jacklin called Kevin Daves, a real estate developer who had overseen the construction of the Ritz-Carlton Hotel in Sarasota, not far from the Jacklins' Bradenton home. Daves had recognized the prime development opportunity in the mid-1990s. Sarasota was one of the top markets in Florida, but it had no five-star hotels. He pitched Ritz-Carlton, which liked his idea, and Daves formed Core Development Inc. to build Sarasota's first five-star resort hotel.

The two men had played golf on a few occasions. Jacklin had learned enough about the developer and his golf interests—Daves was an average golfer at best but had a keen interest in upscale golf properties—to seek him out and present the idea that woke him in the middle of the night. Soon after, the two men met for lunch, during which Jacklin explained the unusual concept. He had found the perfect ear.

"He loved it," Jacklin remembered. "Kevin is a quiet man, but he showed his enthusiasm right away."

His instincts about Daves had been correct. Jacklin had found a key ally. Furthermore, he had won over a savvy developer who could help make things happen.

A vital next move belonged to Jacklin, a passionate man whose life had always been fueled by enormous dreams. He had not been involved in the design of many golf courses, but he did have a special connection and friendship with someone who had, the same man whose historic gesture had given birth to his novel idea. Tony Jacklin needed to arrange a time to meet with Jack Nicklaus.

PART
I

—1—

MUTINY

The Vietnam War was escalating, the first Boeing 747 jet airliner was set to roll off the assembly line, and the Ryder Cup, if not already dead, was on life support. The biennial golf matches between the United States and Great Britain, which except for a ten-year interruption resulting from World War II had been played since 1927, were jeopardized by new and existing forces in professional golf. In the late summer of 1968, the fate of the Ryder Cup rested in the hands of the Americans.

Officials of the United States and British Professional Golfers' Associations (PGA) were scheduled to meet in London during the third week of September to discuss the 1969 Ryder Cup, which was to be played at Royal Birkdale Golf Club in Southport, England. The location of the matches alternated between the United States and the British Isles, and it was the Brits' turn to host. Yet, as *The Guardian* reported on September 19, they were not even able to host an initial meeting. The U.S. PGA representatives weren't coming to London. They faced serious problems at headquarters in Palm Beach Gardens, Florida. It seemed the Ryder Cup was the least of their concerns.

Founded in 1916, the PGA of America was a burgeoning organization of about 5,800 club professionals and 300 year-round tournament players, or tour pros, by the late 1960s. The club pros oversaw golf operations at public and private golf clubs throughout the United States. They gave lessons, sold equipment, promoted golf programs, and, when time allowed, sharpened their own games. Tour pros, conversely, were golf vagabonds, chasing the growing riches on the PGA tournament circuit. Both professional breeds were ruled by pro golf's governing body in Palm Beach Gardens, but in 1968 the tour pros could no longer tolerate governance they felt didn't represent their best interests.

Although the players had fought for and won equal representation on the PGA's Tournament Committee, deadlocks between the committee's four player representatives and four members of the PGA Executive Committee were broken by an advisory panel—and its decisions were final. This didn't sit well with the players, one of whom was Jack Nicklaus, and one of the four players on the Tournament Committee who had sought to resolve philosophical differences with the PGA men and gain more autonomy for the players and the tour.

"Just as we wouldn't presume to tell the P.G.A. how to run its affairs, we think we should have the authority to run ours," Nicklaus said during that period in *The Greatest Game of All*, his first book about his life in golf.

There were several thorny issues, including number of tournaments and tournament schedule, course selection and conditions of play, purse sizes and distribution, sponsors, television contracts, and tour administration. During the previous year, for example, the players wanted to start a new tournament sponsored by singing legend Frank Sinatra to the tune of $200,000, but the PGA brass vetoed the idea. Resentment grew. A lot of money and control were at stake, and the two sides could not bridge their differences. The final straw was two television contracts. The PGA negotiated the rights to the World Series of Golf and Shell's Wonderful World of Golf with no involvement from the tour players. All the resulting TV money went into the PGA's general fund. No money went into tournament purses or to the players. The inevitable split came in mid-August of 1968 when tour players, led by Gardner Dickinson, Frank Beard, Doug Ford, and Nicklaus, among others, voted to establish an organization separate from the PGA named the American Professional Golfers (APG).

Tensions escalated when tour pros arrived for the $100,000 Philadelphia Golf Classic. PGA President Max Elbin met with seventy tour pros on the Tuesday night before the tournament to inform them the PGA didn't recognize their new association. A special entry form was being prepared for future tournaments. "A player who signs it may continue on the PGA tour," Elbin said. "Those who don't sign will be ineligible."

Beard later remembered Elbin and Leo Fraser, who was secretary of the PGA of America, as "the staunch hotheads" on the PGA board at that time. "We were bitter enemies during the two-year period when we tried to break away," Beard said. "We went head-to-head behind closed doors more than once."

Arnold Palmer, the charismatic superstar who almost single-handedly elevated the game of golf in the television age, did not break with the other players, instead pursuing a peacemaker role. "I saw an opportunity to serve as a bridge of sorts to a better world for everybody," Palmer later said in his autobiography, *A Golfer's Life*. Palmer also had business interests with the PGA and its more than five thousand club pros to consider, but, as one golf writer noted, "I think he was principally motivated by a desire to do the best for the professional game and if possible to avoid damaging its image."

It was apparently in that spirit that Palmer met with Elbin to broker peace and resolve differences between tour players and the PGA. It was to no avail. Around that same time, an unnamed PGA executive issued a statement critical of Nicklaus's role in the player mutiny. If it was intended to drive a wedge between Nicklaus and Palmer, it failed. Despite having different approaches to solving the problems, golf's two biggest names had similar interests. In addition, attacking Nicklaus was bad business because the players and the public regarded him as honest, straightforward, and sincere about professional golf and its best interests.

In early September at a meeting in Houston, the International Golf Sponsors Association said it would negotiate with both the players and the PGA and threatened to pull the plug on its tournaments if the talks were unsuccessful. The seriousness of the threat was debatable at a time when U.S. tour pros appeared to have the upper hand—if they could remain united. Corporate money was pouring into professional golf in America. If sponsors bailed, others were likely to take their place.

By mid-September, after legal wrangling and third-party attempts to make peace and reach an agreement of some kind, there was still no resolution to the mess, and, hence, no London meeting to plan the next Ryder Cup.

"If the newly formed association, the American Professional Golfers, gain complete control of tournament golf next year," reported *The Guardian*'s Pat Ward-Thomas, "there is no telling whether they will want to play the [Ryder Cup] match. Even if they do it must be unlikely that the PGA will hand over the trophy, and they themselves can hardly continue the match if they cannot call upon any of the leading players."

Another month passed, and there was still no definitive word from the western side of the Atlantic about the Ryder Cup. British PGA secretary John Bywaters said his organization had expected a U.S. delegation to arrive for a meeting by the third week of October. Once again, they were no-shows.

"There must be some element of doubt about the competition, but we are optimistic," Bywaters said, trying to sound a hopeful tone.

If the rift between the PGA and defiant tour professionals wasn't enough of a problem, there was another potential obstacle to the continuation of the Ryder Cup. In the forty-year history of the event, Great Britain had never won on American soil, and rarely on any soil. To some, the Ryder Cup had become irrelevant. A goodwill match? Sure. A competition between two relatively equal golf superpowers? Absolutely not.

•   •   •

The Ryder Cup was the namesake of Samuel Ryder, the fourth of eight children born to a seed merchant and a dressmaker on March 24, 1858, in Preston, Lancashire, England. Ryder joined his father's business after attending Owens College and working at a shipping concern in Manchester. He studied to become a teacher but didn't graduate due to poor health. It was a theme, for illness would again divert his life in such a way that his name would rest on one of golf's most-famous trophies.

Ryder split with his father after the two disagreed about the business wisdom of selling seed packets through the mail. He moved south to St. Albans in Hertfordshire, near London, and began selling seed packets from his home for a penny apiece. Ryder had a simple motto: "Everything in a penny packet from orchids to mustard and cress." The microscopic price undercut his competitors, and he posted the packets each Friday so his working customers would receive their seeds on Saturday, a day during which they could devote time to their gardens.

With a steady supply of seeds from his garden shed and assistance from his wife and daughter, Ryder's mail-order seeds business grew rapidly. The expansion led to the establishment of a large packaging facility on Holywell Hill where he employed up to a hundred people. He added herbs to the product line and named his small empire Heath and Heather Seed Company. By 1908 Ryder had become a very rich man. He was also exhausted and fell ill from his labor.

Light exercise and fresh air were prescribed for the fifty-year-old seeds tycoon, who had played cricket during his youth but had since become a workaholic with no hobbies or recreational interests that bolstered his physical health. Frank Wheeler, a friend and the minister of Trinity Congregational Church, where Ryder was a devoted member, suggested that Ryder try the game of golf. After initial resistance to the idea, Ryder took up golf and was soon hooked. He hired a local professional to teach him the fundamentals of the game. It marked the beginning of a new obsession. He then retained Abe Mitchell, a famed English golf professional with several tournament victories, as his personal instructor for the sum of £1,000 per year. Ryder, it seemed, had discovered a new vocation, and he worked diligently on his golf game in fair or stormy weather every day of the week except Sunday. He could be seen hitting drives and iron shots on the grounds of his five-acre family residence, Marlborough House. To develop his short game, he chipped over a hedge in the paddock and honed his putting stroke.

Ryder's manic golf immersion paid off. In a year's time, at the age of fifty-one, he played to a 6 handicap, a skill level that most golfers never attain in a lifetime of devotion to the sport. He joined Verulam Golf Club in St. Albans and soon after was elected captain of the club, a post he would again hold in the mid-1920s. Ryder's keen interest in tournament golf led to his sponsorship of the Heath and Heather Tournament in 1923, the first event reserved for professionals. Then, in 1926, he witnessed an informal match between American and British professionals that further stirred his passion for the game, including golf's potential for international competition and goodwill.

The U.S. players were in England for the Open Championship at Royal Lytham & St. Annes Golf Club in Lancashire. Arriving early because they had to qualify for the Open, American pros traveled to the Wentworth Club outside of London for a friendly practice match with the Brits. The U.S. side included the colorful Walter Hagen, Tommy Armour, Jim Barnes, Fred McLeod, Cyril Walker, Joe Kirkwood, and Emmett French. Of that group, only Hagen and French were natives. The other men had migrated to the States from England, Scotland, and Australia to ply their golf trade. The British team, which included 1920 Open champion George Duncan and Ryder's instructor, Abe Mitchell, handily beat the Americans, 13½ to 1½. Gallery member Samuel Ryder was captivated.

"Why can't they all get to know each other?" Ryder wondered. "I will give £5 to each of the winning players, and give a party afterwards, with champagne and chicken sandwiches."

Later, during tea, Ryder, Duncan, Mitchell, Hagen, and French drew up a plan for an official international competition pitting British professionals against American professionals. It would be called the Ryder Cup because Samuel Ryder donated the trophy, a nineteen-inch gold chalice that was crafted by Mappin and Webb for the sum of £250. The trophy bore the likeness of Mitchell, who was forever grateful for the gesture. "Putting me on top of the cup is more distinction than I could ever earn," he said.

While the Ryder Cup was born at Wentworth, the concept can also be traced to 1920, when a *Golf Illustrated* circulation manager named James Harnett sought to raise funds for international matches. The PGA of America approved the funding at its annual meeting in December, and the Americans took on the British at Gleneagles, Scotland, in 1921. Harnett didn't provide a trophy, but he did pick the U.S. team, probably with Hagen's help. The Brits prevailed, 9–3.

The inaugural Ryder Cup was played on June 3 and 4 in 1927 at Worcester Country Club in Worcester, Massachusetts. The British Ryder Cup team was barely able to scrape together the £3,000 needed to make the trip. When an appeal to 1,750 British golf clubs failed to raise the necessary funds, Ryder contributed £500 to help make up the difference. The Stock Exchange Golf Society also made a donation of £210.

Winners of sixteen British Opens and known as the Great Triumvirate, Harry Vardon, James Braid, and John Henry Taylor—selected the nine players for the British team: Aubrey Boomer, Archie Compston, George Duncan, George Gadd, Arthur Havers, Ted Ray, Fred Robson, Charles Whitcombe, and Abe Mitchell, who was chosen as captain. On the train to the ship that would take them to America, Mitchell became ill (later diagnosed as appendicitis) and had to abandon the journey. PGA secretary Percy Perrins selected Herbert Jolly as Mitchell's replacement on the squad, and Ted Ray took over the captaincy. Ray had won both the British and U.S. Opens and participated along with Vardon and Massachusetts amateur Francis Ouimet in the famous 18-hole playoff at the 1913 U.S. Open, which Ouimet won.

Clad in suits, ties, overcoats, and brimmed hats, most of the team appear in a photograph prior to their departure from Waterloo Station. Also pictured are G. A. Philpot, the editor of *Golf Illustrated*, who served as team manager, and Ryder, holding the leash of a stout-looking dog. After a stormy crossing, the money- and fashion-challenged British team stepped off the boat and into another world. American PGA officials had arranged a welcome party hosted by the U.S. captain, the stylish Walter Hagen. The Brits arrived with a police escort at the Biltmore Hotel in midtown Manhattan, where they deposited their bags before heading north to the Westchester Biltmore for a fancy dinner and nighttime putting tournament made possible by floodlights.

Besides Captain Hagen, the U.S. team included Leo Diegel, Al Espinosa, Johnny Farrell, Johnny Golden, Bill Mehlhorn, Gene Sarazen, Joe Turnesa, and Al Watrous. Like Ray, Hagen was a playing captain.

The teams competed in four foursomes matches and eight singles matches over the two days. Foursomes pitted two British players against two American players, each team playing one ball and taking turns hitting the ball until it was holed. Singles were one-against-one matches. Whether foursomes or singles, the object was to make the lowest score on a hole, and thereby win the hole. Tied holes were called "halves." Matches ended when a team or player was ahead by more holes than remained to be played. Teams or players were awarded 1 point for winning a match and $1/2$ point for a tied (or halved) match. All matches were 36 holes, a format that would continue until 1961.

This time, with only native-born players as Ryder Cup rules dictated, the Americans reversed the results at Wentworth. They took a 3–1 lead after foursomes matches on the first day. The second day was no better for the British boys. The U.S. players won the first four of eight singles matches to capture the Cup. Only the final score was in doubt. Prevailing in singles $6^1/2$–$1^1/2$, the United States won the first official Ryder Cup by the score of $9^1/2$–$2^1/2$, a decisive victory.

"One of the chief reasons for our failure was the superior putting of the American team," summed up Captain Ray.

The winning team took possession of the trophy until the matches resumed in two years. Samuel Ryder's prized Cup did not make the return voyage to Southampton, England.

In May 1929, five months prior to the stock market crash that plunged the United States and much of the rest of Western civilization into a deep and protracted depression, the teams met at Moortown Golf Club in Leeds in northern England. Walter Hagen again served as captain of the U.S. team, a role he would assume for the first six Ryder Cups. George Duncan led Great Britain. The era of hickory-shafted golf clubs was coming to a close, although the Royal and Ancient Golf Club, Great Britain's ruling golf body, wouldn't approve clubs with steel shafts until the following year. As a result, U.S. player Horton Smith, a rising star who would go on to win the inaugural Masters Tournament, switched to hickory sticks for the first time.

People streamed to the Leeds course to watch the action, creating a one-mile backup of automobiles. A boisterous gallery of 10,000 saw the visiting Americans take a 2½–1½ lead in dry and fast conditions after the first-day foursomes matches. Most disturbing was the 7 and 5 thumping Captain Duncan and Aubrey Boomer took from Leo Diegel and Al Espinosa. Duncan shook it off as he went out the next day to face Hagen in singles. An excellent match-play competitor, Hagen had won eleven major titles, including his fourth British Open two weeks earlier at Muirfield in Scotland. "Sir Walter," as he was nicknamed, was a brash man, which on this occasion worked to his disadvantage. Word reached Duncan that Hagen had guaranteed a point to his teammates. The captains' 36-hole singles duel resulted in a 10 and 8 rout in favor of Duncan, an enormous upset. It would be Hagen's only defeat in nine Ryder Cup matches. The British team won the day, 5–2, and the Ryder Cup, 7–5.

Returning to the States, the 1931 Ryder Cup was played at Scioto Country Club on the outskirts of Columbus, Ohio. Team selection rules stirred debate and an outcry before and after the matches. The Ryder Cup Deed of Trust declared that team members must be both natives and residents of the country for which they played. This and a team rule that required the players to travel together prevented the selection of three of Great Britain's finest players: Percy Alliss, who was serving as a club professional in Berlin; Aubrey Boomer, who was a member at St. Cloud Golf Club in Paris; and Henry Cotton, who planned to remain in America after the Ryder Cup. Without the three accomplished players, an aging Great Britain squad went down to defeat in stifling June heat by the score of 9–3. The scorching Ohio summer would result in early fall dates for future Ryder Cups played in America.

The 1933 Ryder Cup at Southport & Ainsdale Golf Club on the northwest coast of England was the closest and most exciting to date. The British team was led for the first time by a nonplaying captain, five-time British Open winner John Henry Taylor. An enthusiastic crowd numbering 15,000 watched the home team take a 2½–1½ lead in closely contested foursomes matches. The second-day singles produced high drama, leaving the Cup in doubt until completion of the final match between Great Britain's Syd Easterbrook and America's Denny Shute. Easterbrook had holed three consecutive putts to reach the final hole of the match all square, or tied, with Shute. Both men drove into bunkers and reached the green in 3 shots. Easterbrook lagged his long par putt close, but Shute's 30-footer slipped 4 feet by the hole. He missed the comeback attempt, Easterbrook tapped in, and Great Britain was again Ryder Cup victors, edging the United States 6½–5½.

The 1935 matches were contested in New Jersey at Ridgewood Country Club. Propelled by Captain Hagen in his final Ryder Cup appearance, Gene Sarazen, Paul Runyan, and Horton Smith, the United States won three of four foursomes matches on the first day to take a comfortable lead. The following day the Yanks dominated singles play and recaptured the Cup by the same 9–3 score as four years earlier in Ohio. The home side had won all five Ryder Cups, but the tide would soon turn.

Three months later, on January 2, 1936, Samuel Ryder died from a massive hemorrhage in London at the age of seventy-seven. The man who had sold countless seeds that had been planted throughout England was put into the ground with his favorite mashie, roughly the equivalent of the modern-day 5-iron. It was a blessing that Ryder did not live to see the future of his cherished Cup.

Beginning the following year, in 1937, the British would lose for the first time on their home soil. The victory drought—both at home and in the States—would extend well past World War II. After splitting the first four Ryder Cups with the Americans, Great Britain would win only one of the next thirteen contests. Conceived and meticulously crafted in England thanks to the visionary efforts of a passionate golf convert, the Ryder Cup trophy, for all practical purposes, had migrated to the United States.

·   ·   ·

In December 1968, a month after Richard Nixon had won the White House, the fledgling APG formed by defecting tour players had arranged twenty-eight tournaments for the 1969 season. Except for four holdouts, all existing sponsors were on board. Doral Country Club in Miami would host a qualifying school. The players had strengthened their hand.

Among the APG's first moves was to appoint New York attorney Sam Gates as its acting commissioner. Gates had been tour veteran Doug Ford's lawyer, and the players wanted legal muscle for their ongoing skirmishes with the PGA. Jack Tuthill, an ex-FBI agent and the PGA field man who ran tournaments, jumped ship with the players and was hired as the APG's tournament director. Tuthill occupied a small office in a Manhattan hotel and could not initially be assured of a paycheck, but he nonetheless rallied most of the sponsors that had formerly supported the PGA-sanctioned tournaments.

At the same time, the tenure of PGA President Max Elbin was coming to a close. His successor was Leo Fraser, a PGA member since 1927 and former head pro at New Jersey's Seaview Country Club. The change of leadership provided a new opportunity. Although originally backing the PGA position, which included a "verbal attack" against Nicklaus that the star golfer detailed in a self-penned *Sports Illustrated* article in September 1968, Fraser slowly came around. According to Palmer, who met with Fraser in Atlantic City to discuss the creation of an autonomous players organization within the PGA as the way forward, the incoming president was open to compromise with tour pros. Unlike other PGA officers, Fraser was willing to talk to the "rebels," as the players were sometimes called during that turbulent period. He squashed the public war of words and, in good faith, sat down with the players, listened, and bargained until a settlement was reached. There would be no APG tournaments in 1969. The short-lived organization had helped achieve the players' goal—the formation of the Tournament Players Division of the PGA, which would become known as the PGA Tour in the mid-1970s. (For the sake of uniformity, the tournament circuit will be referred to as the PGA Tour throughout the rest of this book.) Players would now enjoy majority status on policy boards and thereby guide important decisions about their livelihood.

"We could finally get back to playing the game we all loved to play instead of bickering about it," Palmer said.

The deal clincher, as Nicklaus called it, was the naming of Joe Dey as the tour's first commissioner. The sixty-one-year-old Dey, whom *Golf World* called "the most respected golf authority in the world," had been the executive director of the United States Golf Association (USGA) for more than three decades, a period of tremendous growth in the game. The USGA had become synonymous with Dey, who was trusted and admired by virtually all who had a stake or interest in the game. Dey's departure was a surprise to many people, probably even to Dey himself. After turning down many offers through the years, he would pursue a new role in professional golf. "I am ending what has really been my love affair with the USGA," Dey said upon his resignation in January 1969.

Players responded to Dey's hiring with enthusiasm and widespread support.

"I'm so happy we have secured a man of Dey's stature," said 1968 Masters champion Bob Goalby, "but I just couldn't believe he would take the job at first."

Billy Casper asserted, "I don't think professional golf could have picked a better man."

Nicklaus believed "Dey was the only man who could handle the job."

Palmer declared, "I'm as happy as can be."

Despite the ringing endorsements from the locker room and elsewhere, the job as first commissioner would be an enormous challenge. Dey didn't claim to have all the answers to the PGA's problems, and, as *Golf World* noted, he would be "dealing with men who have caused much grief for past administrators." Dey didn't expect trouble from the players, though. "I have known most since they were kids," he said.

In the beginning, Dey would focus on rules uniformity, improvement of tournament courses, and the conduct of tournament play. Splitting time between offices in New York City and Palm Beach Gardens, he would attend some tournaments but not impose himself on Jack Tuthill, who was returning to the PGA to serve as tournament director.

After months of acrimony between tour pros and the PGA honchos in Palm Beach Gardens, the new Tournament Players Division with the highly respected Dey at the headquarters and the able Tuthill in the field was off to a good start. By the end of January, after teeing it up in Los Angeles, Napa, Pebble Beach, and San Diego, tour pros were looking ahead to events in the California and Arizona deserts.

However, the matter of the 1969 Ryder Cup at Royal Birkdale and its many important details had not been settled. More than four months had slipped by since the London postponement and still no meeting between British and U.S. PGA officials had taken place. Based on the most recent history of the matches, one might wonder if the Americans would bother to cross the Atlantic.

—2—

CHAMPIONS

Founded in 1957 on the outskirts of Houston, Texas, Champions Golf Club was the joint vision of Jack Burke Jr. and Jimmy Demaret, two native Texans and golf legends with forty-seven PGA Tour titles between them, including five majors. Designed by Ralph Plummer, the Cypress Creek Course, noteworthy for its tens of thousands of trees, water hazards, enormous Bermuda greens, and snake-infested gorges, opened for play in 1959. After attracting the Houston tour stop in the mid-1960s, Champions, with its spacious, first-rate clubhouse facilities, hosted the 1967 Ryder Cup.

The British team, commonly known as the Great Britain and Ireland team during that period because it was comprised of players from all the British Isles, hoped to reverse a long history of American domination. (The team was also routinely called "Great Britain" and will be referred to as simply "Great Britain" from this point on for ease and consistency.) The Brits had just one victory since 1933, a $7\frac{1}{2}$–$4\frac{1}{2}$ triumph at Lindrick Golf Club in Yorkshire, England, in 1957. Dai Rees, a Welshman and the heroic captain of the winning British side, returned to lead the team for the fourth time at Champions. A feisty competitor, Rees had played in nine Ryder Cups and finished runner-up in the British Open on three occasions. A formidable task lay ahead of Rees and his squad in October 1967. Since the British blip in 1957 the United States had again established a firm grip on the Ryder Cup. In the two most recent meetings, at the Atlanta Athletic Club in 1963 and Royal Birkdale in 1965, the Americans romped 23–9 and 19½–12½, respectively. After five-time major winner Byron Nelson captained the U.S. team at Royal Birkdale, it made perfect sense to turn to another Texas golf legend in the long march of American supremacy.

Ben Hogan, winner of nine majors including a record four U.S. Opens, had been the nonplaying captain of the winning 1949 U.S. team eight months after a head-on collision with a Greyhound bus that nearly killed him. Hogan was considered to be one of the toughest and most determined men to ever play the professional game. Johnny Pott, a player on the 1967 U.S. Ryder Cup team, later recalled his role in recruiting Hogan to his second captaincy.

In May, some players met in the locker room at the Colonial National Invitation in Fort Worth, Hogan's hometown tournament, which Hogan had won five times. Pott sat at one end of the table as he and fellow tour pros reasoned there were several factors that pointed to Hogan as the logical choice. Hogan would follow longtime rival Nelson, Houston was not far from his Fort Worth home, and he was friends with Burke and Demaret, co-owners of Champions. All great reasons, but that didn't mean the aloof and brusque legend would do it. Then someone turned toward Pott. "Johnny, go find Ben Hogan and ask him if he'll be the captain!"

In 1962, Pott had lost to Arnold Palmer in an 18-hole playoff at Colonial. However, in Pott's mind, that didn't mean Hogan would know him any better than the guy handing out tournament programs. Pott located Hogan and introduced himself as a member of the Ryder Cup team. Then he popped the question: Would Hogan be the team's nonplaying captain? The Ryder Cup was in October at Champions, Pott added. Hogan said he would let Pott know the following day. The next day, as Pott left the Colonial locker room and passed through the swinging doors, there was Hogan, on his way in.

"I'll do it," Hogan said.

•   •   •

Each team had ten players plus a nonplaying captain, a slight increase to the nine-man Ryder Cup teams of the early days. Great Britain's team had Peter Alliss, Hugh Boyle, Neil Coles, Malcolm Gregson, Brian Huggett, Bernard Hunt, Tony Jacklin, Christy O'Connor, Dave Thomas, and George Will. Their American opponents were Julius Boros, Gay Brewer, Billy Casper, Gardner Dickinson, Al Geiberger, Gene Littler, Bobby Nichols, Arnold Palmer, Johnny Pott, and Doug Sanders.

A notable absence was Jack Nicklaus, who, with seven major wins in his short professional career, was arguably the best U.S. player and on his way to being one of golf's all-time greats. U.S. pros had to be PGA members for five years to be eligible for the Ryder Cup team. Nicklaus reached the five-year mark that season but was unable to collect enough Ryder Cup points in a relatively short time period to earn a spot on the team.

Tony Jacklin, an eager, dark-haired, twenty-three-year-old Englishman who had turned professional in 1962, was making his second trip to the United States and his first appearance as a member of Great Britain's Ryder Cup team. Famed American golf writer Herbert Warren Wind later wrote that Jacklin, who stood 5'9" and had a medium build, was "a self-confident, bouncy young man, more American in temperament than many Americans."

Teenager Jacklin was at Lindrick with his father in 1957 when Rees and his countrymen took the Cup back. It was Jacklin's first brush with great players from both sides of the Atlantic. "I watched them perform, walked closely along with them, and began to fantasize that one day it was going to be me walking on the other side of the ropes." On the day he and his father returned from the Ryder Cup, there was still enough daylight to play 9 holes. Tony came off the course as darkness fell with his best 9-hole score.

The son of working-class parents—his father was a truck driver and labored in the steelworks; his mother was a strong-willed woman with a fine singing voice showcased in small, local productions—Tony hated his name as a youth. Ben Hogan, Sam Snead, Arnold Palmer—those were great names, he told his parents one night during dinner. Someday Tony Jacklin could also be a great name, they replied.

As Jacklin and his teammates arrived in Houston for the matches, the future of the Ryder Cup was an open question. Great Britain hadn't won in a decade and only once since the Great Depression. The 1967 Ryder Cup was not televised because the U.S. TV networks didn't think it was worth the airtime. Even the American players were thought to be losing interest in the biennial matches. The idea of pitting the United States against the rest of the world was beginning to circulate. Nonetheless, as Jacklin remembered, the Brits touched down in Texas in a mood of "defiant optimism" sparked by their passionate nonplaying captain.

There was considerable fanfare, and it made a lasting impression on Great Britain's players. Gregson recalled the team's ride from the airport to the hotel, a procession of limousines with a police escort, lights flashing. Welcome to America, quite different from merry old England. The team visited NASA's Manned Spacecraft Center, where the Apollo program conceived to send a man to the moon was at full throttle, and enjoyed lavish American hospitality everywhere they turned. It included a memorable gala dinner with both teams and more than a thousand people in attendance. The twenty players and two captains sat at a long table on a stage. When it came time to introduce the respective teams, the guest captain went first. As Alliss later recalled, Rees "made rather a meal of it, going on about the things each of us had won and done." Each British player received polite applause from the large audience.

Then all eyes shifted to the U.S. team as Captain Hogan stood. Alliss noted they wore "beautiful suits" and "looked like a million dollars." Hogan asked the audience to hold its applause until the end of his introductions. One by one, Hogan said the names of his players, and nothing else. One by one, each player stood. When he finished introducing his men and all were standing, Hogan said, "Ladies and gentlemen, the United States Ryder Cup team—the finest golfers in the world."

"The whole place went berserk," Gregson said.

"The British were about ten down before a ball had been hit," commented Alliss.

One of America's "finest," Arnold Palmer got off to a bad start with the skipper. Hogan had told his players to arrive on Monday since the various functions got under way that evening, but Palmer didn't show up until late Tuesday morning. The man a press member once called "the James Bond of golf" did not endear himself to the stoic golf legend.

"Hey, Ben, what ball are we playing?" asked Palmer on the Champions practice tee. (In the Ryder Cup, players could choose to play the American ball or a slightly smaller British ball.)

"Mr. Palmer, when I pair you, I'll let you know," Hogan replied.

Another version of the ball story has Palmer and Hogan in a room with players from both teams. When Palmer asked about which ball they would be playing the next day, Hogan stared at him for an uncomfortable moment. "Who said you were playing tomorrow?" the U.S. captain replied. Still another version has Hogan saying to Palmer, "You haven't made the team yet." Teammate Littler later said the captain's comment was "in jest but it was very timely because everybody laughed and it helped to create a good feeling of being a team."

Jacklin, who channeled Hogan's work ethic as a golf-obsessed lad in Scunthorpe, was awed by his first encounters with the legend at the 1967 Ryder Cup. An incident early in the week revealed Hogan's unusual aura. Players from both teams were sitting in the locker room when Hogan silently appeared. The U.S. players immediately jumped to their feet. Jacklin remained seated and wondered who might be following America's captain into the locker room. Was it the president? The queen? "I was quite perplexed," Jacklin later said, "because it was just Ben Hogan." Maybe so, but Alliss said Hogan could "give you an inferiority complex just walking around." Nor was he above doing it with his words. During long practice sessions, Hogan was heard saying to his men, "I've never seen so many god-awful shots in my life." He told his team to be in bed by 10:30 P.M. Except for official events, socializing was forbidden. Hogan ran his team with military precision and commanded respect.

Gregson witnessed the American players' reverence for Hogan on the practice tee. The teams were practicing at opposite ends of the driving range when Rees alerted his boys to the lack of activity on the U.S. side. No one was hitting balls—except Captain Hogan. His players were intently watching. The scene amused Gregson, as well as the U.S. player standing in the back of the group who feigned boredom—Palmer.

In a way, it made sense. For Palmer, watching the great Hogan strike golf balls was dull compared to buzzing the clubhouse with his Jet Commander aircraft. Jacklin and teammate George Will were hitting practice balls early in the week when a grinning Palmer approached the two players and asked if they wanted to go for a ride in his new jet. "Why he chose us I'll never know, likely because we were the only suckers he could find hanging about," Jacklin later said. A notoriously poor flier, Will should have declined the invitation, but perhaps it was impossible to say no to the magnetic Palmer.

The men departed for a local private airstrip and were soon airborne. Palmer did his best imitation of a stunt pilot. As he later admitted, he raced to 8,000 feet and then peeled off and rolled the plane. At one point during the terrifying flight, a shaken Jacklin turned to his teammate and saw an ashen-faced man who appeared to be on the verge of a panic attack. Jacklin mentioned Will's distress to a gleeful Palmer, who said he would take them down closer to the ground. Palmer pointed the nose of the plane down and rushed earthbound before pulling it up at what seemed like the last second. The golfer-pilot also buzzed Champions and the surrounding area, flying below the legal minimum level according to a local dairy farmer concerned about his frightened cows. The farmer apparently reported the incident to the Federal Aviation Administration (FAA). Palmer landed the Jet Commander and rolled to a stop. Jacklin was now ashen. Will had turned green. A dark wet spot stained the front of his pants. "It was bloody unbelievable," Jacklin said.

When Palmer returned to Champions, a member told him an FAA official was waiting on the phone. The FAA and local police had received several complaints about a low-flying jet that spooked locals. The official was irate and prepared to revoke Palmer's pilot's license. Arnold picked up the receiver and listened patiently as the man blared into his ear. Then the Palmer charm took over. The golfer offered profuse apologies, taking full responsibility, citing his poor judgment, saying it would never happen again, and generally being "ingratiating to the extreme," recalled Jacklin, who noticed Palmer smiling at him while on the phone with the agitated official. It worked. Letters from Demaret and others may also have helped Palmer keep his license. He was a Houdini, able to escape trouble both on and off the golf course.

As the beginning of the matches drew near, Hogan called a team meeting and told his squad that his job was easy because they were all great players. Pairings would make no difference. He would put crooked hitters together and straight hitters together. Just go play your games, men. Forty-seven-year-old Julius Boros would hit the first ball because nothing bothered him, not even playing beneath a waving American flag in the Ryder Cup. Saying he never felt comfortable in others' clothes, Hogan said the players didn't have to wear the team uniforms if they didn't fit or were distracting in any way. If he preferred, Doug Sanders could dress like a peacock, wearing his customary pastel shades. The captain simply didn't care.

"But let me tell you boys one thing," said Hogan, who would look all business in a white dress shirt, striped tie, dark blazer with Ryder Cup insignia, and his trademark white flat cap covering his bald head. "I don't want my name on that trophy as a losing captain."

Beginning on Friday, thirty-two matches, each with 1 point at stake, would be played over three days. Sixteen-and-a-half points were needed to win the Ryder Cup. In the event of a tie, the United States, winner of the 1965 matches, would retain the Cup.

The format had expanded twice since 1959 when the Americans won at Eldorado Country Club near Palm Springs in the California desert. The format in place for the first thirteen Ryder Cups had been four foursomes matches on the first day and eight singles matches on the second and final day. All matches were 36 holes. A total of 12 points was available. A structural overhaul began in 1961 for the matches at Royal Lytham & St. Annes Golf Club in England. First, the number of matches doubled. First-day foursomes matches increased from four to eight. Second-day singles matches went from eight to sixteen. Second, all twenty-four matches would be 18 holes rather than 36 holes.

Another new wrinkle that became a permanent change appeared at the 1963 Ryder Cup at the Atlanta Athletic Club in Georgia. Eight fourball matches (also known as better ball, in which two men play as partners and record their best score on each hole) were added to the competition. Fourball matches were played on the second day. As usual, singles matches were contested on the final day. With foursomes, fourball, and singles matches, the Ryder Cup became a three-day golf event with more matches, more points (32), and hopefully more excitement. The changes did not stop America's domination of the biennial matches. Since Great Britain's breakthrough at Lindrick in 1957, the United States had won four straight. None of the meetings had been close.

On the morning of Friday, October 20, 1967, the Union Jack and the Stars and Stripes were raised at Champions Golf Club. The twenty-four players and two captains stood at attention for the playing of the national anthems by the Rice University band, first "God Save the Queen" and then "The Star-Spangled Banner." Foursomes matches would begin immediately after the opening ceremonies. The gravity of playing for one's country got to players, even experienced Ryder Cuppers such as Billy Casper, who was appearing on his fourth team. Casper would go out first with Julius Boros. Both were fast players, and Hogan wanted to get them on the course first (and hopefully ahead in their match) to set the tone for the other U.S. golfers. They would face Brian Huggett and George Will, two British veterans who had beaten Arnold Palmer and Johnny Pott in foursomes at the 1963 Ryder Cup.

A carefree former accountant with a golf swing as smooth as buttermilk, Boros would not hit the first ball in the 1967 Ryder Cup, as his captain had promised. That honor instead went to Casper. Actually, it was more like a curse. The winner of thirty-four PGA Tour titles, including two U.S. Opens, struggled for air. "Did you ever try to hit a golf ball without any oxygen in your system?" Somehow Casper struck his drive in the center of the 1st fairway. He and Boros lost the first two holes but fought back with birdies at the 4th and 6th holes. The opening match went the distance, ending in a tie.

"Not a bad start for a bunch of no-hopers," remarked Jacklin.

The morning's second foursomes match went to the Americans. Arnold Palmer and Gardner Dickinson beat Peter Alliss and Christy O'Connor 2 and 1. The contest was still in doubt on the 15th hole when Dickinson hooked his drive into the trees. Palmer faced a difficult recovery shot. All paths to the green appeared to be blocked by pines and oaks, but Arnold somehow hooked a 6-iron around and through the trouble, depositing the ball onto the green 10 feet from the hole. Dickinson sank the putt for a birdie and a slim lead the pair didn't relinquish.

Jacklin made his Ryder Cup debut playing alongside Dave Thomas, a large, jovial Welshman who hit the golf ball absurd distances but was an atrocious wedge player and chipper. To minimize his glaring weaknesses, Thomas teed off on all the even holes, which included all four par 3s. If Thomas missed the green, Jacklin hit the chip. Conversely, Jacklin teed off on all the odd holes, which included all four par 5s. This strategy pretty much assured that Jacklin rather than Thomas would be hitting the team's wedge and chip shots onto the large greens.

Flags raised and anthems played, Jacklin's heart pounded as he prepared to hit his first shot in his first Ryder Cup. It was a nasty snap hook, flying sharply to the left. "It might have been the fastest, most ill-tempoed golf swing of my entire career," he later said. Calmed by his good-natured partner, Jacklin settled into the morning match and played inspired golf to help the pair go 2 up after 9 holes against Doug Sanders and Masters champion Gay Brewer. The rookie and veteran went on to a 4-and-3 victory to capture the first point for the British side. While their teammates struggled against the Yanks, Jacklin and Thomas won Great Britain's only point in the afternoon foursomes by beating Gene Littler and Al Geiberger 3 and 2. The American team had holed the putts when it needed them and held a comfortable 5½–2½ lead at the end of the first day.

If Thursday was an inauspicious start for Great Britain, then Friday's fourball matches were a complete disaster. Alliss and O'Connor, one of Great Britain's strongest pairs, were 3 down to Casper and Brewer after 9 holes. Hunt and Coles engaged in a seesaw battle against America's Johnny Pott and Bobby Nichols. Thursday's British stars Jacklin and Thomas faced Littler and Geiberger in the morning and afternoon, both tight matches. Huggett and Will squared off against Dickinson and Sanders.

Palmer, however, sat out the morning session. With ten men on each team and four matches per session, two players on each side would not play. The captains decided the pairings, the order, and which two golfers would sit out the various sessions. Why won't Palmer play? inquired the press. "Because I say he won't," Hogan replied. Reporters wanted more. A reason, anything. They got nothing from the grim captain.

Palmer did play on Friday afternoon with Boros in an American fourball stampede. Early on they were 3 down to Will and Hugh Boyle when Palmer spotted Champions co-owner Burke, who "loved to pull [Palmer's] chain whenever he could." Burke suggested that even Palmer couldn't climb out of the hole he and his partner had dug. Care to wager on that? Palmer asked. Terms were set. If Palmer and Boros won the match, Burke would make Palmer a handsome clock. The rally began on the following hole as the Yanks cut into the deficit and went on to earn a 1-up victory. Palmer won the clock. The Americans won the day.

The scoreboard delivered Friday's brutal verdict. The United States had won seven of eight matches. Half of the matches had gone to the final hole, but Great Britain came away with only a half point. Thanks to their halved match with Littler and Geiberger, Jacklin and Thomas saved their team from the humiliation of a Friday shutout. Heading into the final day's singles matches, the USA led 13–3. It was over. Despite the impassioned Captain Rees and a strong rookie debut by Jacklin, the outcome, it seemed, was preordained. The final day was for pride.

Great Britain won four of sixteen singles matches on Saturday. Two of the victories were authored by Coles, who beat Sanders in both the morning and afternoon sessions. Alliss and Huggett also won matches. Three games were halved. Jacklin watched Palmer sink a 50-foot birdie putt on the 1st hole and was 5 down at the turn, losing to the superstar in the morning and the hot-putting Dickinson in the afternoon.

Mercifully, the matches ended. Palmer had won all five of his games. So had Dickinson. Each notching four wins, Casper, Pott, and Nichols were also undefeated. (Casper and Nichols also halved a match.) Who needed Nicklaus?

"Ever since Samuel Ryder, a British optimist, donated his solid-gold trophy back in 1927, this same one-sided monotony has been going on much too often," reported *Sports Illustrated*'s Alfred Wright.

Captain Hogan was gracious in victory, saying, "This is one of the finest teams you have ever put out against us." If true, then why were the British routed? Jacklin reasoned that he and his teammates stumbled through the closing holes of many winnable matches. Their short games let them down. The Yanks, on the other hand, were demons around and on the greens. They had the killer instinct.

Hogan's remarks may have been a small concession, but the final score effectively drowned out his well-intentioned comments and others' insightful postmortems. With the stinging $23\frac{1}{2}$–$8\frac{1}{2}$ defeat at Champions Golf Club, Great Britain had suffered one of the three most lopsided losses in Ryder Cup history, another being an 11–1 drubbing in Portland, Oregon, in 1947. That U.S. team was also captained by Hogan, although through the years it didn't seem to matter who was in charge—the result was the same. The future of the Ryder Cup was shaky at best.

—3—

TOUR DIVIDE

In early February 1969, around the same time the Boeing 747 jet airliner made its maiden commercial flight, British PGA secretary John Bywaters traveled as a one-man delegation to Palm Beach Gardens, Florida, to meet with U.S. PGA officials. Leo Fraser and Max Elbin, the current U.S. PGA president and his predecessor, were on hand and later appeared in a magazine photograph with Bywaters that showed the three men standing beside a bronze casting of the Vardon Trophy, an annual honor bestowed on the PGA Tour player with the lowest scoring average. Also present at the February meeting were former PGA president Harold Sargent, secretary Warren Orlick, treasurer Bill Clarke, executive director Robert Creasey, and executive secretary Lloyd Lambert. The purpose of the meeting was the 1969 Ryder Cup, which, after some uncertainty in the preceding months, would be played after all.

The matches would be contested on September 18, 19, and 20 at Royal Birkdale Golf Club in Southport, England, the same course that had hosted the most recent Ryder Cup in Great Britain. In 1965 Bryon Nelson led the U.S. team to a 19½–12½ victory over Harry Weetman's British squad. A links course on the edge of the Irish Sea, Royal Birkdale had hosted three British Opens in addition to the Ryder Cup, making it an ideal venue for the thousands of visitors and spectators the biennial event would attract. Despite Great Britain's abysmal record, the Ryder Cup was much more popular in the British Isles than in the United States, where fewer spectators attended the matches and television companies didn't bother to pursue the broadcast rights.

The allure of the Ryder Cup on his side of the Atlantic likely helped Bywaters fend off some drastic changes discussed in Palm Beach Gardens. One idea put forth was to adopt a new scoring system that would ensure that each match went the full 18 holes, creating heightened excitement and thereby making the event more attractive for TV. Bywaters countered that such a change was unnecessary in Great Britain. The British Broadcasting Corporation (BBC) would provide extensive TV and radio coverage of the 1969 Ryder Cup. The British PGA secretary requested that no change to the scoring system be implemented for the 1969 matches, and U.S. officials agreed. In addition, the format would remain unchanged. There would be a total of thirty-two matches—eight four-somes matches, eight fourball matches, and sixteen singles matches—as there had been since 1963.

Team composition was also a topic of discussion. In recognition of America's Ryder Cup dominance, might it be time for Great Britain to field a team that included players from the Commonwealth Nations? It would allow them to draw talent from countries such as Australia, Canada, and South Africa—all with rich golf histories—and perhaps make the matches more competitive. Variations of this idea had already been circulating. Again, Bywaters resisted, asking that no change be made for the upcoming matches. The Great Britain team would go it alone against the mighty Americans on the windswept shores of the Irish Sea. There was, however, one significant modification that resulted in bilateral agreement. For the first time in a Ryder Cup, both teams would have twelve players instead of ten, plus a nonplaying captain. On the surface, the increase might favor the Brits, who could put out their eight strongest players at any given time in the sixteen foursomes and fourballs matches, sitting four men instead of only two. However, so could the Yanks. Which team would benefit more from twelve-man squads was certainly debatable.

The U.S. team would be announced on August 17 following the PGA Championship, and the golfers would stay at the elegant Prince of Wales Hotel upon their arrival in Southport in mid-September. The twelve British players would be named in July following the British Open at Royal Lytham & St. Annes Golf Club.

Playing on their home soil, and with two more men to aid their cause, would the Brits rise to the challenge presented by "the finest golfers in the world"? Bywaters could only hope so as he returned home to England. Thanks to his insistence on such things as scoring and team composition, the Ryder Cup, as conceived by Samuel Ryder and other forebears, was still largely intact. Three days in September would determine whether it was wisdom or folly.

.   .   .

Also in early February, on Groundhog Day, Jack Nicklaus was putting the finishing touches on his first win of the 1969 season at the $150,000 Andy Williams–San Diego Open Invitational. Starting the final round 2 strokes behind San Diego native Gene Littler, Nicklaus shot a mediocre 73 at Torrey Pines, but it was good enough to edge the faltering Littler by a stroke. Nicklaus was awarded the trophy and a first-place check for $30,000. The PGA Tour was by far the best and richest tournament circuit on the planet. The popularity and economics of the sport had skyrocketed in the 1960s, thanks in large part to the power of television and superstar players such as the charismatic Arnold Palmer and the dominant Jack Nicklaus.

The early-season win in San Diego was Nicklaus's twenty-eighth tour title in seven seasons as a professional. Only once in that span had he won fewer than three events in a calendar year. It happened to be during the previous season, when he managed only two wins—the Western Open and the American Golf Classic. In addition, more than a year had gone by since he won his seventh major championship, the 1967 U.S. Open at Baltusrol in New Jersey.

As was his ritual, "the Golden Bear"—a nickname given to Nicklaus by Australian sportswriter Don Lawrence because of Jack's blond hair and stocky physique—came out of hibernation during the latter part of January rested and ready to play golf. The off-season began in late November after fall events such as the Australian Open and World Cup and after filming golf TV shows that aired in the winter months. Nicklaus relished his time away from the game. He slipped out of his golf spikes and into his sneakers. He slept in and went fishing. He spent time with his wife, Barbara, and their three young children, traveling to his hometown of Columbus, Ohio, for the holidays. Then he said, "I have to rouse myself for . . . another tournament season."

The first tournament on his schedule was the Bing Crosby Pro-Am. There was much that Jack liked about the annual event on the Monterey Peninsula: the convivial host, the clambake, and certainly the breathtaking Pebble Beach and Cypress Point golf courses. After the Crosby, he would play one or two more West Coast events before returning to his home in North Palm Beach, Florida. Nicklaus would rejoin the PGA Tour when it arrived in the Sunshine State a few weeks later, beginning his preparation for the year's first major, the Masters, played in Augusta, Georgia, during the first full week of April. Tournaments following Augusta were Nicklaus's preparation for the U.S. Open, which he later rated as the most important major championship and the most difficult to win. In July, his focus turned to the British Open, where he would arrive a week early to adjust to the unique playing conditions on Scotland's and England's famous links courses. Lastly, the PGA Championship, the season's final major, was played in mid-August.

While Nicklaus was home in Florida for his customary early-season break, the 1969 PGA Tour caravan journeyed from the Palm Springs area to Phoenix and Tucson, with satellite events played concurrently in Bogotá, Colombia, and Maracaibo, Venezuela. There were more than forty events on the 1969 schedule, totaling about $6 million in prize money. With the exception of satellite and other smaller events, most of the tournament purses were six figures, ranging from the $100,000 offered at the L.A., Phoenix, and Tucson Opens to the $150,000 to $250,000 doled out at tournaments such as the Doral Open Invitational, the Masters, the U.S. Open, and the Westchester Classic. The tour was swimming in corporate money. The previous year, Frank Beard was the first player to haul in nearly $100,000 in a season—without winning a tournament. The Kentuckian did it with consistent play: nineteen top 15 finishes, including three times as runner-up, in a total of thirty-two tournaments. Beard, who would keep a diary of his 1969 season for a book with sportswriter Dick Schaap, was destined for even greater riches.

Tommy Aaron, two years older than Beard and a teammate at the University of Florida, marveled at Beard's transformation. "In college [Beard] was a skinny little thing and had a crew cut," Aaron said decades later. "The biggest thing about him was these big plastic horn-rimmed glasses he wore."

When Aaron next saw Beard on the PGA Tour, his former teammate was about fifty pounds heavier and had a long, upright swing. "His game had completely changed in the two years I hadn't seen him. I asked him how that came about but he never gave me an answer."

However his game changed, Beard recalled a seminal moment early in his tour career. "I saw [Nicklaus] hit some balls just after we turned pro," Beard later said about the powerful, 5'10" golfer, "and I remember thinking, 'What am I doing out here with this guy?' I couldn't even clean his wedge, if you just looked at the games. So somewhere in there I realized that, if I was going to make this a goal, I was going to have to go with what I had, and just stick to it."

With big money at stake, there was plenty of competition and pressure. British golf writer Ben Wright wrote that "stomach ulcers are a by-product of the American professional tour, and young men grow to look old before their time." The PGA Tour's top 60 money winners enjoyed exempt status, which allowed them automatic entry into most tournaments. Other players had a difficult time earning a spot in the field of a tour event. For many PGA Tour wannabes, Monday qualifying was their only slim hope—slim because they typically had to compete against a hundred or more other pros for a few available spots. If they got into a tournament and made the 36-hole cut, they could enter the next event without going through Monday qualifying. If they somehow broke through and won, they earned a one-year tour exemption and joined the ranks of the elite players. It was a Darwinian system. Only the strong survived.

At the Bob Hope Desert Classic in Palm Desert, the strong man was Billy Casper. The two-time U.S. Open champion fashioned a 66 in the final round to overtake Beard, who led after 54 holes. The following week Gene Littler, another U.S. Open champion, won in Phoenix. Reigning U.S. Open champion Lee Trevino captured the title in Tucson. All three winners received checks for $20,000.

Life was good on the PGA Tour for tournament winners such as Casper, Littler, and Trevino who enjoyed exempt status, as well as for players who had a healthy bankroll or sponsor backing while they tried to board the gravy train. Superstars Palmer and Nicklaus flew in their private jets. Other top players flew on commercial airlines and drove the interstate highway system. The best golfers were given courtesy cars to use during tournaments, and in some cases for the entire season. All others drove their own cars, often with their wife and kids, crisscrossing the country. Grier Jones, a successful rookie and All American at Oklahoma State University whose wife sometimes traveled with him, estimated that it took about $400 a week to play on the PGA Tour. The ideal setup for a family was a motel suite or small apartment with a kitchen—a place with at least two rooms, especially if a baby or small children were traveling along. This type of lodging cost $100 or more per week. Sometimes a discounted rate was arranged for or by tour pros. Cheap rooms went for as little as

$6 a night, but they were generally found at shabby motels beside busy highways or in run-down neighborhoods. The cut-rate rooms often did not provide a basic level of comfort, though, so they were undesirable for tour players, who needed good rest. Food for a small family with access to kitchen facilities ran at least $50 per week. There were also gas-guzzling cars to fill up, and other expenses.

One regular expense was the caddie fee. A rule of thumb was $10 a day plus 3 percent of a player's winnings. For example, Beard's ninth-place tie in San Diego netted $3,325. He paid his caddie $150 for the week—$50 for five days of work plus $100, 3 percent of his check. The PGA Tour was a tremendous financial opportunity. It was also a financial drain.

On February 27 the $150,000 Doral Open Invitational teed off at Doral Country Club in Miami, the first of five tournaments on the Florida Swing. Nicklaus reappeared, and Beard was paired with him in the first round. On the first tee, the Golden Bear wrapped his arm around Beard and said, "How's the family, pro?" Beard didn't warm to Nicklaus's friendly greeting. "I just don't feel comfortable with him," he explained. "Jack's never been just another pro. From his first day on the tour, he's been in the superstar class." Comfortable or not, Beard bested Nicklaus on the opening 18 by 1 stroke, 71–72. Doral was a breakthrough for Tom Shaw, the first tour win for the University of Oregon All American who had joined the tour in 1963.

At the $115,000 Florida Citrus Open Invitational in Orlando, Ken Still, an angular Tacoma pro who had been toiling on the circuit since 1953, captured his first PGA Tour title, a 1-stroke victory over Miller Barber, a bridesmaid for the third time in the early season. Second was still good money, and, besides, Barber had won the Kaiser International Open Invitational in January. Nicknamed "the Mysterious Mr. X," Barber was stockpiling high finishes with an unorthodox golf swing and eyes shielded with aviator sunglasses.

The first-time winner parade continued the following week at the $100,000 Monsanto Open Invitational in Pensacola. Jim Colbert collected the trophy and $20,000 winner's check. Then Raymond Floyd, known as a playboy with immense golf talent, collected his third tour title and $20,000 at the $100,000 Greater Jacksonville Open. It was back to first-time winners as the PGA Tour returned to Miami for the $200,000 National Airlines Open Invitational, the final and most lucrative stop on the Florida Swing. Two days after former U.S. president and avid golfer Dwight Eisenhower died at the age of seventy-eight, Bunky Henry earned the largest winner's check of the season thus far—$40,000.

The five-event Florida Swing concluded with four first-time winners, a testament to the deep talent on the PGA Tour. As players emptied their lockers and packed their belongings for the next event, eight hundred miles to the north in Greensboro, North Carolina, the season for the pro circuit that would supply players for the 1969 Great Britain Ryder Cup team was still not under way.

· · ·

In the spring of 1969, the formation of the European Tour was still nearly three years away. In its inaugural season, the European Tour would hold twenty events, thirteen in the British Isles and seven on the Continent. Many of the same tournaments existed in the late 1960s, but they were essentially played as separate pro circuits and organized by separate golf bodies until unified by the British PGA in the early 1970s.

The money was awful, which discouraged extended travel to the Continent and elsewhere. Playing for professional pride against top talent was exciting and honorable, but it didn't pay for weeklong stays in Paris, Berlin, and Barcelona. As U.S. tour pros headed to the North Carolina Piedmont for the Greater Greensboro Open—already with a dozen tour events completed—the Penfold Tournament, the season's first big event on the British tour, was still weeks away. No one would mistake Wales, England, Scotland, or Ireland for California or Florida. Consequently, the British season only lasted about six months.

If Great Britain's pros wanted to get in some tournament competition before their PGA Championship teed off in late April, then they could play the tour in South Africa (known today as the Sunshine Tour), home to golf legend Bobby Locke and Gary Player, one of "the Big Three," a moniker given to Palmer, Nicklaus, and Player in the 1960s. Two British pros who made the journey in early 1969 were Brian Barnes, a twenty-three-year-old pupil (and son-in-law) of Max Faulkner, the colorful Englishman who won the 1951 British Open, and Bernard Gallacher, a twenty-year-old Scottish wunderkind. Barnes played alongside Player in the third round of the South African PGA Championship and matched Player's 68. Barnes later visited the eventual winner's spacious home outside of Johannesburg, a residence that included two swimming pools and a gymnasium for the fitness-crazed golfer. Over dinner Player told Barnes to work on his short game and to remain patient—a first professional win would soon come. For young Gallacher, a trip highlight occurred in Rhodesia, where he tied for sixth in the Dunlop Masters after a 62 in the final round.

Faulkner also coached Gallacher, and good results followed. "He really helped with my game," Gallacher later said, "and I had a good season in '69."

Subsistence may have been the perfect word to describe the average tour pro's pay and travel and living conditions on the eastern side of the Atlantic, whether playing in South Africa, on the Continent, or even in Great Britain. Tony Jacklin called purses on the British tour "ridiculously low." As he pointed out, Neil Coles, the top money winner during a five-year period that began in 1962, earned slightly more than £25,000, roughly equivalent to $69,000. Not per year, mind you, but for half a decade. During the 1950s and 1960s, the British tour often resembled a "genteel garden party," according to Jacklin, with players "content to make a comfortable living without too much travel and the inconvenience it brings."

Jacklin affectionately recalled his early years traveling the circuit with Alex Caygill—the questionable automobiles, the humble digs, the fish and chips, and barely meeting expenses on winnings of £1,000. In a letter to his parents, Tony shared how he had touched Dai Rees's driver, retrieved a divot for Peter Alliss, and actually carried on a conversation with Harry Weetman. Jacklin was thrilled to be playing alongside the stars in the British golf galaxy. Yet none of the players, however rich from their tour experiences, were getting rich.

In 1968, Peter Townsend, a promising twenty-one-year-old English pro, topped the British money list with £9,593, a considerable haul by tour standards. Still, it was the equivalent of about $28,000, a minuscule amount compared to Billy Casper's 1968 PGA Tour–leading total of $205,169. While other events and exhibitions offered income opportunities not included in the official money list (also the case for U.S. players), it was clear that British tour pros were grossly underpaid when measured against their American counterparts. That wasn't going to change anytime soon. The 1969 British money leader would fall well short of Townsend's 1968 mark.

There were obvious reasons for the stark difference in money on opposite sides of the Atlantic Ocean. Sponsors lined up in the United States, where many of the tournaments were organized and supported by the chambers of commerce of cities. Thanks to Palmer, Nicklaus, Casper, and a strong supporting cast of talented players, U.S. television was also pumping generous amounts of money into professional golf. This was not the case in Great Britain, where often a single sponsor and a golf club would put on a tournament without much outside assistance. The BBC had cut back on its televised golf coverage in the latter half of the 1960s, calling the game played by approximately 1.5 million Brits a minor sport. While televised golf flourished in the United States, the BBC only planned to televise three British golf events in 1969: the Open, the Piccadilly Match-Play, and the Ryder Cup.

Great Britain was the home of golf. It was a different brand of golf in the British Isles, though, and it started with the golf courses. Historic links courses blended into the coastlines of Scotland, England, Wales, and Ireland, where golf traditions were celebrated and fiercely preserved. The weather was always a factor, pot bunkers were numerous and penal, the uneven terrain meant the bounce of the golf ball was left to chance, and the greens were uneven and slow in speed. Conversely, in the States, many of the tour courses were lush and manicured, often with wide fairways and large, receptive greens, such as the ones at Champions Golf Club in Houston. Unlike the scruffy links across the ocean, U.S. courses were drenched with water. PGA Tour pros aimed directly at the flagsticks on the greens—a reckless strategy on British courses because of the erratic conditions—and stuck their bold approach shots like darts. Target golf, some critics of the U.S. game called it. Whatever the label, and despite criticism from those who preferred golf as played in the old country, there was no argument about which nation was producing the world's best and richest players. The difference in golf courses was but one of several explanations.

Writing for *Sports Illustrated* in May 1967, British golf writer Ben Wright shed light on the shortcomings of British pros. "It has been said that the British swings are old-fashioned, that they are graceful and elegant but not effective. The inability to play the year round has been blamed, and the lack of different kinds of courses. Finally, it has been argued that the British are bad putters under pressure because they use a wristy stroke, which is, again, aesthetically satisfying, yet does not seem to hold up under the strain of an 8-footer worth $10,000." Wright offered a telling anecdote about highly touted amateur Clive Clark. Clark traveled to Australia for three months in 1965 to practice under the tutelage of Norman Von Nida, an Aussie who had won dozens of tournaments Down Under and recorded third- and fourth-place finishes at the British Open in the late 1940s. "Glad to have you," Von Nida said to Clark, extending his hand. "There is only one thing that can keep you from becoming a champion—you are English!"

During an era when transcontinental air travel was increasing but still not frequent or economical, tour pros on both sides of the Atlantic mostly played in their home countries. With the exception of top players and a handful of others—Palmer and Nicklaus, to name two—U.S. tour pros didn't bother to play in the British Open, golf's oldest major championship, which engraved the winner's name on the famous Claret Jug.

"It was a long way to come," Jacklin later said. "By and large, they preferred to play their golf in good weather conditions and in their own country, where they knew what it was about."

Nor did many British players tee it up in the States. Travel, cost, and depth of competition were big obstacles. A foreign player had to advance through the PGA Tour qualifying school and be among the few dozen professionals out of hundreds to secure tour membership. The only thing a hard-earned PGA Tour card assured him was the chance to qualify for a spot in a tournament when the tour started in January in Los Angeles and then hopped from event to event through the fall. There were few British players with the sturdy game and heady ambitions to leave the comforts of home and test their skills against America's finest.

Jacklin was one such player. After victories at the Dunlop Masters at Royal St. George's and the Pringle at Royal Lytham, he left the British tour at the end of the 1967 season and set his sights on the PGA Tour. As Jacklin insisted, his departure for America was not an act of disloyalty. In his estimation, the United States was the obvious destination for any tour pro who wanted to raise his game to the highest level and win tournaments that fielded the world's best players. In explaining why he never tried the U.S. tour, Peter Alliss passed along wisdom that Jacklin would remember. Alliss thought it was a long-term commitment, three or four years, which meant uprooting his English life, moving to the States, and living like an American. Alliss offered Jacklin this nugget: "There is no good going there and thinking of yourself as an outsider . . . To beat them, you have to join them."

Jacklin took the advice to heart. "America it was," he later said, referring to the decision made with his wife, Vivien. "We packed up for the [1967] Ryder Cup, but we also knew we were packing up to try and make the U.S. Tour."

After an encouraging debut on a Ryder Cup team that suffered a humiliating loss, Jacklin headed to West Palm Beach, Florida, to the PGA Tour Qualifying Tournament, an eight-round marathon. His game was clicking, and he earned his tour card by firing a pair of 68s in the final two rounds.

Jacklin became friends with U.S. players Tom Weiskopf and Bert Yancey, and the three young pros put in long hours working on their games. "We were all trying to become better players. It started to pay off for me," he later said. Nicklaus also befriended the Englishman. "When he first came over here, I had him at the house," Nicklaus said in 2013. "We spent a lot of time together. Tony was a good friend."

A breakthrough came early in the 1968 season during the Florida Swing. "Young Tony Jacklin cooly fought off Arnold Palmer and Doug Sanders in the final 18 holes of the Greater Jacksonville Open Golf Tournament," reported the Associated Press, "finishing with a 15-under-par 273." Jacklin had done what no other British player had accomplished—win on the PGA Tour. "That gave me a lot of confidence," he said.

While Jacklin was accepted by his American practice buddies and treated well by star players such as Nicklaus and Palmer, there were others who resented him. They considered Jacklin a foreigner who was dipping into U.S. purses—their purses. It was not like today's PGA Tour that is stocked full of international players. "There was always a bit of animosity that you felt," he remembered.

Beard, who later called Jacklin a friend but didn't consider himself close to the Englishman, admitted PGA Tour rules and player attitudes were tough on international golfers. "To be very honest with you," Beard later said, "foreign players were not really welcome in America. We made it very difficult on them."

Jacklin also caught flak at home, especially early on. Switching tours seemed as far-fetched as going to the moon, soon to be the destination of the Apollo astronauts. Jacklin's defection was covered in minute detail by British newspapers, the underlying question always "Why go to America?" Some admired his ambition; others thought he was "big-headed."

The spoken and unspoken expectations of his fellow Brits would tug at Jacklin in the years to come. As his success grew in the United States—a country big enough to produce larger-than-life sports heroes like Arnold Palmer—pressure grew at home, where the press had few stars to latch on to, a dynamic that Jacklin called "intensely claustrophobic."

Tony and Vivien relished their new American way of life. It was big and wide open. Compared to the English, most Americans had a prosperous lifestyle. There was little not to like about the United States. The food was good, and to the amazement of a young couple accustomed to the capricious infrastructure of centuries-old England, services and creature comforts were abundant and reliable. Wherever they went, the power switched on, water flowed from taps, and the phones—my goodness, the phones!—worked instantaneously and clearly.

There was no looking back for the Jacklins. While the Ryder Cup and PGA Tour qualifying school were a huge boost, Jacksonville proved that Tony could win playing against the world's best players. It was a turning point.

Jacklin, however, was not the lone Brit to storm the American shores. Peter Townsend, a fellow Englishman who turned pro in December 1966 after an impressive amateur career that included a starring role in the 1965 Walker Cup, was also determined to play on the PGA Tour. Townsend was such a coveted golf prospect that he was the first European player to sign with Mark McCormack, the superagent who represented the business interests of Palmer and Nicklaus. Jacklin joined McCormack's growing stable not long after Townsend. Thanks to McCormack, Townsend secured contracts with makers of clothing, golf balls, and golf clubs. He also had deals with *Golf World* magazine and Coca-Cola and drove a BMW 1800 sports car that he felt sheepish about parking in the players' lot at tournaments. Shy or not about outward signs of success, Townsend, like Jacklin, had loftier ambitions than most. They were part of a new and small contingent of British tour players who didn't regard Great Britain as the sole planet in the golf universe.

"I no longer think of playing just in Britain, as did the older brigade of professionals," Townsend said in 1967. "Britain is only one of the stops we'll have to make on a worldwide, year-round tour from now on."

Townsend advanced through the same PGA Tour Qualifying Tournament as Jacklin. Besides Townsend and Jacklin, the 1967 PGA Tour qualifier class featured Bob Murphy, Deane Beman, Lee Elder, Orville Moody, Bobby Cole, and Gibby Gilbert. PGA Tour card in hand, the going didn't get any easier for Townsend. Unlike Jacklin, who entered PGA Tour events thanks to an exemption as a Ryder Cup player, Townsend faced the long odds posed by the Monday qualifiers that preceded the full-field tournaments that began on Thursdays. The twenty-one-year-old Englishman was a "rabbit," the term for players who hopped from event to event hoping to sneak into the field. If a player qualified for a spot in the field and made the cut, he could enter the tournament the following week and bypass Monday qualifying. It was a big if, though, as Townsend discovered on the West Coast in early 1968.

"They had some 120 guys teeing up for four or five places," he later said. "And you needed to shoot 66, 67 to even think about getting into the tournament. I do remember in California—I went something like six weeks—all I did was play on a Monday."

Malcolm Gregson, a member of the 1967 Great Britain Ryder Cup team, and Clive Clark, the young man who had gone to Australia, were two other British players who also tested their games in the United States. Both earned their tour cards in 1968 but found it difficult to earn spots in tournaments and win money.

Both Gregson and Clark played in the 1968 Masters, won by Bob Goalby when Argentine Roberto De Vicenzo signed an incorrect scorecard to lose by a shot. Gregson finished in a tie for thirty-fifth, while Clark missed the cut. It was the only Masters appearance for the two men, both soon to be cast off the PGA Tour. Jacklin finished in a tie for twenty-second at the same Masters and went on to earn nearly $60,000, which put him in twenty-ninth place on the 1968 PGA Tour money list. Safely within the top 60 and the winner at Jacksonville, Jacklin was a rarity, an exempt tour player from Great Britain.

Despite facing the Monday qualifying blues, Townsend persevered. He liked America, even though he also sensed negative vibes. "It was never spoken to your face," Townsend later said, "but you heard things that were going on." He befriended U.S. players Hale Irwin, Randy Wolff, and Mac McLendon. They played Tuesday practice rounds, ate together, and played cards. "I had Tony [Jacklin]," he added. "We used to go out to dinner quite a bit. I had no regrets whatsoever about being [in America]. It was a good experience."

Despite the difficulty of getting established on the PGA Tour, 1968 was a successful year for Townsend. He won three events—two in Great Britain and one in Australia—and ended the year as the leading money winner on the British circuit. In early January of 1969, Townsend headed to California for the start of another PGA Tour season. A photograph in *Golf Illustrated* showed him at Heathrow Airport being sent off by his fiancée, Lorna Hogan. The couple would marry that April. A "Townsend in America" photographic collage later showed a typical day in the life for the twenty-one-year-old pro on "the American Tour, the toughest circuit in the world." Townsend is shown reading his mail in a locker room—golf shoes strewn everywhere—eating a hot dog and drinking a Coke near the practice area, and talking with 1967 Masters champion Gay Brewer on the practice putting green. He also is photographed sitting alone in his motel room, a small kitchen in the background. Surely the Brits were fascinated as they flipped through their golf magazines and peered into the strange tour life in faraway America.

· · ·

The PGA Tour rolled into North Carolina in early April for the $160,000 Greater Greensboro Open, the prelude to the Masters Tournament in Augusta, Georgia. Fifteen-year tour veteran Gene Littler, who had won in

Phoenix, prevailed at Sedgefield Country Club in a sudden-death playoff against Julius Boros, Orville Moody, and Jacklin practice partner Tom Weiskopf. Prior to Phoenix, Littler had only won once on tour since 1962, so the two early-season victories marked a comeback for the quiet San Diegan.

During the same week, a story appeared in *Golf Illustrated* detailing a minor controversy concerning U.S. Ryder Cup hopeful Charlie Sifford. Titled "Negro Sifford in Ryder Rumpus," the article reported that Sifford, the first black man to play on the PGA Tour when the tour rescinded its Caucasian-only membership clause in 1961, had been shorted on Ryder Cup points for his victory at the season-opening Los Angeles Open. By his own calculation, Sifford was ranked tenth in the Ryder Cup points standings after Los Angeles. (Twelve men would earn spots on the U.S. Ryder Cup team, which had never included a black man.) Sifford was surprised to learn he was in seventeenth place on the list rather than tenth. Tournament wins typically garnered 70 Ryder Cup points, but Sifford had only received 35. A PGA representative said the points were cut in half because two PGA-sponsored tournaments took place during the same week. (The other event was the Alameda County Open in Northern California, won by Dick Lotz.)

The explanation didn't satisfy some of Sifford's pro friends. They appealed to PGA headquarters, and Sifford was awarded the full 70 points for his L.A. win. A month later, Sifford would slip to fifteenth in the Ryder Cup points standings. After completion of the Greater New Orleans Open Invitational on May 4, the points totals were as follows:

U.S. RYDER CUP TEAM POINTS STANDINGS

1.	Jack Nicklaus	293.03
2.	Lee Trevino	289.34
3.	Billy Casper	249.84
4.	Gene Littler	238.30
5.	Miller Barber	202.84
6.	Dan Sikes	188.88

7. Raymond Floyd	170.68
8. Ken Still	165.20
9. Frank Beard	157.35
10. Julius Boros	146.99
11. Dale Douglass	143.95
12. Chi Chi Rodriguez	132.00
13. Arnold Palmer	119.50
14. Tommy Aaron	110.91
15. Charlie Sifford	105.00

•   •   •

During the second week in April, eighty-three golfers rolled down Magnolia Lane at Augusta National Golf Club to play in the thirty-third Masters Tournament. Billy Casper, a two-time U.S. Open champion and winner of the Bob Hope Desert Classic two months earlier, opened with a 66 for a 1-shot lead over George Archer, a 6'5½" Northern California native known for his deft putting touch. Archer had won the $125,000 Bing Crosby Pro-Am in late January. Casper continued his solid play with a pair of 71s that kept him atop the leaderboard at the end of the second and third rounds. One more good round and Billy, a player with more wins than Nicklaus during the decade, would slip into his first Green Jacket. It wasn't to be. Carding a 74 that included a dismal 40 on the outward 9, Casper was nipped by Archer, who shot a 72 to claim a 1-stroke victory.

Archer continued a Masters trend. From 1960 through 1966, the Masters was dominated by the Big Three: Arnold Palmer (three wins), Gary Player (one win), and Jack Nicklaus (three wins). Beginning in 1967, three journeymen—Gay Brewer, Bob Goalby, and Archer—donned Green Jackets. The Masters would be the only career major for each man.

Nicklaus, the man atop the U.S. Ryder Cup team points list, finished in a tie for twenty-fourth after starting off with a promising 68. Other

Ryder Cup team contenders fared better. Kaiser winner Miller Barber finished seventh. Greensboro winner Gene Littler and Tommy Aaron tied for eighth. Dan Sikes was twelfth. Tucson winner Lee Trevino, Frank Beard, and Dale Douglass tied for nineteenth. Arnold Palmer finished a stroke behind Nicklaus in twenty-seventh.

A handful of British players were also at Augusta: Tony Jacklin, Peter Townsend, Brian Huggett, and Peter Butler, making his sixth consecutive Masters start. Huggett and Butler missed the cut. Jacklin, who had finished in a tie for twenty-second and sixteenth the previous two years, also missed the cut. In his first Masters appearance, Townsend opened with a 75, followed by a 71 in more difficult conditions, to be the only British player to qualify for the final 36 holes. His 73-79 weekend resulted in a forty-second-place finish.

"If the British contingent [at the Masters] can be said to have comprised the spearhead of this year's Ryder Cup team as I suppose it must," wrote Peter Dobereiner, "then the prospects for the match are not exactly encouraging."

If it was any consolation to members of the British press and anyone else who pinned their often-dashed hopes on Great Britain, the Ryder Cup was still five months away. Whatever the team makeup, at least this time Britain's best would face the Yanks on their home soil. At Royal Birkdale in Southport, England, the famed links on the Irish Sea, the British boys would be able to play their kind of golf. However, as they were soon to find out, they wouldn't be able to play their kind of golf ball.

—4—

THE BIG BALL

Pat Ward-Thomas was a pilot for Great Britain's Royal Air Force during World War II. After being shot down over Holland in 1940, Ward-Thomas was imprisoned at Stalag Luft III in Poland until the end of the war. The long incarceration led to a new career for the prisoner of war. Ward-Thomas reported on the golf matches played by his fellow prisoners, who fashioned golf balls from scrap materials and knocked them around on an improvised golf course. The POW determined that writing about a game would be an enjoyable way to make a living. A 1950 audition with *The Guardian* went well, and Ward-Thomas began his new line of work, which became a long love affair with the game of golf.

During the third week of April in 1969, shortly before the British tour season got under way in earnest at the Penfold Tournament, Ward-Thomas filed the briefest of stories in the *Guardian* sports section. In three short paragraphs, the British golf writer explained that the large ball would be used by both teams at the upcoming Ryder Cup.

The "large" ball was the American golf ball approved for play by the USGA. The "small" ball was the British golf ball sanctioned by the Royal and Ancient Golf Club, also known as "the R&A," golf's ruling authority throughout the world with the exception of North America. The two golf balls were virtually identical. If they were set side by side, the average person would be hard-pressed to tell them apart. They were constructed of the same materials, and both were white and covered with dimples. The weight, as dictated by the USGA and the R&A, was the same for both: 1.62 ounces. The diameter of the two golf balls was the sole difference— and it was a very slight one. The British golf ball measured 1.62 inches in diameter. The American golf ball was 1.68 inches wide.

The departure from a standard international golf ball had begun earlier in the century when golfers wore knickers and swung clubs made of hickory. In 1920 the two governing bodies agreed to a weight of 1.62 ounces, but in the early 1930s the USGA abandoned the agreement, creating what would become known as the big ball, 1.68 inches wide and with a lesser weight of 1.55 ounces. The USGA-stipulated weight returned to 1.62 ounces a year later, but the new wider diameter remained as the U.S. standard.

What that meant during the biennial Ryder Cup matches was that players on both teams could choose which ball they wanted to play in the matches. Many chose to use the smaller British ball. Fred Hawkins, a player on the 1957 U.S. Ryder Cup team that lost to Great Britain, had mostly fond memories of the small ball. "I played the small ball over [in England] because I could drive it so much farther," Hawkins said. "I like the way it putted, too." It worked out for the slender Illinois native, who enjoyed a long career on the PGA Tour. Hawkins was the only U.S. player to win in singles, beating Peter Alliss 2 and 1.

The small ball wasn't just for the windswept links courses of the British Isles. It also was the preference at Ryder Cups played in the United States. As Ward-Thomas noted, except for one brief instance every man on both 1967 teams put the British ball into play at Champions Golf Club in Houston.

"Sure we had to choose the little ball for the matches at Houston,"

Arnold Palmer said shortly after America's largest Ryder Cup victory margin. "We couldn't give the British that much of an advantage and expect to win."

It would be different at Royal Birkdale in September 1969. "Now, for the first time, one size of ball is compulsory," wrote the man who had watched fellow POWs hit homemade golf balls made from junk.

That one-size-fits-all golf ball, as agreed to by both the British and U.S. PGA for the upcoming Ryder Cup, would be the larger 1.68-inch-diameter ball. Eric Brown, the recently named Great Britain Ryder Cup captain, said the mandatory use of the large ball would make no difference. The men who would form Brown's team had been using the big ball for a year or more in tournaments in Great Britain and the United States. Certainly, part of learning how to compete with and beat the Americans was adapting to their golf ball.

The minuscule difference (six one-hundredths of an inch) in the diameter of the two golf balls was, in fact, a rather big deal for the British. In the exhaustive search for reasons why they couldn't win the Ryder Cup, the role of the golf ball came into sharper focus in the late 1960s. One theory held that U.S. players were superior shotmakers because they had been playing the harder-to-control big ball since the Great Depression. Consequently, beginning in 1968, the British PGA took the extraordinary step of making the large ball mandatory for tournament play, a three-year experiment designed to help British players catch up with U.S. pros.

Anecdotal evidence suggested higher scores after the switch to the big ball. At the 1967 Agfa-Gevaert Tournament at Stoke Poges Golf Club near London, Peter Alliss posted a winning 72-hole score of 270. The following year at the same course, Clive Clark, using the 1.68-inch-diameter ball, won the tournament with 288. It appeared that the British pros had a ways to go in learning how to play the big ball. If it required 18 more strokes at Stoke Poges, an inland course, what might players expect at the windy links of St. Andrews, Carnoustie, and Royal Birkdale?

The wind might not be the only loud noise, offered a newspaper report.

"Indeed, before the year [1968] is out there may be considerable howling for a return to that bullet-like little British pellet." Howling wind or howling golfers notwithstanding, the big-ball experiment continued into the 1969 season.

No less an authority than former British Ryder Cup captain Dai Rees addressed the issue in a *Golf Monthly* column titled "How to Play the Big Ball Well." Some British tour pros, initially in favor of the ball switch, were finding it more difficult than they expected. Although there were those who second-guessed the wisdom of the British PGA, Rees wasn't one of them, suggesting players "plug on" with the experiment. It would be worthwhile in the end.

The British golf hero opined that swing technique was a major determinant of success with the large ball. Some of the older-generation British players who had honed their games using the small ball were what Rees called "flickers." They "are fast on and off the ball at impact," he noted, employing a wristy action that was effective with the British ball. That type of action, however, was not an optimal method for striking the large ball. Rees believed that a player needed to drive through the big ball by extending the right arm through the hitting area. The big ball was thought to stay on the clubhead slightly longer. Using it all their lives, U.S. players were therefore adept at plowing through the larger ball with sturdy golf swings powered by arms and shoulders.

Rees also fingered an underlying concern. For many years, the Americans had come to Britain, switched to the smaller ball, and won the British Open, British Amateur, Ryder Cup, and Walker Cup. Going from the big ball to the small ball wasn't a problem for them. "Their technique for hitting the larger ball worked equally well with the smaller ball," Rees explained.

The same could not be said for old-school British professionals, whose small-ball game didn't translate as well. Yet some of the new British tour breed were figuring it out. Rees offered Brian Huggett and Alex Caygill as examples, two players who possessed solid techniques for striking the larger golf ball. A long hitter with the British ball, Caygill was also producing monster drives with the American ball. The seven-year tour veteran won the Penfold Tournament and the winner's check of £750 in early May, his first victory in six years and only his second pro title. It represented a comeback for the twenty-eight-year-old Caygill, who had battled an ulcer five years earlier that put him into a Yorkshire hospital and kept him off the golf course for nearly six months. The man from Cleckheaton had worked hard on his game all winter, and it paid off at the first big tournament of the 1969 season. (The fifty-six-year-old Rees was also in action at the Penfold Tournament, but it was what happened to him off the course that made news. A burglar broke into his Totteridge home through a French window and stole all of his golf trophies. Rees's sleeping wife didn't hear a thing.)

Bernard Hunt, a veteran of seven Great Britain Ryder Cup teams, was also singled out by Rees for his big-ball work. Hunt practiced diligently with the larger ball throughout the winter months and won springtime tournaments in Portugal and Italy—using the small ball. Hunt confirmed the conventional wisdom. The small ball was easier to play after putting in long work with the large ball.

Not mentioned by Rees were Tony Jacklin and Peter Townsend, who, along with Malcolm Gregson, were toiling on the PGA Tour in the spring of 1969, continuing their education on American golf—the big ball, the long courses, and the abundance of good players.

"The ball issue was not huge for me," Townsend later said. He did notice differences, though. The bigger golf ball was harder to putt. Chipping was easier. Looking back on the golf-ball evolution and switch, he said "the majority of professionals were happy when the R&A and USGA agreed to adopt use of the same golf ball and the USA-size golf ball became the standard."

Rees hoped the big ball wouldn't be a problem for the British team come September. "One thing is certain," he concluded in *Golf Monthly*. "If we are to have any chance of winning this year's Ryder Cup match at

Royal Birkdale, then those who are in the running for places in the team must eliminate from their thinking any doubts about their ability to play the larger ball."

After congratulating his successor, Eric Brown, on assuming the Ryder Cup captaincy, Rees said it was up to Brown's team members to meet the challenge of playing on British soil with the American ball. In typical Rees fashion, he closed with an inspiring thought. "And what a wonderful fillip it will be for British golf if we can beat the Americans in this country using THEIR size of ball!"

In truth, any win over the Yanks with any ball would surely drive Britons into a patriotic frenzy. To their dismay, Samuel Ryder's cherished Cup had been parked on the far side of the Atlantic for most of the last four decades.

—5—

JACKO

Jack Nicklaus was not on his game. Yes, he had won in San Diego in February, but since then, except for a pair of fourth-place ties at Doral and the Colonial National Invitation, his 1969 tournament record was uninspired as the U.S. Open approached. The disappointing results included a four-event stretch during which the Golden Bear finished in a tie for twenty-eighth in Jacksonville, missed the cut at the National Airlines Open in Miami, finished ten strokes behind winner George Archer at the Masters, and tied for thirty-sixth in Chicago at the Western Open, where he was the defending champion.

"As for Nicklaus," wrote Joe E. Doan midway through the 1969 season, "outside of his respectable showing in the Colonial, he may as well have been out of the country. Or, maybe he was."

"What's wrong with Jack Nicklaus?" was the perennial question on the lips and minds of sportswriters when Nicklaus went through a season without winning a major, and whenever other victories stopped piling up. It had been nearly two years since Nicklaus had won his last major title, the U.S. Open at Baltusrol in New Jersey, where he posted a 275 total that broke Ben Hogan's nineteen-year-old record by a shot. It had been three years since Nicklaus had slipped into his third Green Jacket on the 18th green at Augusta National Golf Club, the same season he also won his first British Open. There was a simple explanation for what was wrong with Jack in the late 1960s, as he later revealed in his autobiography. He was in a slump, a common occupational hazard for tour players, but a surprising development in a meteoric amateur and professional career that had drawn comparisons to the greatest golfers ever to play the game. After watching twenty-five-year-old Jack Nicklaus win the 1965 Masters in record-setting fashion, Augusta National Golf Club and Masters founder Bobby Jones, a lifelong amateur who amassed thirteen major wins, said Nicklaus "was playing a game with which I'm not familiar."

Other pros would have been elated to be in a slump that had produced six PGA Tour titles since the 1967 U.S. Open. This was Jack Nicklaus, though, a player who had won his first of two U.S. Amateurs at the age of nineteen, and who as a twenty-two-year-old tour rookie whipped Arnold Palmer in an 18-hole playoff at the 1962 U.S. Open in Palmer's western Pennsylvania backyard. Wins had multiplied at a rapid rate throughout Nicklaus's career, but so, too, had the myriad distractions that came with unrivaled success and commitment to family life, which Nicklaus made top priority when he married Barbara Bash. After family, golf came second, business third, and recreation fourth—fishing, hunting, and tennis, to name a few of Jack's favorite pastimes. By 1969, the great Nicklaus had reached a point in his career where his natural talent could no longer carry him to new, or perhaps the same, heights.

The son of a pharmacy owner in the Columbus, Ohio, suburb of Upper Arlington, Nicklaus said the rich-kid articles that popped up in his late amateur and early pro career were "bull." His family may have had a membership at prestigious Scioto Country Club, but they certainly were not wealthy on Charlie Nicklaus's $15,000 annual income. Young Jack understood the importance of hard work. Beginning at the age of ten, he channeled his energy into the game of golf, practicing and playing every day, often until dark, throughout the hot, muggy Ohio summer. Jack shot 51 for his first 9 holes, a harbinger of uncommon golf talent. At thirteen, he broke 70 at Scioto and overcame a mild case of polio. (His joints would ache off and on from that point forward.) Jack never went off to camp, and his family didn't take summer vacations, so it was golf, golf, and more golf. His regimen was to hit balls for an hour or two and play an 18-hole round. After a sandwich break, he returned to the practice range, followed by another 18 holes and pounding more balls or honing his short game until he ran out of daylight. Sometimes Jack made three full loops in a single day, a 54-hole expedition on foot with his carry bag slung over his shoulder. Other times the stocky teen spent all day at the driving range and hit hundreds of balls. Citing hardworking golf champions such as Ben Hogan, Sam Snead, Arnold Palmer, and Gary Player, Nicklaus said, "I was certainly in their league."

After the powerful young golfer had built a game that could fill trophy cases, he backed off the rigorous practice schedule. He still worked on his game, but only as required to maintain his precision or, if necessary, to correct a problem. There was no point expending the time and energy to beat balls all day long when he had come so far so fast, dominating golf at every level—high school, college, regional and national amateur events of all kinds, and, finally, the professional ranks. Still, by the mid-1960s, the game had begun to teach Jack Nicklaus an important lesson. He would not be able to coast through his professional years on his immense natural talent and by putting Band-Aids on a swing built with the help of Scioto club pro Jack Grout. The game that had come easily since the age of ten became hard in his mid- and late twenties.

"I . . . did not fully learn how difficult the game is until after I turned professional," Nicklaus said.

His motivation suffered as this sobering reality set in. In addition, demands on his time and energy placed limits on his practice schedule and adversely affected the quality of golf sessions. Weaknesses popped up in the Golden Bear's game. He was still unusually long off the tee, but not as straight. His putting was unpredictable—good one day, atrocious the next. Most alarming were the mental lapses. Nicklaus's concentration had always set him apart in tournament golf, the ability to think his way around the golf course and outperform competitors when the pressure was the greatest. With his sturdy golf mind and practice regimen in a weakened state, uncharacteristic mental mistakes creeped into his tournament rounds. It made him angry, which tended to perpetuate the problem.

"All in all, the game of golf over most of that period was not a lot of fun," Nicklaus later admitted.

After shooting 71-72-75-73—291 at Midlothian Country Club in the Western Open, a tepid title defense, Nicklaus might have wondered what kind of game he would have in Houston at Champions Golf Club, site of the 1969 U.S. Open.

•   •   •

Tony Jacklin was thinking about golf half the time. The other half he was thinking about his home in England. His house near Scunthorpe in Lincolnshire was undergoing renovations, and Jacklin's waking thoughts that spring on the PGA Tour often turned to home. His divided mind was not helping his golf, and it showed. Two weeks after missing the cut at the Masters, Jacklin missed another cut at the Byron Nelson Classic in Fort Worth. That was it. He needed a break.

"My concentration had been so bad recently that it has become pointless playing," Jacklin told *Golf Illustrated*'s Peter Willis.

It was a case of burnout. Despite his commitment to compete full-time on the PGA Tour, "Jacko," as Willis and other British scribes called him, was "sick and tired" of living in motels. It was also a case of homesickness. He missed England, so he and Vivien hopped on a plane to London and headed home for a rest from tournament golf. It did wonders. Jacklin took notice of things about English life that he had sorely missed while away—the lush green countryside, authentic fish and chips, and the relaxed pace in Lincolnshire. While his fellow British pros teed off at the Penfold Tournament, Jacko settled in at home for a respite from the hectic tour lifestyle in the States, a content man.

His golf game, he decided, was not in such bad shape, even though he was not enjoying the same results as the year before. Jacklin's only top 10 finish in 1969 was an eighth-place tie at Doral. Putting was partly to blame for his slow start. Long putts were not dropping into the hole with the same regularity. Tony also suspected that he might be pressing. With his win at Jacksonville and a twenty-ninth-place finish on the money list that made him an exempt player on the PGA Tour, 1968 had been a very successful year. Now he was trying to improve upon that impressive debut. Tony Jacklin wanted to be one of the game's best players.

Tony and Vivien's house wasn't the only thing being renovated. Although not yet fully incorporated, important changes to Jacklin's golf swing were in process. He had studied the leg action of American players— Tommy Bolt, Jack Nicklaus, Arnold Palmer, Bert Yancey, and Tom Weiskopf, in particular—and sought to adopt their technique. The method differed from how Jacklin learned to play the game in Great Britain, which was to strike the golf ball with a firm, or locked, left side. Playing conditions at home didn't help matters either.

"In Britain," Jacklin later said, "all those guys that I played with . . . were competitive but their swing techniques were less than perfect because they had the compromise of the weather. You were getting buffeted around in winds all the time."

Through observation and trial, he recognized the new leg action would unleash greater power. Better yet, working his legs in the new manner would allow for more control under tournament pressure, the ultimate win-win.

"I always had a tendency to be a little quick, especially under pressure. I knew I had to come get that controlled."

It was still many years before the era of full-time swing gurus on tour and detailed video analysis. Jacklin, mostly on his own, was seeking answers "in the dirt," as golf legend Ben Hogan had said. Although progressing, the move that could take his ball striking to a whole new level was still under construction.

While on his ten-day break in the north of England, Jacklin, perhaps influenced by the mental and physical strains of the PGA Tour season, said he would consider a different schedule in 1970. Upon further reflection about his golf game that spring, he told Willis, "Anyhow, it may well be that I come good later in the year."

·　　·　　·

The day following the premiere of *True Grit,* a Western movie that would do well at the box office and deliver his only Best Actor Oscar to film legend John Wayne, the 1969 U.S. Open teed off at Champions Golf Club outside of Houston. Deane Beman, a thirty-one-year-old short-game artist who had notched his first tour win at San Antonio a month earlier, led by a shot over first-round leader Bob Murphy and Miller Barber at the tournament's midway point. A small player who only averaged 233 yards off the tee, Beman recorded rounds of 68 and 69 for a 36-hole total of 137 on the long Champions layout. The man who would become the second commissioner of the PGA Tour had to use a wood on his approach shots to reach six par-4 holes. He also teed off with a wood on three of the course's four par 3s. It was no handicap for Beman because he regularly put his golf ball on the large greens and often sank putts.

Returning to the scene of the humiliating 23½–8½ loss in the 1967 Ryder Cup, Tony Jacklin got off to a solid start with rounds of 71 and 70. The trip home to England had rejuvenated Jacko and his golf game. He had played a few rounds with friends during the break and begun feeling better about his swing and putting. Good results followed a few weeks later in Chicago at the Western Open, where Jacklin finished in a fifth-place tie.

Tied with Jacklin at Champions after a 74 and a 67, Jack Nicklaus was also within 4 strokes of Beman's 36-hole lead. Arnold Palmer was 2 more shots back at 143. Defending champion Lee Trevino missed the cut. Nicknamed the "Merry Mex," Trevino appeared on the June 9 cover of *Sports Illustrated* wearing a black sombrero, a red bandanna, and with bandoliers crossed over his chest. U.S. Open champions Gene Littler and Ken Venturi also failed to qualify for the final 36 holes. Peter Townsend, playing in his first U.S. Open and the only British player besides Jacklin in the field, also missed the cut. Townsend was coming off his best finish on the PGA Tour, a fourth at the Western Open the preceding week, but Champions roughed up the young Englishman.

In the third round, while Beman slipped to a 73, Barber carded a 68 to take a 3-shot lead over former army sergeant Orville Moody into the final round. Mr. X faded on Sunday, though, shooting a dismal 78 that landed him in a tie for sixth place. The eleven-year tour veteran had also faded in the final round of the Masters in April. "Every time I get in a contending position, something happens," Barber said. "It looks like I can't win."

With no one making a move—Champions played tougher on Sunday, and the wind came up—Moody, a long-shot qualifier who was a sublime ball striker and lousy putter, emerged as the surprise winner. Trevino somehow foresaw the result. He picked the man nicknamed "Sarge" early in the week, saying, "He's one helluva player." It was Moody's first and last PGA Tour victory.

Lodged in a six-way tie for twenty-fifth 8 shots behind Moody's winning total of 1-over 281, both Nicklaus and Jacklin lost ground in the final two rounds.

Across the ocean on the same weekend Moody was crowned U.S. Open champion, Alex Caygill was celebrating his second win of the season on the British tour. Caygill came to the final hole of the Martini International needing a birdie to win outright, but he left his 15-foot putt short of the hole, resulting in a tie with South African Graham Henning. There was no playoff. The two players would share the title, unusual for tournament golf but not for the Martini, which also ended in a tie in 1963, 1966, and 1967.

Although Caygill was impressing onlookers with his pair of comeback victories, it was a young Scottish player who was attracting massive attention from British golf writers, and for good reason. Bernard Gallacher, barely twenty years old, had three wins (two of them in Zambia on the South African Tour) and had also collected a second, a third, and a fourth by the third week of May. The Bathgate native and former amateur star had banked £3,000 since January 1 and was the leading money winner on the British circuit with £1,125. Gallacher would visit the United States in the winter with his manager, Derrick Pillage, to play in the occasional event and receive advice from Julius Boros and Lee Trevino, both represented by the same agency. There would be no rushing the young star, Pillage said.

Golf Illustrated had seen enough of Gallacher to rush to its own verdict. The weekly golf publication could hardly contain its enthusiasm for the Scottish golf prodigy after he won the Schweppes Open in South Wales on May 18, the youngest player to capture a major British title since Gary Player won the 1956 Dunlop Tournament at the age of twenty years and five months. "Gallacher," wrote the magazine, "who has the face of a choir boy and a heart of a lion, has a bright future ahead before him." The magazine added Gallacher to its editorial staff, and his first byline appeared the same week Orville Moody surprised the golf world with his U.S. Open win in Houston.

As the PGA Tour traveled to Charlotte, North Carolina, for the Kemper Open Invitational, where Dale Douglass would win his second title of the season, both of them coming in the Tar Heel state, the British circuit headed to Parkstone, the home course of Peter Alliss, for the Pains Wessex Tournament. The run-up to the world's oldest golf championship had begun. The ninety-eighth British Open, to be played at Royal Lytham & St. Annes Golf Club, was less than a month away.

•   ·   •

Keith Mackenzie of the Royal and Ancient Golf Club received the cable more than a week ahead of the championship. It read: "Dear Mr. Mackenzie, I regret very much that I will be unable to participate in the Open Championship this year and request that my entry be withdrawn." The sender was Arnold Palmer.

Palmer, one of the few players to win the British Open in consecutive years (1961 and 1962), had not won a tournament during the 1969 season; nor had he performed particularly well at Royal Lytham & St. Annes the last time the Open had been played there in 1963, finishing in a tie for twenty-sixth. It had been five years since his last major victory at the 1964 Masters, his fourth Green Jacket, and some questioned whether Palmer's inner drive had stalled.

"Obviously he has great difficulty in summoning enduring concentration," wrote Pat Ward-Thomas in *The Guardian* about Palmer's withdrawal from the British Open, "not to mention the depth of his desire that once drove him to the heights."

Palmer's subpar year had another implication—he was in jeopardy of not making his fifth consecutive Ryder Cup team.

Former champions Palmer and Nicklaus aside, Americans not turning up for the British Open was common during the era. Few Yanks made the trip. There were several reasons why they stayed home. Once U.S. (and other) players arrived in the British Isles, they had to play in qualifying tournaments to earn a spot in the field, a significant challenge in itself. In addition, playing overseas was a foreign expedition in almost every conceivable way—the food, the accommodations, and the golf, which was played with the smaller British ball on windswept links courses, sometimes in foul weather.

There was another critical factor, as Raymond Floyd explained. "There wasn't any money over there at all. I guess you might have broke even if you won, but it was an expense to go to the British Open just to play golf, the time and the travel. So American players didn't go there and their players didn't come to the U.S."

For most U.S. players, the payout, if there was one, didn't justify the cost. Why play in the British Open in mid-July when you could drive from

Michigan to Minnesota and tee it up in the Minnesota Golf Classic for a $100,000 purse? That's where Frank Beard would be playing as Jack Nicklaus, Billy Casper, and Lee Trevino clashed with a field of British and international players in Lancashire, England. Beard's chances of winning in Minnesota were far better with the biggest U.S. guns out of the country. Besides Beard, there were scant top money winners in the Minnesota Golf Classic field—Tommy Aaron, Dan Sikes, and Dave Stockton, to name a few.

Despite the many drawbacks of the overseas adventure, there was still a notable, if small, U.S. contingent at Royal Lytham & St. Annes. In addition to Nicklaus, Casper, and Trevino, American entries included 1967 Masters champion Gay Brewer, current Masters champion George Archer, current U.S. Open champion Orville Moody, Raymond Floyd, Miller Barber, Bert Yancey, Gardner Dickinson, and Davis Love Jr.

Eager to vie for the Claret Jug, the best players from Great Britain and Ireland were also on hand: Christy O'Connor, Peter Alliss, Neil Coles, Tommy Horton, Eric Brown, Brian Huggett, Peter Townsend, Bernard Hunt, Alex Caygill, Brian Barnes, Guy Wolstenholme, Peter Butler, and the last Brit to win the Open Championship, Max Faulkner, who prevailed at Royal Portrush Golf Club in Northern Ireland in 1951. For most of these players, the Open was their only major championship because few of them traveled to the States to play in the Masters, U.S. Open, or PGA Championship.

Not so for Tony Jacklin, who also was on the scene at Royal Lytham & St. Annes. Jacklin had missed the cut at the Masters, had tied for twenty-fifth at the U.S. Open, and would play in the PGA Championship in August. He was the rare Brit who teed it up with the world's best players in all four of golf's majors. How would he fare in his sixth British Open? His putting had troubled him throughout the season, but his revamped golf swing with new leg action and controlled tempo had rounded into form. Jacklin had two recent fifth-place finishes on the PGA Tour, including the Kemper Open Invitational. Despite his commitment to playing in America, it felt good to be back in England playing in front of his countrymen.

"I could literally feel their support," Jacklin later said. "It was a palpable, physical presence, and made me feel valued."

Top players from Australia, South Africa, New Zealand, and Argentina also filled the Open field: five-time champion Peter Thomson, two-time and defending champion Gary Player, 1967 champion Roberto De Vicenzo, 1963 champion Bob Charles, 1960 champion Kel Nagle, Bruce Devlin, and Harold Henning.

The only course in the British Open rotation to begin with a par-3 hole, Royal Lytham & St. Annes Golf Club would be a strong test. Surrounded by houses and bordered by a railway line, the par-71, 6,848-yard layout was considered to be a true links course influenced by weather and buffeted by winds despite being situated a half mile from the Irish Sea. It was tough, with a difficult closing stretch of par 4s. Famed English golf writer Bernard Darwin called Lytham "a beast of a course, but a just beast." On the eve of the championship, *The Guardian*'s Eddie Musty suggested a successful playing style for the beast. "The course favours the long, accurate driver who draws the ball and who pitches and putts boldly."

The 1969 British Open showcased innovations. Leaderboards erected throughout the course displayed the scores of the top 10 players. Closed-circuit television projected on large screens allowed spectators to watch tournament action as it took place on the course. There was another exciting development: For the first time, the BBC broadcast the Open Championship in color.

New Zealander Charles, who had won his Open the last time it visited Lytham in 1963, opened on Wednesday with a course-record 66 to take the lead. The southpaw called it one of the best rounds of his life. Beginning with four birdies in the first six holes, Jacklin carded a 68 and was tied for second with fellow Englishman Hedley Muscroft. Barber was low American with a 69. Charles continued to set the pace with a 69 in the second round that gave him a 36-hole total of 135. Irishman O'Connor fired a 65 to break Charles's one-day course record and move within 1 shot of the halfway lead. Jacklin shot a steady 70 to trail by 3 strokes.

Charles faltered in Friday's third round. Poor driving resulted in a 75. With another 70, Jacklin moved to the top of the leaderboard. He was putting well, and his bunker play "seemed magical." Four times during the third round Jacklin got up and in from greenside bunkers for pars. He would take a 2-shot lead over Charles and O'Connor into the final round. Three other British Open champions were lurking. De Vicenzo (66) and Thomson (70) were 3 back. Nicklaus, the 1966 winner at Muirfield, was within 5 after a 68. Welshman Brian Huggett was tied with the Golden Bear.

On the cusp of achieving his dream of winning the Open, Jacklin anticipated a long and fitful Friday night. So he swallowed a sleeping pill and fell asleep watching a movie with wife Vivien and tour pal Bert Yancey, who, at 214, trailed by 6 strokes. Yancey carried the 54-hole leader up the stairs and put him in bed beside his wife. A well-rested Jacklin awoke at 9:00 A.M. and faced the frightening dual reality of leading the Open and a seven-hour wait until his final-round tee time. Slowly, agonizingly, the time passed, and Jacklin arrived at the first tee for his 2:00 P.M. pairing with Charles and, hopefully, destiny.

The leader got off to a wonderful start. Birdies at the 3rd and 4th holes widened the margin to 5 shots, but he gave 1 back with a bogey at the 5th. Jacklin held steady, and Charles was unable to further cut into the lead until making a birdie at 10. The gap was 3 strokes with 8 holes to go. No one else was mounting a charge.

On the tee of the short par-4 13th hole, Charles discovered the binding on his persimmon driver had come undone. Not wanting a long delay, the former assistant pro and club repairman at Potters Bar offered to help. Jacklin rethreaded the whipping on Charles's driver, tied it off, and, borrowing a pocketknife from a spectator, trimmed the excess. On they went.

Jacklin owned a 3-shot lead when he reached the 17th hole, but he took 3 putts—his first 3-putt green of the championship—and made a bogey. His lead had shrunk to 2 shots with 1 hole to play. Moments later the Englishman and the New Zealander arrived at the home hole. The large British gallery was electric, anticipating the end of an eighteen-year victory drought.

Charles hit first and deposited his golf ball into the right-hand rough. Jacklin, trusting the new swing, drilled a driver that split the 18th fairway. Understated Henry Longhurst could not contain himself. "What a corker!" exclaimed the BBC TV announcer. "My word, that was a fine drive. Look at it! Miles up the middle." Jacklin would call his final tee shot in the 1969 Open "one of the best of my life." In recent years, he said, "That was a real test, actually, for my new swing, as it were. I got by then to control the speed of my swing."

All Jacklin had to do was hold on to the club—and his shoe. From a perfect 7-iron distance, he hit his second shot onto the green. As he walked through the excited crowd that rushed onto the 18th fairway, an Open tradition, someone stepped on his heel and his left shoe came off. He slipped it back on but left the lace untied until nearly reaching the green. Charles missed his birdie attempt, allowing Jacklin 3 putts from 12 feet to claim a historic win. Clad in matching lavender sweater and slacks, Jacklin nearly sank the birdie and then carefully tapped in from less than an inch away. Tony raised his arms in triumph and threw his Dunlop 65 golf ball into the appreciative gallery. He was the Open champion.

A short while later Jack Nicklaus appeared and congratulated the winner.

"I said to him I couldn't believe I could be that nervous and still play," Jacklin later said.

Nicklaus put his arm round the first-time major winner. "I know, isn't it great?" Nicklaus replied, as Jacklin recalled.

During the trophy ceremony, as the twenty-five-year-old Briton stood at the microphone, spectators sang "For He's a Jolly Good Fellow."

The press and headline writers heralded the truck driver's son from Scunthorpe:

AT LAST, OUR VERY OWN OPEN CHAMPION (*The Observer*)

TONY THE GREAT (*Golf Illustrated*)

THE NEW TONY JACKLIN (*Golf Monthly*)

JACKLIN—CONQUERING HERO! (*The Observer*)

JACKLIN ON OPEN ROAD TO GOLD (*The Guardian*)

HAIL KING TONY (*Golf World*)

For his historic victory, Jacklin received a check for £4,250 ($10,200). In the upper Midwest, Frank Beard cruised through Sunday's back 9 to win the Minnesota Golf Classic, worth nearly twice that amount—$20,000— illustrating the oceanic divide between golf's oldest championship and a run-of-the-mill stop on the PGA Tour. Nevertheless, Tony Jacklin had his name etched on the Claret Jug and received the worldwide acclaim that went with it, including the adulation of a proud empire. The greatest moment of his life, as Jacko called it, was also a turning point in his life. Nearly everything was about to change.

•　　•　　•

Within days of Tony Jacklin's victory came the announcement of six players earning spots on the Great Britain Ryder Cup team: Christy O'Connor, Brian Huggett, Peter Butler, Peter Townsend, Neil Coles, and Brian Barnes. As the top six points holders in the British PGA Order of Merit, the half-dozen men automatically qualified for the 1969 team. The other six players would be discretionary picks to be made by Captain Eric Brown and two helpers, O'Connor and former captain Dai Rees. One pick would surely be the new British Open champion. Jacklin had spent most of the 1968 and 1969 seasons competing in America, forgoing British tournaments and their corresponding points opportunities that determined standings in the Order of Merit.

The twelve players for the U.S. team, based entirely on a points system (no captain's picks), would be finalized after the PGA Championship.

•   •   •

In mid-August, a month after the euphoria at the British Open in Lancashire, England, civil rights demonstrators threatened the PGA Championship in Dayton, Ohio. *Professional Golfer* later reported that a spokesman for the demonstraters submitted twenty-three demands to the sponsoring chamber of commerce, which included declaring the birthdays of Martin Luther King Jr. and Malcolm X national holidays and providing three thousand free tickets to allow poor people to attend the championship. They apparently got nowhere. The protesters would soon turn their focus to Gary Player, a native of South Africa, an apartheid state with a rigid system of racial segregation.

A field of 139 players teed off at the National Cash Register Country Club, a hilly, wooded, par-71 layout with numerous doglegs. Nine players were tied for the lead at 69 after the first round. Arnold Palmer shot an 82 and withdrew.

"I love to play golf, but I just can't go on playing like this," Palmer said in the locker room. Suffering with inflamed bursitis in his right hip, Arnold needed to fly home, talk to his doctors, and rest the ailing hip—perhaps until the start of the 1970 season.

One of the nine players who opened with a 69, Raymond Floyd fired a 66 on Friday to take a 1-shot lead over Player at the midpoint of the year's final major. Jack Nicklaus and Orville Moody trailed by 3 strokes after 68s.

The plot thickened in the third round as protesters infiltrated Saturday's gallery of more than 20,000 people. So did three hundred uniformed and plainclothes policemen. The main target of the protesters was the South African golf superstar, Player. The first sign of trouble was on the 8th tee. While Player was preparing to hit, a protester threw a program that landed at the South African's feet. Then as he and playing partner Nicklaus were walking from the 9th green to the 10th tee, someone threw a cup of ice at Player. A short while later a few men charged toward the 10th green. One picked up Nicklaus's golf ball and threw it. Another

71

stomped through a bunker heading in the direction of the Golden Bear. Raising his putter, Nicklaus assumed a defensive posture. Police tussled with the demonstrators and took them away.

The episodes rattled Nicklaus. "I just wanted off the golf course," he said. He made a triple bogey on the last hole for a 74, announcing, "I'm out of it now." Player fought through the adversity. At the 13th, a woman rolled a plastic golf ball onto the green as he was getting ready to putt. He proceeded to sink the 12-footer for a birdie and went on to shoot an even-par 71, a remarkable score under the circumstances. "That was the toughest round I've ever played," Player said.

Floyd, meanwhile, shot a 67 to build a 5-stroke lead heading into the final round. It almost wasn't enough. The tenacious small man who had ice thrown at him and received death threats shot a 1-under 70 on Sunday. Player was escorted through the final 18 holes by six large deputies. Floyd's 74 nipped the determined South African by 1. It was Floyd's second victory in three weeks—he won the American Golf Classic at Firestone Country Club in late July—and third title of the season.

The four majors had produced four first-time major winners—George Archer, Orville Moody, Tony Jacklin, and Raymond Floyd. It was the first time in a dozen years that none of the Big Three (Palmer, Nicklaus, Player) had won a major championship. Only two of the new quartet of major champions—Jacklin for Great Britain and Floyd for the United States—would play in the Ryder Cup at Royal Birkdale, a month away.

The two twelve-man teams were set, but there were still a few more tournaments with attractive purses on the PGA Tour schedule before the U.S. players and their captain, Sam Snead, departed for England. National pride could wait. Besides, the United States had possessed the Ryder Cup for all but two of the previous thirty-four years. In the summer of 1969, there was little reason to think Samuel Ryder's trophy would change hands.

—6—

THE TEAMS

As the summer days grew shorter, twenty-four players and two nonplaying captains representing their respective nations prepared to depart for Southport, England, for the eighteenth playing of the Ryder Cup.

It wasn't merely another golf tournament during a long season that had begun for many of the players in January or February. These men would be competing as a team rather than as individuals, playing for their captain and country rather than for prestige and money. The matches still mattered, even to the Americans, who had waltzed through all but three of the seventeen Ryder Cups dating back to 1927, the same year Charles Lindbergh made the first solo nonstop transatlantic flight in a single-engine monoplane called *Spirit of St. Louis.* Six weeks earlier, eight days after Tony Jacklin captured the Claret Jug, Apollo 11 astronaut Neil Armstrong was the first man to walk on the moon. "It's good country for golf up here," Armstrong said. "You could drive a ball 2,000 feet."

For the Americans, especially the ten Ryder Cup rookies, Southport was plenty far enough to go for a game of golf. They would fly to England in a Pan Am jet airliner—and in the confident hope they would return home in possession of the Ryder Cup trophy. Great Britain, on the other hand, was in no mood for another goodwill match that ended in another loss. Led by their fiery captain, Eric Brown, they were in the mood for a fight, a fight that, this time, they believed they could win.

· · ·

1969 GREAT BRITAIN RYDER CUP TEAM

"This team," wrote Pat Ward-Thomas in *The Guardian,* "is probably as strong as British golf can muster, and must be one of the youngest ever." Of the seven team members with Ryder Cup experience, only Christy O'Connor was over forty. The five rookies were, indeed, youngsters. Alex Caygill was the only first-timer over the age of twenty-four. Seven of the twelve players shared a first name: There were three Peters, two Brians, and two Bernards. Half of the players automatically qualified for the team by occupying the first six places in the Order of Merit. The other six were chosen by a committee of three: current captain Eric Brown, former captain Dai Rees, and Ryder Cup veteran and Order of Merit leader Christy O'Connor.

Picking half of the twelve-man team was arguably the most important job for Brown and his lieutenants. The generous number of picks was intentional. Tony Jacklin was ranked ninety-second in the Order of Merit because he spent nearly all of his time playing in the United States. It would be absurd to leave the new Open champion and Great Britain's best player off the Ryder Cup team. The picks, in theory, afforded the captain and his men maximum flexibility for assembling the strongest team. Besides Jacklin, the chosen players were Alex Caygill, Bernard Gallacher, Maurice Bembridge, Peter Alliss, and Bernard Hunt.

"There were a number of young players under consideration," Alliss said decades later, "but I was only thirty-eight years of age and a very experienced Ryder Cup player. Although I was having problems with my putting, I had played pretty well that year. I would have been surprised if I had not been chosen particularly as I had done well four years before when the matches were played at Birkdale."

Not all of Great Britain was satisfied with the selection method and the picks. A member of the 1967 team, Malcolm Gregson thought discretionary picks should be kept to a minimum, two at most. He also disagreed with basing the automatic selections on the previous year's Order of Merit because it wasn't a reliable measure of a player's current form. "In the Ryder Cup a man's future livelihood is at stake," said Gregson, who believed he would return to the team but had played in his only Ryder Cup.

Of the six picks, Hunt's selection was likely subject to the most scrutiny. The seven-time Ryder Cupper was outside the top 12 in the Order of Merit, whereas Tommy Horton stood in the ninth spot and had tied for eleventh in the British Open. Horton had made a solid case, but Hunt was presumably chosen for his experience. He had played a total of twenty-six matches in his seven appearances, second only to teammate Alliss. Some, however, including at least one letter writer in *Golf Illustrated*, thought Horton had earned a spot on the team. Mrs. R. Anderson of Selby, Yorks, expected Horton to be a "certain selection" and called his omission "a rough deal." Another letter writer called the selection process "very strange and weird" and suggested that it would "make the Americans think we are very amateurish."

Peter Dobereiner, Ward-Thomas's colleague at *The Guardian*, said the survival of the current selection system depended on what happened at Royal Birkdale. "Winning will be the complete justification, of course." Ward-Thomas offered a cautious endorsement of the twelve men who would carry the fragile golf hopes of a nation. "The side may give a far better account of itself than many people imagine."

Following are short profiles of Captain Brown and the twelve players on his 1969 team.

ERIC BROWN, CAPTAIN
Fifth Appearance

Brown, forty-four, nicknamed "the Brown Bomber," played on four consecutive Great Britain Ryder Cup teams from 1953 to 1959. During a postwar period when Great Britain was losing to the United States with regularity, Brown posted a respectable 4-4-0 record, including a perfect record in singles play. In head-to-head competition, the Scot beat Lloyd Mangrum, Jerry Barber, Tommy Bolt, and Cary Middlecoff. On this occasion at Royal Birkdale, Brown would serve as Britain's nonplaying captain for the first time. "If sheer determination is enough to win the Ryder Cup for the first time since 1957," read the official program for the 1969 matches, "then Great Britain has it in plenty both in the captain and in the team."

PETER ALLISS
Eighth Appearance

Alliss, thirty-eight, rallied in the summer of 1969 to make his eighth consecutive Ryder Cup team. A 66 vaulted Alliss to an eighth-place finish at the British Open. The following week the tour veteran defeated former Ryder Cup teammate George Will in a final that went 37 holes to capture the Piccadilly Medal, Alliss's first win in two years. Alliss was the famous son of a famous father. Percy Alliss was a four-time Ryder Cup player who made his final appearance in 1937. When twenty-two-year-old Peter appeared in his first Ryder Cup sixteen years later, they became the first father and son to have competed in the international matches. With a 10-13-4 record during a span of American dominance, Alliss was the points leader on the British side, a respected match-play competitor who, in singles, had beaten U.S. Open champions Arnold Palmer, Billy Casper, and Ken Venturi, the latter two on the same day. Alliss always seemed to produce his best golf when the Union Jack traveled up the flag pole.

BRIAN BARNES

Rookie

Barnes, twenty-four, standing over 6' tall and weighing nearly 200 pounds, was described as the giant and longest hitter of the twelve-man squad. With his maiden victory at the 1969 Agfa-Gevaert Tournament at Stoke Poges, Barnes, born in Surrey, England, but representing Scotland, had gotten the monkey off his back. A string of high finishes without a win in the previous two years had put increasing pressure on the son-in-law of 1951 British Open champion Max Faulkner. Barnes credited his success, in part, to *The Power of Positive Thinking*, a bestselling book by American pastor Dr. Norman Vincent Peale. A second win for Barnes would come later in the 1969 season at the Coca-Cola Young Professionals tournament, a play-off triumph over Ryder Cup teammate Bernard Gallacher.

MAURICE BEMBRIDGE

Rookie

Bembridge, twenty-four, was a globetrotter whose forays to South Africa, Asia, Australia, and New Zealand had accelerated his rise in British golf. The humorous nine-year pro from Worksop won the 1968 Kenya Open. With a solo fifth at Carnoustie, Bembridge also recorded the highest finish of any British player at the 1968 British Open. More success followed in 1969 as he successfully defended his Kenya title and teamed with Angel Gallardo to win the Sumrie Better-Ball Tournament. He would go on to notch another 1969 victory at the *News of the World* Match Play. Bembridge was looking forward to his Ryder Cup debut. "It was one of the first things I had in mind," he said, "and I am very grateful to be in it this year."

PETER BUTLER

Second Appearance

Butler, thirty-seven, born in Birmingham, England, was coming off his most productive season in more than two decades as a professional. In 1968, Butler collected three wins on the British circuit and one across the

English Channel—the French Open near Paris. Fellow English pro Clive Clark compared Butler's game to Australian great Peter Thomson, saying, "[Butler] hits it very straight and has a sharp short game." That short game was aided by a "lucky" putter Butler acquired many years earlier in Bombay. Butler co-led the 1966 Masters at the halfway mark before finishing in a tie for thirteenth. At the 1965 Ryder Cup, also played at Royal Birkdale, Butler lost three matches and halved two, taking Arnold Palmer and Tony Lema to the final hole of singles matches before losing.

ALEX CAYGILL
Rookie

Caygill, twenty-nine, a close friend of Tony Jacklin's from the early days when they traveled together, made a comeback in 1969. A promising pro career that began in 1962 and included a win at the 1963 Rediffusion Tournament was interrupted by what was termed "nerves" followed by stomach ulcers. "I used to worry a lot in those days and drove myself too hard," Caygill said. He left the game for six months after an ulcer put him in the hospital. The Appleby native recovered and returned to golf, posting top 20 finishes at the British Open in 1964 and 1966. In 1969, Caygill had won twice—at the Penfold Tournament and the Martini International (a tie with Graham Henning). Caygill's hard-earned form had put him on the Ryder Cup team for the first time.

NEIL COLES
Fifth Appearance

Coles, thirty-four, described as "a natural player with a flair for the big occasion," had played on every British Ryder Cup team since 1961. Except for Peter Alliss, Coles had posted the best British record during the period: seven wins, ten losses, and three halves. The London-born pro was not a big winner—he had not won since collecting two victories in 1966—but was a steady player whose name consistently rose to the top of tournament leaderboards. Coles's considerable Ryder Cup experience, including a proven ability under pressure, was regarded as a strong asset to Brown's squad. In addition, Coles was especially fond of Royal Birkdale, where in the 1965 Ryder Cup he teamed with Bernard Hunt to win two matches and also beat Billy Casper in singles.

BERNARD GALLACHER
Rookie

Gallacher, twenty, which made him the youngest man ever to play on a Great Britain Ryder Cup team, was causing a stir in British golf. The dark-haired Scot looked innocent enough, but he played with an inner resolve that betrayed his years. Thanks to two wins in South Africa and two wins (the Schweppes Open and W. D. and H. O. Wills Open) and three runner-up finishes on the British tour, 1969 was a breakout season for the third-year pro from Bathgate. A long hitter despite a slight 5'9" frame, Gallacher would finish the year at the top of the Order of Merit (Britain's official PGA money list) and also capture the Harry Vardon Trophy for lowest stroke average. Great Britain's young lion was ready to bring his bold play to Royal Birkdale, later describing himself as "confident but not cocky" as a player columnist for *Golf Illustrated.*

BRIAN HUGGETT
Third Appearance

Huggett, thirty-two, was small in stature but a tenacious competitor, which earned him the nickname "Welsh Bulldog." The 5'6" native of Porthcawl, Wales, won three titles in 1968 on his way to topping the Order of Merit. In 1969, Huggett edged Gallacher to win the Daks Tournament and shared victory with Tony Grubb at the Bowmaker Tournament. Huggett's first Ryder Cup was the 1963 matches in Atlanta. The Welsh Bulldog teamed with George Will to defeat the U.S. duo of Arnold Palmer and Johnny Pott in the opening match. Huggett also bested Pott in singles on the final day. After sitting out the 1965 matches, Huggett played on the 1967 British squad that suffered one of the worst defeats in Ryder Cup history.

Nonetheless, Huggett had won 4 points out of a possible 10 in his two Ryder Cup appearances, a respectable showing during an era of U.S. superiority.

BERNARD HUNT
Eighth Appearance

Hunt, thirty-nine, began his Ryder Cup play at Wentworth in 1953. After one interruption in 1955, the tall Englishman made six consecutive appearances, including Great Britain's lone postwar victory at Lindrick in 1957. With a 6-15-5 record, Hunt had borne the brunt of Britain's dark Ryder Cup years. Hunt, who won the Algarve Open in Portugal in April 1969, was at his best in singles competition. He beat Doug Ford in 1957, Jerry Barber in 1961, Dow Finsterwald in 1963, and Gene Littler in 1965 and halved matches with Bobby Nichols and Julius Boros at Champions in 1967. Known for his three-quarters swing, Hunt recorded several high finishes during the 1969 season in the lead-up to Royal Birkdale.

TONY JACKLIN
Second Appearance

Jacklin, twenty-five, fresh off his British Open victory that seemingly sent all of the British Isles into a tizzy, nearly rivaled Her Majesty Queen Elizabeth II in popularity in the summer of 1969. The first Englishman to win the Claret Jug since Max Faulkner in 1951, Jacklin pointed to his two seasons in America as the reason for his transformation into a world-class player. In early 1968, a few months after joining the PGA Tour, the man from Scunthorpe won the Jacksonville Open, making him the first British pro to win an important title in the United States in nearly a half century. Posting a 2-3-1 record in the 1967 Ryder Cup in Houston, Jacklin made an impressive debut in a lopsided loss. As the 1969 Ryder Cup approached, Captain Eric Brown expected great things from Great Britain's new and brightest golf star.

CHRISTY O'CONNOR SR.

Eighth Appearance

O'Connor, forty-four, the oldest player on either team and the lone Irishman, was continuing a Ryder Cup run that began in 1955 at Thunderbird Ranch & Country Club in Palm Springs. He and Peter Alliss were the most seasoned Ryder Cup players on the British side. In twenty-three matches, the Galway native had built a record of 7-15-1. All but 2 of his points had come on British soil. O'Connor was regarded as one of the game's best bad-weather players; despite his advanced golf age, he was still a force in 1969. Although winless, the Irishman was a serious contender at the British Open after a record-breaking 65 in the second round. He finished fifth. Royal Birkdale would be welcome ground for O'Connor, where in 1968 he won the Alcan International.

PETER TOWNSEND

Rookie

Townsend, twenty-two, a Cambridge-born amateur standout who turned pro in 1966, had devoted himself to the PGA Tour for the majority of the 1968 and 1969 seasons. Often mired in Monday qualifiers, Townsend found the going much tougher in America than Tony Jacklin. He fought on after temporarily losing his PGA Tour card to record top 5 finishes at the Western Open and the Greater Milwaukee Open. In 1968, Townsend returned to England from the PGA Tour and raced to the top of the Order of Merit after wins at the Coca-Cola Young Professionals tournament and the Piccadilly PGA Close Championship. He also had a runner-up finish to American Gay Brewer at the Alcan Golfer of the Year Championship. The team's second-youngest member, Townsend had strong playing credentials that boded well for his first appearance. "I was just thrilled to be on the Ryder Cup team," he said in 2012.

• • •

1969 U.S. RYDER CUP TEAM

On the opposite side of the Atlantic, if there was any concern about the composition of the U.S. team, including its ten rookies, it was muted. The PGA of America used a points system to determine all twelve players, end of story. Captain Sam Snead had no picks, so there was no lengthy deliberation or serious debate about his team, if anyone was even paying much attention. Many observers might have figured any twelve U.S. players would do. Snead and company would win—just as they had in twelve of the last thirteen Ryder Cups.

Following are the final points standings.

1969 U.S. RYDER CUP TEAM POINTS STANDINGS

1.	Frank Beard	429.85
2.	Raymond Floyd	355.68
3.	Billy Casper	347.84
4.	Lee Trevino	337.34
5.	Jack Nicklaus	325.03
6.	Dave Hill	292.81
7.	Tommy Aaron	278.85
8.	Gene Littler	257.80
9.	Dan Sikes	247.88
10.	Miller Barber	242.01
11.	Ken Still	237.20
12.	Dale Douglass	223.61

Noticeably absent was Arnold Palmer, a veteran of four Ryder Cup teams. Palmer had finished a distant fifteenth on the list. Still, the points system was an efficient and equitable way to identify the top U.S. players. There could be no hand-wringing over picks since there were none.

"The teams were not easy to make because you had to finish in the top 10 [in tournaments] to acquire any points toward making the team," recalled Tommy Aaron. Victories, especially majors, racked up a lot of points.

It was a system that produced competition-hardened players, even if they were a bunch of Ryder Cup rookies. Despite being heavily stocked with rookies, the U.S. team, on average, was nearly three years older than their British opponents. Masters winner George Archer and U.S. Open champion Orville Moody didn't make the squad. Turning pro in 1967, Moody wasn't eligible. Archer didn't earn enough points.

Clearly, the twelve U.S. players and their captain had strong golf credentials:

SAM SNEAD, CAPTAIN
Eighth Appearance
Snead, nicknamed "Slammin' Sam" and "the Slammer," had competed in the Ryder Cup in 1937, 1947, 1949, 1951, 1953, 1955, and 1959, more appearances than any other American. Still active and competitive at the age of fifty-seven, Snead would be captain for the second time, but this time he wouldn't play. In 1959, Snead was a playing captain at Eldorado in California, where the United States team won 8½–3½. The golfer *Sports Illustrated* said wore his trademark straw hat "with more aplomb than any other man alive" knew about links golf after a handful of Ryder Cups and British Opens, one of which he won, the 1946 Open at St. Andrews. There was nothing to suggest the Slammer was concerned about the upcoming skirmish at Royal Birkdale.

TOMMY AARON
Rookie
Aaron, thirty-two, was coming off his first tour win at the Canadian Open, an 18-hole playoff victory over his esteemed captain, Sam Snead. It had been a long time coming for the lanky, bespectacled Georgian, who played collegiate golf alongside Frank Beard at the University of Florida. Aaron was "thrilled" to make the team "because that was one of my goals."

Possessing a "silky-smooth" golf swing that struck shots with "an authoritative ease," the 1959 Walker Cup player (he competed at Muirfield along with teammate Jack Nicklaus) and runner-up in the 1958 U.S. Amateur had piled up second-place finishes and won a considerable share of the growing tournament purses since joining the PGA Tour in 1960. Still more was expected from the mild-mannered Ryder Cup rookie. Teammate Lee Trevino, for one, predicted great things from Aaron.

MILLER BARBER

Rookie

Barber, thirty-eight, had collected one win in each of the last three PGA Tour seasons coupled with sizable checks for his consistent high finishes. The Shreveport, Louisiana, native was the 54-hole leader at the 1969 U.S. Open before finishing in a tie for sixth. A bachelor who got his "Mr. X" nickname because players never knew his off-course whereabouts, Barber had one of the most unusual golf swings on tour. It included a loop on the backswing that looked "like a man opening an umbrella in the wind." The swing remarks didn't bother the stocky veteran. "The downswing is all that matters," he would say.

FRANK BEARD

Rookie

Beard, thirty, collected his seventh and eighth PGA Tour wins during the 1969 season, including the lucrative Westchester Classic in August, which helped propel him to the money title. A family man who looked more like an accountant than a golfer, Beard turned pro in 1962 after being named a two-time All American at the University of Florida. He fell into a coma for three days in 1964 after contracting encephalitis and was given his last rites by a Catholic priest. After his recovery, Beard refused to be considered for the Ben Hogan Award, saying he did nothing. "I just got well." The son of a former golf pro, and the half brother of an All-American basketball player at the University of Kentucky, Beard was keeping a diary during the 1969 season that would become *Pro: Frank Beard on the Golf Tour*, a first-of-its-kind tour memoir created with sportswriter Dick Schaap.

BILLY CASPER

Fifth Appearance

Casper, thirty-eight, had played on every U.S. Ryder Cup team since 1961 at Royal Lytham & St. Annes in England. With a 12-3-4 record coming into the 1969 matches, Casper was a formidable match-play competitor. A devout Mormon who spoke at religious gatherings as he traveled on tour, Billy had won twice in 1969 after a phenomenal 1968 campaign during which he captured six titles and led the money list with $205,168. He earned his nickname of "Buffalo Bill" because of an unusual diet that included buffalo steaks, honey, and other specialty foods that allowed him to shed fifty pounds from his 5'11" frame in the months leading up to his win at the 1966 U.S. Open. The genius of the two-time U.S. Open champion was most evident in his short game. Hall of Famer Johnny Miller would say, "Billy has the greatest pair of hands God ever gave a human being."

DALE DOUGLASS

Rookie

Douglass, thirty-three, often a Monday qualifier during a PGA Tour career that began in 1963, was having a breakthrough season in 1969. The tall, rail-thin journeyman—"so lean he casts a shadow like a placement pin," said one writer—collected his first two tour wins, the Azalea Open, a satellite event played opposite the Tournament of Champions, and the Kemper Open Invitational. Both victories came in the state of North Carolina. An Oklahoma native who resided in Denver, Colorado, the shy Douglass was an excellent ball striker with a distinctive upright golf swing.

RAYMOND FLOYD

Rookie

Floyd, twenty-seven, a fun-loving tour pro with vast potential, was in the midst of his best season in a six-year PGA Tour career. The bushy-haired bachelor with a deep affection for women and champagne picked up wins at the Greater Jacksonville Open and the American Golf Classic before claiming his first major title, the PGA Championship in Dayton, Ohio. Harboring dreams of a pro baseball career in his youth, Ray, as he was called on tour, was a passionate Chicago Cubs fan who occasionally worked out with the team. In spite of his partying ways—once when asked the color of his eyes, he said, "They're usually pretty red"—the son of a career army man had set lofty goals for the 1969 season: win $100,000, win a major, and earn a spot on the Ryder Cup team. The talented Floyd achieved all three.

DAVE HILL

Rookie

Hill, thirty-two, a dark-haired, slender pro who stood a shade under 6' tall, had a fine golf swing, a quick temper, and a biting tongue. The ten-year tour veteran was famous for his tantrums and moodiness, which sometimes resulted in fines and suspensions, such as the one-week suspension and $250 fine Hill received in March of 1969 for abusing a tour official because of a ruling. The Michigan native collected three titles during the 1969 season, in Memphis, Grand Blanc (Michigan), and Philadelphia, and by year's end would finish as runner-up to Frank Beard on the money list, earning more than $150,000. Hill was colorful and unfiltered, which made him a press favorite.

GENE LITTLER

Fifth Appearance

Littler, thirty-nine, a fifteen-year tour player, was the only Ryder Cup veteran besides Billy Casper on the U.S. team. Like Casper, "Gene the Machine" had appeared in every Ryder Cup since 1961, posting a record of 6-4-8. A man of few words, he said in 2012, "You wanted to make the team." The 1961 U.S. Open champion had broken out of a four-year drought with two victories in 1969, the Phoenix Open Invitational and the Greater Greensboro Open. As *Golf World* reported after the slight San Diegan took the Phoenix title in February, "The quiet one makes some noise." Littler would seek to make more noise at Royal Birkdale in September with one of the most admired golf swings in the game.

JACK NICKLAUS
Rookie

Nicklaus, twenty-nine, after waiting the mandatory five years for full PGA membership and narrowly missing a spot on the 1967 squad, was the most celebrated rookie on the 1969 U.S. team in his eighth tour season. Nicklaus was one of only four men to win all four majors—the Masters, U.S. Open, British Open, and PGA Championship—and the only player to win consecutive Masters, a feat he accomplished in 1965 and 1966. Nicklaus won his second U.S. Open in 1967, breaking the scoring record set by Ben Hogan in 1948, and was named 1967 Player of the Year on the PGA Tour. By the late summer of 1969, tour wins were coming at a slower rate, and major victories had dried up since he surpassed Hogan's U.S. Open mark. Some wondered if the Golden Bear was losing his growl.

DAN SIKES
Rookie

Sikes, thirty-eight, was a lawyer who discovered that his golf talent could make him more money on the PGA Tour than he could earn in the nine-to-five world. Sikes hauled in more than $100,000 in each of the 1967 and 1968 seasons. The Florida native received a law degree and All-American honors in golf from the University of Florida before turning professional in 1960. Beginning in 1963 at Doral, "the Golfing Lawyer," as he was sometimes called, had collected six tour wins, including a pair of victories in both 1967 and 1968. Sikes had contended at the 1969 Masters before falling off the pace and finishing alone in twelfth.

KEN STILL
Rookie

Still, thirty-four, a bachelor 6' tall weighing 160 pounds, was described as "a great moving panorama of fun and games" because of his eccentric behavior on and off the golf course. The Tacoma, Washington, native, who turned professional in 1953, was known to carry a transistor radio at tournaments to keep abreast of his beloved Los Angeles Dodgers, and he might pause along the gallery ropes to kiss an attractive female spectator. His mind was like a computer, and his emotive style had produced tears in the heat of competition. Still broke through in 1969 with wins at the Florida Citrus Open and the Greater Milwaukee Open, a victory that cemented his spot on the U.S. Ryder Cup team.

LEE TREVINO
Rookie

Trevino, twenty-nine, burst onto the golf scene in 1968 when he won the U.S. Open at Oak Hill Country Club in Rochester, New York. In the process, the "Merry Mex" tied Jack Nicklaus's U.S. Open scoring record of 275 and became the first player in tournament history to shoot four scores in the 60s. The talkative, clownish Trevino was a U.S. Marine Corps veteran who learned the game as a caddie, on driving ranges, through betting and hustling, and by developing his skills on a military golf course in Japan. After growing up in a three-room shack with no plumbing in Dallas, Texas, Trevino was enjoying the riches of the PGA Tour, having earned close to a quarter of a million dollars since joining in 1967. In addition to the U.S. Open, he had won in Hawaii and Tucson.

•   •   •

Using two different selection methods, the two teams—the first twelve-man squads, as decided in February by British and U.S. PGA officials—were set and would soon meet in the eighteenth Ryder Cup. The U.S. team and delegation were scheduled to depart for England on Sunday, September 14. On the following Thursday at Royal Birkdale, Great Britain and the United States would resume what had mostly been a one-sided battle.

Samuel Ryder, were he alive, would hope for a spirited competition, displays of sportsmanship, and a cherished victory for Great Britain on its home soil. The upcoming matches, however, would turn out to be quite different than he might have imagined when he first conceived the Ryder Cup at Wentworth more than four decades earlier.

PART
II

— 7 —

ROYAL BIRKDALE

The American golf invasion began on a Sunday morning at 9:35 A.M. when the U.S. Ryder Cup team (minus Billy Casper, who was already there, having played in the Dunlop Masters) touched down at Ringway Airport in Manchester in northwest England, arriving on a British European Airways flight from London. The eleven players and their captain looked sharp in their dark blazers, slacks, dress shirts, and ties, stopping to pose for a photograph on the tarmac, the giant wing of their jet airliner in the background. On hand to greet the Americans, British captain Eric Brown, wearing a bucket hat that covered his bald head, beamed at someone out of camera range. Lee Trevino waved to onlookers, then picked up a small boy and offered him a piece of chocolate. Lee knew how to work the crowd as surely as he knew how to work his golf ball.

Soon after, the U.S. team was whisked away in silver-gray Vauxhall Viscounts, the four-door luxury sedan of the Vauxhall line that served as the official courtesy car for Ryder Cup week. That evening both the U.S. and Great Britain teams would gather informally with the press corps at the Prince of Wales Hotel in Southport.

Tony Jacklin wasn't at Ringway to welcome the Americans. The new British Open champion and his Ryder Cup teammate Brian Huggett were playing an exhibition match that afternoon at the Glamorganshire Golf Club in the seaside town of Penarth, Wales. A week earlier, Jacklin, still showing solid form after having his name etched on the Claret Jug, had finished in a tie for third at the World Series of Golf in Akron, Ohio. At the completion of his exhibition in Wales, Jacko and Huggett were to fly to Southport, where the other ten players were required to report to the team hotel by 5:00 P.M. The two teammates hoped to arrive at the hotel an hour or so later than the others, exceptions that didn't sit well with their serious-minded captain.

"I say that if you're a member of any team you must be a team man and accept the rulings laid down," Brown said.

The captain's official letter about the Ryder Cup arrangements had arrived at Jacklin's home after he departed for America, exposing the scheduling conflict. The Wales exhibition had already been arranged, with tickets sold, so Mark McCormack's hot new property kept his commitment. "I cannot let the organizers down as they have spent a lot of money," Jacklin said. Despite well-choreographed arrangements, Jacklin and Huggett's arrival at the team hotel that Sunday evening was even further delayed due to fog.

There were prematch festivities in the days leading up to the eighteenth Ryder Cup, but it was nothing like the hoopla surrounding the present-day competition, which includes such things as a red-carpet arrival, extravagant dinners and parties, high-profile entertainers, elaborate opening ceremonies with lengthy speeches, endless media conferences, and more. Nonetheless, even in 1969, a good time was had before the golf began.

Case in point: British player Peter Townsend, tall glass in hand, is shown in a photograph with his attractive wife, Lorna, who is wearing a minidress and go-go boots. The couple, along with other players and their wives, attended a Tuesday night party hosted by Roland Hill, the captain of Royal Birkdale. The previous evening, British PGA President Lord Derby hosted a cocktail party at his home at Knowsley Hall. Wives and friends were treated to their own special outings. On Wednesday, event sponsor Senior Service Limited arranged for the ladies to tour the ancient city of Chester and also invited the press to a buffet luncheon at Royal Birkdale. One other notable guest was Rosalind Scarfe, the granddaughter of Samuel Ryder, on hand for the matches and confessing she knew nothing about golf.

Jacklin recalled a variety of events prior to the flags being raised on Thursday, including those for corporate sponsors and the large press contingent. Many if not all of them involved "copious amounts of alcohol." Teammate Maurice Bembridge asserted that one had to be a scratch drinker to make it through Ryder Cup week. Jacklin did his part to uphold that tradition for "team solidarity."

•   •   •

While the players and others engaged in all forms of revelry, Royal Birkdale silently awaited. Set beside the Irish Sea, Royal Birkdale had hosted numerous championships in its eighty-year history, including the 1946 British Amateur, the 1948 Curtis Cup, the 1951 Walker Cup, three British Opens (1954, 1961, and 1965) and the 1965 Ryder Cup. It was a traditional links course with all the requisite features: sand dunes, firm and uneven terrain, pot bunkers, bumpy greens, scruffy vegetation wide of the fairways, and certainly wind, which blew off the sea to the west.

With the growing popularity of American golf and a heightened interest in moving British championships to lush, manicured inland golf courses where luck of the bounce was virtually nonexistent and the wind was not much of a factor, "dyed-in-the-wool traditionalist" Nicholas Tremayne felt the need to defend links golf in an article about Royal Birkdale and the upcoming Ryder Cup. "Seaside courses," he wrote, "are an important part of our golfing heritage and worthy of both our respect and admiration. Great deeds and great championships have been performed over them, and long may that continue to be so."

That certainly pertained to Royal Birkdale, but in 1927 when the Ryder Cup began it was simply "Birkdale." Wrote British golf writer Geoffrey Cousins, "No one who looked at those majestic sandhills then could have foreseen the days when the eye would range over acres of canvas, thousands of parked cars, and all the trappings and trimmings of modern golf promotion."

The development and routing of the holes that became the modern Royal Birkdale began in the early 1930s. New owner Southport Corporation retained Hawtree and J. H. Taylor Ltd. to redesign the primitive golf course. F. G. Hawtree, a renowned course architect, and Taylor, a five-time Open champion, were an impressive design team that turned Birkdale into a challenging seaside masterpiece. They wisely laid out the course's 18 holes in the narrow valleys that cut through the numerous and sizable sand hills. Not only had Hawtree and Taylor set down a golf course without unduly disturbing the natural landscape, they had unwittingly created a spectator-friendly venue that would be greatly appreciated in the ensuing decades. The tall sand dunes formed ideal vantage points for the large galleries that would flock to the grounds to watch future championships.

Great Britain team member Brian Huggett affirmed the architects' wisdom forty years later. "Royal Birkdale is the best tournament venue in our country. Along with having a magnificent links course, playing between the avenues of sand dunes was very special." U.S. team member Billy Casper agreed. "Royal Birkdale was a great golf course to play on." "I know all the championship courses," said caddie Alf Fyles, who grew up in Southport, "and I like a lot of the Scottish layouts. But, to my mind, Birkdale is the toughest, the most testing of the lot."

Not far away on the other side of the railway, the Southport and Ainsdale Golf Club hosted the fourth Ryder Cup in 1933. Cousins recalled an excited woman along the boundary fence during one riveting match, a child in tow.

"Where is he?" she breathlessly asked.

The woman hoped to catch a glimpse of the Prince of Wales. The crowds mobbed him, so the marshals sometimes encouraged His Royal Highness to walk unhindered down the middle of the fairways. Great Britain won the Cup on the last day, in the last match, on the last hole. The Prince of Wales handed the trophy to Captain J. H. Taylor, the same man who had labored nearby to make Birkdale a worthy championship course. The Ryder Cup returned to Southport and Ainsdale in 1937, with a sad ending for the hosts, the first British loss on native soil.

"It was perhaps just as well that we had no inkling of the future," wrote Cousins about the 1933 triumph, "and so were spared the knowledge that Britain would not win again for nearly a quarter of a century."

At Birkdale, a new, two-story clubhouse, a white monument to the architecture of the period, opened in the summer of 1935. Birkdale's reputation grew, and in November 1951 the golf club earned the "Royal" appellation, given by King George VI. Then, in 1965, the Royal Birkdale Golf Club pulled off a first-time double—it hosted both the British Open and the Ryder Cup. That July Australian Peter Thomson captured the Claret Jug for his fifth and final time. Led by Byron Nelson, the Yanks arrived in October to take on a British squad captained by Harry Weetman. With a team that included two-time British Open champion Arnold Palmer, 1964 British Open champion Tony Lema, and Littler and Casper, both U.S. Open champions, the Americans beat the Brits 19½–12½. Prime Minister Harold Wilson watched as Great Britain kept the matches fairly close until the final day, when the U.S. team dominated the singles. It didn't help that course conditions aided America's style of play. An unusually wet summer made Royal Birkdale's fairways green and lush. The Yanks took advantage with their dartlike iron games and strong putting.

Course conditions would not favor the U.S. team in 1969 if Eric Brown could help it. Captain Brown promised that Royal Birkdale would be set up to give the British players their best chance to win the Ryder Cup. One might imagine that if Brown could stop excessive rain from falling on Birkdale, he would. He badly wanted that Cup.

The Daily Telegraph's Leonard Crawley wrote that Royal Birkdale was "laid out in . . . the finest natural country for the game." In Crawley's mind, that included spectacular Cypress Point on California's Monterey Peninsula. No one, it seemed, doubted that Royal Birkdale, one of the premier seaside golf courses in all of England and perhaps anywhere, would be a good test for the twenty-four men competing in the eighteenth Ryder Cup.

•　　•　　•

The man primarily responsible for bringing the first Ryder Cup to Royal Birkdale was a businessman named Brian Park. Park was the fifth generation to head the family business, William Park and Company Forge-masters Limited. He also was a proud member of Royal Birkdale, serving as club captain and also as the chairman of the Green Committee for the 1961 British Open. Arnold Palmer won the first of his two consecutive British Opens that summer, but, as Park wrote in a December 1965 letter to *Golfdom*'s Herb Graffis, "Royal Birkdale got a bad press after the Open Championship . . . which was wrecked by rain and storms and there was criticism of the arrangements generally."

Park said he "wanted to restore Royal Birkdale's good name." In April 1963, the forgemaster decided to dedicate his efforts and finances to the 1965 Ryder Cup and "show the world that Royal Birkdale could do things properly after all." Park had come to the rescue.

"The British PGA could not find a sponsor quickly for the 1965 Ryder Cup matches and it was then that Dad stepped in with his bid in 1963," recalled Graham Park, Brian Park's son.

The British PGA price tag to guarantee the match was £12,500. Park promised the amount and then turned to Royal Birkdale for its approval to host the sixteenth Ryder Cup. The club agreed, and Park's ambitious plan began to fall into place. He didn't only want to bolster Royal Birkdale's reputation; the businessman wanted to turn Southport into the top golf destination in England.

Retiring from the family business, Park threw himself into preparation for the 1965 Ryder Cup with the industriousness of a blacksmith. He traveled to East Lake Country Club in Atlanta to observe all facets of the 1963 Ryder Cup, another one-sided U.S. victory. Park returned to England with the belief that he, in partnership with his club, the British PGA, and others, could stage a better Ryder Cup than the Americans. They went to work preparing the golf course for the players. For example, they toughened the four finishing holes, three of which exceeded 500 yards in length. They also improved the grounds for the spectators, putting in two miles of walking paths and building grass amphitheaters behind several greens.

A small army of club members and others—mostly unpaid volunteers—supervised and helped out with catering, stewarding, scoring, course ranging, gatekeeping, press and public relations, parking, and program selling. Park endeavored to create a Ryder Cup program unlike any other. The result was a 160-page souvenir program with a color pullout of the golf course, player profiles, feature articles, photography, and maps. It cost five shillings and was only one of Park's innovations.

Another was the introduction of hospitality tents, which became commonplace at the British Open and later at other golf events. In their original form at Royal Birkdale, Park's hospitality areas were actually wooden shacks, according to *Golf Monthly*. In addition, there was a massive tented village made of white canvas, a large trade exhibition area featuring the latest golf equipment, a first aid station, a post office, a lost-and-found, and a wooden press structure that contained more golf media than ever before assembled in one place in Great Britain. Another novelty was small motorized cars called Mini Mokes driven by young women golfers. They served as mobile scoreboards that displayed how each match stood.

The pro shop was expanded to give home pro Bobby Halsall additional space to sell Dunlop golf clubs and other merchandise. The caddies were outfitted in maroon tracksuits supplied by the British PGA. The players, their wives, and officials lodged at the luxurious Palace Hotel, which hosted the traditional victory dinner on Saturday night. In so many ways, Brian Park's vision had been fulfilled.

Great Britain again lost the Ryder Cup in 1965, but Park and company had won back respect for Royal Birkdale. Park's many improvements had required an additional outlay of £17,500, bringing his total commitment as sole sponsor to £30,000. Fifty thousand people had paid to attend the matches. There was a profit of £18,000, more than enough to return the guaranteed sum of £5,000 to Royal Birkdale, give £6,000 to the British PGA, and provide a substantial amount of money for the promotion of golf in northern England. The retired forgemaster had succeeded, and his legacy would influence the next Ryder Cup on British soil, also hosted by Royal Birkdale.

The 1969 Ryder Cup would be the first one solely sponsored by a commercial enterprise, a company called Senior Service Limited already connected to the international golf event.

"Senior Service were brought into my father's 1965 Ryder Cup and were a great help to him," said Graham Park.

The first-time commercial sponsor assured the British PGA that the eighteenth Ryder Cup would set even higher standards.

•　　•　　•

Eric Brown was fired up. Judging from his comments to the British press throughout the spring and summer, Brown had been burning bright ever since he was named as the new captain. Nothing stoked the Scot's competitive fire like the Ryder Cup.

Born on February 15, 1925, in Edinburgh, Eric Chalmers Brown played football during his youth, but golf, he said in his autobiography,

Knave of Clubs, was "my first choice in sport almost since I was able to understand what a golf club was." After working on the railways and then failing a physical for the Edinburgh City Police because of a scarred lung, Brown became a golf professional in 1946. His first professional victory came in the 1951 Swiss Open while on his honeymoon with his wife, Joan. Several more wins followed during the 1950s, his best competitive decade in golf, but the title Brown coveted most—the British Open—eluded him. He co-led with Dai Rees in 1953 at Carnoustie after 36 holes but fell off the pace and finished in a tie for ninth. Ben Hogan won the Claret Jug that year in his only appearance in the British Isles. Brown's best Open finishes were a pair of thirds in 1957 and 1958, the latter year being a bitter disappointment. Brown made a double-bogey 6 on the last hole at Royal Lytham & St. Annes after driving into a bunker. A routine par would have given him victory. Instead, he lost by a single stroke.

Brown would achieve golf fame on a different path—the Ryder Cup—and would be considered by many as the greatest British match-play golfer of his generation. His Ryder Cup career got off to a rocky start at Wentworth outside of London in 1953. Brown and John Panton were manhandled by Americans Sam Snead and Lloyd Mangrum in foursomes, losing 8 and 7. Afterward, Captain Henry Cotton remarked that he didn't expect Brown to win his point in singles play, which, according to Brown's wife, ignited the Scot. He beat Mangrum the next day in a match that went to the final hole, beginning an undefeated streak in singles that spanned four Ryder Cups. While his teammates often lost, Brown mowed through the Americans, three of whom were future Hall of Famers. In 1959, his last Ryder Cup appearance as a player, he beat Cary Middlecoff at Eldorado Country Club in Palm Desert, the only singles match won by a player on the British team. It was another remarkable performance by Brown, especially considering the terrifying experience he and his teammates had endured traveling to the matches.

Encountering severe turbulence, the airplane carrying the Great Britain team plunged from 13,000 to 9,000 feet before returning to Los

Angeles and landing safely. Some of the shaken passengers kissed the ground when they stepped off the plane. The British team boarded a Greyhound bus for an uneventful two-hour ride to the California desert.

It was Brown's 1957 singles match, however, that lodged in the memories of his countrymen, an infamous battle at Lindrick with the ill-tempered Tommy Bolt. The Brown Bomber was pitted against "Thunder Bolt," as Bolt was widely known, in a juicy matchup that attracted a large, boisterous gallery. To set the stage, Brown and teammate Christy O'Connor were throttled by Bolt and Dick Mayer in foursomes, 7 and 5. With eight singles matches ahead on the final day, another U.S. victory seemed to be at hand. Playing captain Dai Rees confidently sent Brown out first in singles against the talented and tempestuous Bolt.

"He had supposedly the same type of temper I had," Bolt later said. "We drew a lot of spectators out there because they expected us to get into a fistfight, I guess."

The Brown Bomber built a 4-hole lead during the first 18 holes. After the lunch break, he held steady and beat Bolt 4 and 3. True to his reputation, Thunder Bolt was a bad loser, telling Brown in colorful language that he hadn't enjoyed a single minute of their match. The Brown Bomber, also using profanity, told Bolt he never had a chance and could expect a similar result if they ever met again on a golf course. Brown later heard U.S. players Ed Furgol and Doug Ford lecture their teammate on his sorry display of sportsmanship.

"I guess I got a little frustrated," Bolt recalled, "and Eric and I might have had a couple of words. I lost control of my concentration, and that's the name of the game."

Rees, as it turned out, had assigned a critical task to the right man. Great Britain went on to shock the United States that October day by winning six singles matches and halving one. The Brits took back the Cup for the first time in twenty-four years.

"I've never seen so many delighted folk on a golf course," Brown said.

• • •

Eric Brown would bring the same fiery determination to his Ryder Cup captaincy. "We are going to play this Ryder Cup my way," he said in May of 1969. "If a fellow's only been playing five minutes and I thought he could beat an American, I would want him in my team."

The course would also play his way. Royal Birkdale was groomed as prescribed by the captain, "semi-rough on the edge of the fairways and real high behind that." Jacklin recalled that Birkdale's fairways were narrowed and the rough was tall and thick, but did it give the captain's team any advantage? Jacklin thought not. Actually, tight fairways, such as those found on the PGA Tour, were a good setup for the Americans, who, as Jacklin had witnessed, were adept at driving the golf ball straight down the middle when the pressure was on.

"I certainly don't think the fairways were brought in much," Jacklin said in 2012. "There's only so far you can go on a links course. It's the weather that creates the difficulty. The mere fact that we were playing links golf was an advantage, and in front of a home crowd, of course."

Brian Barnes also put stock in home-course advantage. "We were far more used to links-type golf than the American boys were."

Peter Townsend thought any focus on Captain Brown's course setup was "more propaganda than reality. You could say this," Townsend later said. "If the Americans were used to extremely quick greens, [Brown] would have deliberately said to the greenskeeper don't make them too quick because it's more to our advantage to play on slightly slower greens. The same went on when we went over there to America . . . but in reality it made no difference."

Brown did not prepare Royal Birkdale unassisted. Dai Rees and Arthur Crawley-Boevey, a member of the Ryder Cup Committee, accompanied the captain on visits to Birkdale prior to the matches. Rees and the committee were in charge of the hole positions and tee placements for the three days of competition. Course setup would long be viewed as an advantage for home-side Ryder Cup captains in the decades to come, but as Jacklin observed, "If you couldn't handle that pressure, fixing up the course won't make a spot of difference."

Brown also imposed his will in other ways. There was an array of team rules, some of which Jacklin thought "were bloody ridiculous and even unsporting." For example, once the matches began, Captain Brown instructed his players not to search for their opponents' golf balls in the rough. The Brown Bomber did not want his players to incur a penalty for accidently stepping on, touching, or in any way moving an opponent's golf ball.

Bernard Gallacher supported his captain. "Eric only made the point not to be unhelpful to the Americans, but this was because, if in looking for a ball we accidentally trod on it, we could lose the hole."

No matter, it did not go over well with Britain's star player. Jacklin defied his captain's instruction about ball searches and dismissed any other counsel that he thought deviated from a sporting approach to the matches. He thought Brown was trying to use intimidation, and he would have none of it.

The two men had butted heads in the past. At the 1964 *News of the World* Match Play, Jacklin saw Brown lean on his club and feign an exaggerated yawn while he was waiting for Jacklin to play out of a bunker. It angered the young pro, who went on to give Brown a sound beating.

"It was one of the most satisfying things I ever did," Jacklin said. "He paid the price for that."

Many of Jacklin's teammates were either tolerant or completely supportive of Brown's combative approach.

"Eric Brown was a good captain," Peter Alliss later said. "He didn't do anything really to cement Anglo-American relations, but he had a wonderful Ryder Cup record and he did the job very competently." Citing the long rough and Brown's ball-search edict, Alliss acknowledged that there were "silly things going on," part and parcel of the Ryder Cup experience. "There was always something," he said.

"I'd been under several different captains," Neil Coles said, "and, to that point, Eric was probably the best captain I was under. Great passion about winning. Really sort of geed you along. I felt most of the players appreciated his passion to win, and that seemed to rub off on the players."

"Eric was a super captain," remembered Brian Huggett, "all fire just as he was a player in Ryder Cup matches. His outlook was similar to mine."

"Eric was my hero because he came from the same golf club," Gallacher said. "He took me under his wings, so to speak, and made me feel a million dollars."

"Obviously, he wasn't anti-American," Townsend said, "but he did really very much want to beat them. He didn't think the Americans were unbeatable. He was a good captain because I think he had a good spirit about him."

If Brown tried something to gain an upper hand, it would have absolutely no effect on his counterpart, Captain Snead, according to *Professional Golfer.* "Sam," reported the magazine, "will not be intimidated by any amount of gamesmanship that might be coming his way from the fiery Scot Brown." Henry Longhurst, who also wondered if the captain might cross any lines in his zeal for the Cup, coined a term for it— "Brownsmanship."

"He was called 'the Brown Bomber,'" Jacklin later said. "That was his whole thing. He didn't mind upsetting people."

Like Jacklin, Brian Barnes was uncomfortable with his captain's aggressive approach. "Eric was one of these guys that I felt believed that you tried to win at all costs, which wasn't quite my idea. I felt that, yes, by all means, you let the clubs do the work. It is only a game, after all. You try to beat your opponent with the clubs that you have at your disposal, and gamesmanship shouldn't come into it. But I honestly felt that Eric was a bit that way inclined, as I thought Sam Snead was. I found him very difficult, I must admit. Eric and I didn't really get on particularly well."

Snead was unlikely to be surprised or fazed by Brownsmanship. No doubt, the wise old country boy from Virginia's Allegheny Mountains had seen gamesmanship in all its forms in his long golf career—and probably had tried much of it himself on unsuspecting opponents.

.   .   .

Jack Nicklaus was familiar with Royal Birkdale, a par-74 layout, unusual in tournament golf. (Most championship golf courses have a par of 70, 71, or 72.) Royal Birkdale's two 9s had pars of 36 and 38, respectively. The incoming 9, featuring four par 5s, was long for that era, a total of 3,674 yards. The full course measured 7,140 yards. Nicklaus had played Birkdale in the 1965 British Open and finished in a tie for twelfth. It was his worst Open finish since his first appearance in 1962, when he opened with an 80 and finished in a tie for thirty-fourth. From 1963 through 1969, the Golden Bear had one victory (at Muirfield in 1966), three runner-up finishes, and a third. A high-ball hitter, he had always seemed to play well in the unpredictable conditions found in the British Isles.

Two days before the start of the Ryder Cup, Nicklaus was trying to find some form that he could take into the matches. Playing a practice round with Dan Sikes, Jack shot a fat 4-over-par 40 on the outward 9. Former PGA president Max Elbin suggested a slight grip change. It worked. Nicklaus fired a 6-under-par 32 on the inward 9. "It enabled me to get my left side through the ball better and made a lot of difference," he told the press.

Sikes shot a 73 and moaned about his putting. "I didn't make a decent putt in the entire 18 holes." Captain Snead liked the thirty-eight-year-old rookie's length off the tee, calling his driving action a "sling shot." Foursomes pairings were of no great concern for Snead, although he would consider pairing players who hit the golf ball similar distances because it would make club selection easier for approach shots. "They're all good players," Snead said. "At any time any one of them might beat the rest."

The larger American golf ball would be in play for both teams, but Snead did not consider it to be an advantage for his side. The U.S. captain pointed out that Great Britain's players had been using the big ball for two years and expected their pitching had improved. This was one of the reasons why Snead predicted the outcome "will be closer than people think." Perhaps trying to lessen Ryder Cup pressure on his inexperienced team, he added, "Some of my guys have never played match play. It'll be a little strange to them." Snead said that any distance advantage his long hitters had would be negated by Birkdale's par-3 holes, which "will be the crunch, not the par 5s."

Putting would also determine the outcome. *The Guardian*'s Eric Wadsworth snapped a photograph of three of the British players stroking short putts on the practice green: Bernard Hunt, Tony Jacklin, and Maurice Bembridge. In addition to newspaper photographs, there was a variety of team photos that appeared in publications. One, taken at an angle, shows the respective teams standing beside their large leather Ryder Cup golf bags. The British players are outfitted in long-sleeved V-neck sweaters; their handsome white golf bags sporting an emblem with a lion, a symbol of Great Britain. In the photo of the American team, the men are wearing navy blue blazers with the Ryder Cup insignia, red-hued ties, and gray trousers. Many players are smiling; others look serious, as if they were going into battle. Great Britain's team also sat for several team photographs in front of the white Royal Birkdale clubhouse. In one photograph, they are wearing powder blue long-sleeved sweaters with white polo shirts underneath, dark slacks, and black and white leather golf shoes. Half the players are seated with hands on knees; the other half, arranged by height with the tallest, Hunt, in the middle, are standing. These men are short and tall, young and aging, bushy haired and balding. On their cashmere-clad shoulders rested the golf hopes and fears of a proud empire.

Captain Brown was pleased after sending his players out in three-somes during Tuesday's practice session. "My team is playing so well it's frightening," Brown told reporters. *The New York Times*'s Fred Tupper described the British as "cock-a-hoop," meaning boastful or prideful, and their captain as "the militant Scot."

Frank Beard noticed. A U.S. Ryder Cup rookie in unfamiliar surroundings, Beard detected a brash attitude and what he regarded as open
rudeness upon his arrival in England.

"I'd never been treated like that," Beard said decades later, admitting
that it made him uncomfortable the entire week. "They came into that
on their home turf with great expectations, not only from them but from
the people there. There was a bit of arrogance, cockiness—and you could
feel it. While it was my first one, I just knew things had changed. It was
like, 'You better watch out boys, this is a whole different scene.'"

"There was back in that day quite a bit of bravado on the British
team," Jacklin later said. "We could do this, but there was no genuine
substance to some of the talk. Of course, we were getting a lot of support
from the home crowd as well, which always helps, even today. We all dug
very deep."

No matter how bullish Brown or Snead might have been about their
troops, practice was one thing, but the actual matches were something
altogether different, as Ward-Thomas pointed out in a story published under
the headline BRITISH OPTIMISTIC. The *Guardian* scribe did suggest that
Great Britain's youth movement probably held one important advantage—
"stronger nerves." Barnes, Bembridge, Caygill, Gallacher, and Townsend
could play boldly, uninhibited. There was no mental scar tissue from past
failures, no Ryder Cup nightmares to haunt them and steal their confidence.

Many players on the U.S. team practiced as partners to simulate actual match situations when play opened on Thursday with foursomes, a
format in which two players on the same team alternate hitting shots
with the same golf ball until the ball is holed. Partners golf was rare on
the pro circuit, and the alternate-shot format was virtually nonexistent.

"We had an occasional team championship, you and your partner
playing," Beard later said, "but they didn't work real well with television.
We'd never played as a team except maybe since college golf."

PGA champion Raymond Floyd and Miller Barber were among the players who teamed up to play alternate shot during their Tuesday practice session.

"I didn't know much about match play," Floyd later said. "Yeah, I played some local [and] some state tournaments that were match play, but once I turned pro and had gone to the tour, there was no such thing as match play."

For Floyd, alternate shot resembled the back-and-forth nature of a game of catch, something he occasionally did with his beloved Chicago Cubs. Less than a week earlier he had joined the National League team for its warm-up before a game with the Philadelphia Phillies. "He loves the Cub players, and we love him," said star shortstop Ernie Banks.

Floyd wasn't a total imposter. At the age of seventeen, he was a top baseball prospect who nearly signed with the Cleveland Indians to pitch in their farm system. Now twenty-seven, with 200 pounds on his 6' frame, including some thickness around the middle, Floyd didn't look major-league fit as he tossed the baseball alongside southpaw pitcher Rich Nye. Phillies coach Billy DeMars pointed at Floyd, who wore his own Cubs uniform with the number 23. "Who is that? Boy, he's really out of shape," DeMars said. It wasn't a joke. The coach didn't recognize the PGA champion.

As he headed into his first Ryder Cup, Floyd's golf was in good shape. "I could do it all," he later said about his 1969 season. "And to have a year like that, everything was clicking. I was a good putter, and my confidence level was there."

The other eight U.S. players toured the links in two groups. Lee Trevino, Dave Hill, Tommy Aaron, and Ken Still formed one; Frank Beard, Gene Littler, Billy Casper, and Dale Douglass were in the other.

Beard recalled being closest to Douglass, Still, and the veteran, Littler, who "was one of those guys who kind of took us under his wing." Beard also was friendly with Nicklaus, but "Nicklaus was Nicklaus. He knew he was better than we were, we knew he was better than we were, and we knew he knew. But he was a nice guy. He wasn't snotty. He was Jack, and that was it."

Veterans of the victorious 1965 team, Littler and Casper knew their way around Birkdale. It was foreign soil for most of the others, although Trevino and Aaron had both played tournament golf in Britain. So had Still, who later said, "I loved Royal Birkdale. It was a links course, but I didn't have any problem with a links course."

Hill was one of four U.S. players—the others being Sikes, Beard, and Douglass—who had never played golf on a British links course. The mercurial American had mock-warned the British about his arrival on their shores after winning the Philadelphia Classic in late July in a sudden-death playoff against Gay Brewer and R. H. Sikes (no relation to Dan Sikes). Hill's third win of the 1969 season and his tour-leading earnings assured him a spot on the Ryder Cup team.

The blunt Michigan man made light of it. "When they see me leading the money list, why it's just gonna make some of those cats sick. I can think of about fifteen of them who are gonna cut their throats." Then he added, "I might set England back forty years. They're gonna send two special guards along with me just to see I don't get in trouble."

Whether or not Hill would alienate the entire host country remained to be seen, but one thing termed a "minor controversy" was resolved on Tuesday, according to a press report. Captain Eric Brown would now allow his players to search for the golf balls of their U.S. opponents when the matches began on Thursday. Pat Ward-Thomas wrote that it "was much ado about a triviality which stemmed from a misunderstanding concerning the rule covering searching for a ball." The matches could proceed minus at least one distraction, although the small controversy would serve as an example of Brown's confrontational nature for the rest of his days. It was an unfair characterization, according to the captain's wife, who sought to correct the story years later.

"What actually happened," Joan Brown said, "is that the PGA secretary approached Eric and said, 'Could you make the boys aware of the fact that if they look for the Americans' balls and accidentally stand on one, or interfere with one in any way, we lose the hole.' Eric told the players to be careful but the story came out twisted."

Whatever one's interpretation of the captain's instructions and motive, there was no disputing that Eric Brown had a special talent for provoking strong feelings and reactions, whether they be negative or positive, and whether they burst forth from his opponents or spilled out of his own players.

—8—

THE CAMPAIGN

The British press had reached a Ryder Cup fever pitch. It had begun months earlier, and no one was more vocal and unapologetically partisan than Paul Trevillion, a writer and illustrator for *Golf Illustrated*. "Ryder Cup Reggie," a mascot sketched by Trevillion, first appeared in the publication in May 1969. Inspired by England's "World Cup Willie" mascot, Reggie was a cartoonish tiger who wore a cap emblazoned with the Union Jack, Great Britain's flag. WE WILL WIN THE RYDER CUP—AND "REGGIE" AGREES! read the headline in Trevillion's May 22 column.

Trevillion wrote that big money on the U.S. tour bred complacency rather than champions and boldly predicted that "the hungry young lions" of Great Britain would rise up to dominate world golf in five years' time. Then he offered this in all capital letters: "THEY FEAR NO MAN AND THEY WILL START THE BALL ROLLING AT BIRKDALE THIS YEAR WHEN WE WIN THE RYDER CUP."

Trevillion had, in effect, assumed the role of head cheerleader for Captain Eric Brown and his young lions. He reveled in the captain's "fighting words" and wrote that "every golfer in these Isles is behind you." Trevillion had picked up on Brown's combustible tone and gleefully ran with it like a pyromaniac. Ryder Cup Reggie reappeared in the July 24 issue, in which the Great Britain team was named and profiled, and also returned in September before the start of the matches. Reggie's stripes were unchanged, his enthusiasm unflagging.

Yet there were those in Great Britain and beyond who thought Trevillion was a raving lunatic and that *Golf Illustrated*—the world's oldest golf magazine and the same august publication that helped finance Great Britain's first Ryder Cup team in 1927—had gone off the rails with its hyperbolic coverage of the upcoming matches at Royal Birkdale. One only needed to look at Great Britain's dismal Ryder Cup history.

For reasons only they could know, Trevillion and a *Golf Illustrated* team that included editor Tom Scott and deputy editor Peter Willis had turned their backs on reality. If Trevillion was, in fact, a lunatic, then Scott and Willis had been duped, because by the summer of 1969 they were becoming convinced that Trevillion was, instead, a genius.

．　　．　　．

Earlier that year, Scott and his twenty-four-year-old deputy editor had, at best, a small ray of hope for the British boys. The Ryder Cup certainly mattered to *Golf Illustrated*, but the one-sided nature of the 1967 matches could not be ignored. The year 1969 looked no different to Willis. "The USA had, on paper, one of its strongest Ryder Cup sides," he later said. "The Great Britain team looked extremely weak by comparison."

Then one spring day a man walked into the *Golf Illustrated* offices at 8 Stratton Street in central London. It was Paul Trevillion, a well-known sports artist and illustrator, who, among other projects, was collaborating with Gary Player on a golf-skills cartoon strip that was syndicated worldwide.

"[Trevillion] delivered a message that Tom and I didn't expect when we sat behind our typewriters that day," Willis remembered. " 'We will win the Ryder Cup in September. Let's get behind the boys, stop the defeatist talk, and start the campaign as soon as we can.' "

Decades later Trevillion also recalled those early days in the top-floor offices in Mayfair. The *Golf Illustrated* editor laughed at the home side's chances. "The Great Britain team should hoist a white flag at the opening ceremony," Scott said. "I fear for my great friend and fellow countryman Eric Brown."

"Are you going with those headlines in the magazine?" Trevillion asked.

"Can you think of a better one?" the editor replied.

Trevillion took the pencil out of Scott's hand. On a piece of paper on Scott's desk, Trevillion wrote in large letters: GB WILL WIN THE RYDER CUP.

Scott was momentarily speechless.

"I can't believe you're serious. If you really believe that, you must be off your head."

Scott turned toward Willis. "Do you agree, Peter?"

"I think we should give it some serious thought," Willis replied. "Everything is possible in golf. It could be a good idea to get behind the Great Britain team. They will need all the support they can get."

The campaign began.

"From that moment to the beginning of the match, we ran a nonstop campaign in the magazine insisting that this time it was going to be different. This time we would win the Ryder Cup," Willis said.

It was as if Trevillion had cast a magical spell. The young deputy editor was captivated.

"It was a brave call for the magazine to make," Willis admitted in 2013, "but there was a feeling of revolution in the air at Stratton Street because of the remarkable charisma and sheer force of personality displayed by Trevillion on his regular visits to see us. Waiting for his entry into the office was like a child anticipating Christmas morning. Each visit contained a motivational talk so powerful that Tom and I would want to produce the best magazine in the world after he left. Trevillion believed in *Golf Illustrated* like no one we had ever met, and he believed in British golf when few others did."

Trevillion set out to recruit a key ally for the bold campaign—Great Britain Ryder Cup captain Eric Brown. The artist-writer and the player-captain already knew each other. Trevillion had worked in Brown's native Scotland during the 1960s at the *Scottish Daily Express, The Sunday Mail,* and the *Evening Citizen.* Trevillion sketched and wrote about soccer, boxing, and golf, and had frequent encounters with "the firebrand Scot with the Rob Roy spirit," as he later described Brown. "Eric Brown could have played the Mel Gibson role [of William Wallace] in the film *Braveheart.*" Scottish golf hero Brown was "great copy" for Trevillion's golf stories. "We often met and always the sparks would fly, but we enjoyed each other's company." Brown knew about Trevillion's mark in golf: the popular instructional cartoon strip featuring Gary Player; *Easier Golf,* a bestseller that Trevillion coauthored with Peter Alliss; and Trevillion's successful opposition to legal claims made by IMG, the U.S. sports agency headed by Mark McCormack.

When Brown was announced as the British Ryder Cup captain for the 1969 matches, the opportunistic Trevillion wasted no time. He arranged a meeting with the new captain and made his pitch. "Eric, will you back up the *Golf Illustrated* campaign that Britain's Ryder Cup team will beat the Americans and will win the Ryder Cup?"

Brown reached out and firmly shook Trevillion's hand. "Yes," he replied, "because losing is not an option."

"We both laughed," Trevillion recalled. "War had been declared."

·   ·   ·

Born in London in 1934, Paul Trevillion was a child of the Blitz, the relentless eight-month bombing campaign by Germany during the World War II. More than a million London homes were destroyed or damaged, and tens of thousands of civilians were killed. Never evacuated from

London, the young boy survived. He remembered sitting in a schoolyard shelter with his classmates during German daytime bombing raids. As bombs exploded in the city and throughout England, the children recited a famous rallying speech of Prime Minister Sir Winston Churchill:

> *We shall go on to the end, we shall fight in France, we shall fight on the seas and oceans, we shall fight with growing confidence and growing strength in the air, we shall defend our island, whatever the cost may be, we shall fight on the beaches, we shall fight on the landing grounds, we shall fight in the fields and in the streets, we shall fight in the hills; we shall never surrender.*

In 1955, by then a young man of twenty-one, Trevillion recited the last two lines of the speech with Churchill himself. The artist had drawn a portrait of the retired British prime minister. The eighty-one-year-old Churchill was so enamored with the image that he called Trevillion and arranged a meeting in Berkeley Square. The two men shared a cup of coffee and war memories. Then Churchill reached for his pen and signed Trevillion's drawing, the only time Churchill would ever sign a drawing or painting of himself.

Trevillion later said he felt ten feet tall when he shook the great man's hand and got up to leave. "The voice of Sir Winston followed me as I walked through the door. 'Treat every obstacle as a hurdle to be overcome. No matter how big the obstacle or how high the hurdle, it must be overcome.'"

. . .

The campaign was mocked by the golf establishment in Great Britain, which was virtually impossible to ignore since, at the time, *Golf Illustrated* was the lone weekly golf publication in the British Isles, a staple of golf clubs throughout the land. It didn't matter. The *Golf Illustrated* team relentlessly carried on with its sunny Ryder Cup coverage week after week after week. Willis later recalled a photo of the Great Britain team appearing in an issue preceding the match. The photo heading read: "This is the team which WILL WIN the Ryder Cup."

Letters poured into the *Golf Illustrated* offices. The phone rang off the hook. Willis recalled that out of every one hundred letters received by the magazine only two or three might have said Great Britain would win the Ryder Cup. Few even considered victory a possibility. The majority of letters implored the golf weekly to provide more balanced and believable coverage.

"The campaign," remembered Willis long after, "was attracting a massive amount of media reaction . . . with many thinking Trevillion and the *Golf Illustrated* magazine had gone mad."

Perhaps they had.

As Ben Hogan had steadfastly declared and his team had emphatically proven at the 1967 Ryder Cup, the United States possessed "the finest golfers in the world." How could any sane person dispute that obvious fact?

"To win the match, even make a contest of it, was beyond the wildest dreams of the British golfing public," Willis said.

A few *Golf Illustrated* letter writers did express mild optimism and good wishes for the home side. Noting that Ryder Cup selection would always be a "bone of contention," Dennis Mullins of Frimley wrote, "As a betting man, I am ready to lay a share of odds that Alliss and Hunt come out of the Birkdale fray better than many of the players above them in the Order of Merit. In any case, let us anticipate a British victory." R. D. Hakanson of Sweden wished "much luck to the British boys when they play their Ryder Cup match."

During that time, Trevillion met with editor Scott and Henry Cotton, the legendary English golfer who won three British Opens and was a member of four Ryder Cup teams, playing three times and captaining twice, in 1947 as a playing captain and also in 1953. In 1969 Cotton was a

Golf Illustrated contributor, as was 1951 British Open champion Max Faulkner.

"In truth," Trevillion recalled, "it was Cotton who inspired the idea for the '69 Ryder Cup campaign. I never let an opportunity go by when talking to Cotton to ask about the great golfing legends of the past. Cotton's information never disappointed."

Trevillion remembered Cotton outlining the strengths and weaknesses of both Ryder Cup teams. Cotton felt that of all twenty-four players, British Open champion Tony Jacklin was the "main man." He bravely put Jacklin down for 5 points. The brash Trevillion did Cotton one better— Jacko, 6 points.

"During our discussion," Trevillion said, "Tom Scott dropped an autograph page down on the piece of paper, and both Scott and Cotton laughed." The page, dated 1929, bore the signatures of Cotton and Samuel Ryder, recalling Great Britain's 7–5 Ryder Cup victory at the Moortown Golf Club. Cotton remembered how his side, captained by George Duncan, set up the golf course to favor the British team. "[Cotton] then, hole by hole, indicated how, if he was team captain, he would prefer the course to be set up at Royal Birkdale." Trevillion later passed Cotton's course assessment on to Captain Brown, but "Brown didn't take it all aboard."

According to Trevillion, Cotton also passed along another strategy he had learned in his Ryder Cup battles. "Needle the U.S. captain," Cotton said. "Play mind games, get him worried and you have half his team. I lost heavily in 1947 when Hogan was the captain, but it almost worked for Whitcombe in 1949. He lost by 2 points. Then in 1953 I lost again, but this time by only 1 point."

"When I left Cotton," Trevillion said, "I thought, 'Get the captain and you get half the team. Jacklin can take care of the other half. Great Britain can win the Ryder Cup.'"

A week ahead of the matches, Trevillion's column said what was at stake for Great Britain. "They [the British team] do not have to be reminded that this Ryder Cup match is being played under a sentence—the sentence of death. For should we lose the Americans will put an end to the series." By winning, often by wide margins, the United States had lost interest in the Ryder Cup, wrote Trevillion. It was do or die.

The BBC's Henry Longhurst, also a *Golf Illustrated* contributor, promised a reward to the twelve men and their captain if they managed to beat the Americans. Calling himself a realist, Longhurst did not think it would happen. Through the years when the Ryder Cup was played on British soil he had heard his countrymen say, "This at last is our turn." With the exception of 1957, it never was, and, as Longhurst wrote, "not even the naivest of commentators could suggest that we are likely to win it in America." Longhurst hoped that when the matches concluded at Royal Birkdale, the British players could say they did their best and accept the result. If they somehow did the unthinkable, he would help supply the celebration. "I hereby undertake to stand each and every one of them a bottle of champagne," Longhurst pledged.

Not long after, Trevillion ate lunch with U.S. players Lee Trevino and Ken Still. Trevillion asked the 1968 U.S. Open champion about Great Britain's chances. Erupting in laughter and looking down at his plate of turkey rolls, Trevino said, "Just like these rolls here, boy, we're going to gobble them up." After the Merry Mex left half of his food on his plate because it was too salty, Trevillion suggested that the British team would also be hard to digest. "No, baby, no!" Trevino exclaimed. "You've been knocking our team all season, so I'll be looking for an apology in six-inch-high letters after we give your team a whopping." Trevillion promised Trevino an apology—if the Yanks won. It was an apology he desperately hoped not to make.

Remaining in London to produce the next issue of the magazine, Willis received daily phone calls from Trevillion at Southport during the early part of Ryder Cup week. "The campaign was making its mark not only with the players, but also the fans. Even more pleasing was the news from Trevillion that he had set up a close relationship with home team captain Eric Brown. As soon as I heard this, I knew we were in for something special because as a motivator Trevillion was simply the best."

Trevino was child's play compared to Trevillion's first encounter with U.S. captain Sam Snead. Forty-three years later Trevillion recounted the "run-in" with "one of my all-time golfing heroes." The campaigner was talking with Captain Brown when Captain Snead appeared.

"Sam, over here!" Brown said. "Meet Paul Trevillion, *Golf Illustrated*."

Snead wore a broad smile and a cold stare.

"It told me at once he had read the magazines," Trevillion later said.

The American captain walked over and extended his hand to Trevillion—not a friendly handshake but a strong gripping one. Snead had something to say to Trevillion, and he was not going to release Trevillion's hand until he had said it.

"So you're Trevillion?" Snead began.

"That's the name I answer to."

Snead leaned in close, the two men's noses practically touching.

"Have you ever heard of Jack Nicklaus? Billy Casper? Lee Trevino? Ray Floyd? Gene Littler?"

Trevillion nodded.

"Check the American team sheets," Snead said.

He unclasped hands and momentarily turned to leave before turning back to deliver the punch line. Snead's smile was gone, only a deadly stare on his face.

"They are all playing," the U.S. captain promised.

Then he walked away.

• • •

At Southport on Wednesday, Pat Ward-Thomas worked on his last report before the start of the eighteenth Ryder Cup. Paul Hahn, the world's greatest trick-shot artist, had arrived that afternoon to conduct an exhibition. That evening the press, officials, and sponsors would attend a civic reception.

"One of the hardest tasks facing the golf correspondent is the final article on the eve of one of the great contests between Britain and the United States," Ward-Thomas wrote. "All supposition, assessment, hoping and fearing are as nothing when battle is joined and lengthy discussion of probabilities as to individual matches is a futile exercise."

The Daily Telegraph's Leonard Crawley anticipated greatness. "Great deeds and great moments there have been at Royal Birkdale," he wrote in the official Ryder Cup program. "There will be more to come. Perhaps this week."

If there was any concern about, or interest in, the Ryder Cup from the western side of the Atlantic Ocean, it was not evident in U.S. sports pages or golf magazines. There were preview articles, but nothing like the frenzied ink spilled in *Golf Illustrated* and other British publications. Fred Tupper was at Royal Birkdale to report on the matches for *The New York Times*. Gwilym Brown was on the scene for *Sports Illustrated* and would soon call the Ryder Cup "one of those neglected waifs of international sport, more of a diplomatic hands-across-the-sea ritual . . . than a hot-blooded athletic event."

For the American public—if any part of it was paying attention—this was not sport. That September a riveting baseball pennant race was one of several exciting distractions in the United States. Floyd's beloved Chicago Cubs were in the midst of an epic collapse. The once lowly New York Mets had raced past Chicago in the National League East standings and would go on to win the pennant. The "Miracle Mets" would then shock the Baltimore Orioles and most everyone else by winning the World Series in five games. Golf was mostly relegated to the back pages of American sports sections.

"[It was] a very very big event for this country," Great Britain team member Neil Coles later said, "whereas in those days the Ryder Cup was of less importance in the States."

On the grounds at Royal Birkdale, Ward-Thomas typed the concluding paragraph of his story on the eve of the Ryder Cup. The former prisoner of war's closing lines would sweep into the pages of the next morning's *Guardian* like a few grains of sand from the seaside dunes.

"As I write, a light easterly breeze is across the links, beneath lightly overcast skies through which the sun has faintly appeared. Thus far, Birkdale has not been a fearsome place. It waits in peace for what should be a memorable three days, come what may."

—9—

THURSDAY: MORNING FOURSOMES

Page 19 of the Official Souvenir Programme explained how the eighteenth Ryder Cup would unfold over the three days of competition. A total of thirty-two matches would be played as follows:

THURSDAY, SEPTEMBER 18
Morning: four 18-hole foursomes matches
Afternoon: four 18-hole foursomes matches

FRIDAY, SEPTEMBER 19
Morning: four 18-hole fourball matches
Afternoon: four 18-hole fourball matches

SATURDAY, SEPTEMBER 20
Morning: eight 18-hole singles matches
Afternoon: eight 18-hole singles matches

A total of 16½ points was needed to win the Ryder Cup. In the case of a tie, the United States would retain the Cup since it had won in 1967. However, in the seventeen previous matches that spanned more than four decades, the Ryder Cup had never ended in a tie. Despite the fervent hopes of British fans, press members, and a first-time captain, there was a sober recognition of history and a sense of realism when it came to the important matter of wagering. Leading British bookmakers had installed Great Britain as up to a 4–1 underdog. Transported by U.S. PGA president Leo Fraser, the Ryder Cup trophy would make a weeklong visit to England, its origin, but it required a kind of sunny optimism that money interests wouldn't risk to believe the Cup's brief homecoming would turn into a more permanent stay.

In addition to the program, the Daily Draw Sheet was available for sale to spectators for a shilling as they arrived at Royal Birkdale on Thursday, the same day pop-culture phenom Tiny Tim, famous for his falsetto-and-ukulele rendition of "Tiptoe Through the Tulips," got engaged in America. The draw sheet listed the captains and players of both teams. More important, it listed the "draw," the four morning foursomes matches and the first points at stake in the three-day event:

MORNING FOURSOMES

Neil Coles–Brian Huggett (GB) vs.
Miller Barber–Raymond Floyd (USA)
Bernard Gallacher–Maurice Bembridge (GB) vs.
Lee Trevino–Ken Still (USA)
Tony Jacklin–Peter Townsend (GB) vs.
Dave Hill–Tommy Aaron (USA)
Christy O'Connor–Peter Alliss (GB) vs.
Billy Casper–Frank Beard (USA)

The draw for the four Thursday afternoon foursomes matches would be announced at midday. The draw sheet was tantalizing, for it not only listed who would play the opening matches but also revealed which play-ers would sit out the first session. Brian Barnes, Peter Butler, Alex Caygill, and Bernard Hunt would be idle for Great Britain. The sidelined Americans were Dale Douglass, Gene Littler, Dan Sikes, and the greatest surprise, if not a total shock, Jack Nicklaus. The Golden Bear had waited seven years to make his Ryder Cup debut. Captain Snead had seen to it that Nicklaus would have to wait a bit longer.

"Sam, as a person, I loved," Raymond Floyd said decades later. "We became really close friends through the years."

At the time, though, Floyd was stunned that Captain Snead didn't have Jack Nicklaus in the lineup that first morning. "For a man to bench the best player in the world . . . because he wasn't playing good in practice—that was just Sam's way. Jack didn't play that opening match, and we all looked at each other like, 'What the hell is going on here?' "

According to *Sports Illustrated*'s Gwilym Brown, Nicklaus was "shocked" to be sitting out on Thursday morning. When someone joked that he was washed up at age twenty-nine, he returned the jab, saying he indeed was finished if being 12 under par for his last 27 holes in practice meant he was through. Ryder Cup veteran Littler was also a nonstarter.

What was Snead thinking?

• • • •

Sam Snead had certainly been around his share of Ryder Cups, seven to be exact, including a pair of appearances as a playing captain in 1951 at Pinehurst, North Carolina, and in 1959 at Eldorado in Palm Desert, California, two more in a string of decisive U.S. victories. Snead's Ryder Cup career had begun in 1937 a short distance from Royal Birkdale. The 8–4 triumph at nearby Southport & Ainsdale Golf Club was America's first Ryder Cup win on British soil. Rookie Snead, like Nicklaus, sat out open-ing foursomes. The next day, in singles, he handily beat Englishman Dick Burton 5 and 4. Snead played in two more Ryder Cups in England—at

Ganton Golf Club in 1949 and at Wentworth in 1953, where he and Lloyd Mangrum humiliated Eric Brown and John Panton in foursomes. The Slammer's Ryder Cup playing record was a splendid 10-2-1. As a player and a captain, he had never been on a losing team.

Snead was also one of the few American golfers of his era to venture across the Atlantic for the British Open. In 1946, playing in the first Open after a six-year interruption due to World War II, Snead captured the Claret Jug at the home of golf, St. Andrews. Sam knew links golf, and he knew about winning.

"[Snead's] knowledge of English courses and style of play in years of competition should give a technical edge in planning a winning strategy," *Professional Golfer* wrote in September 1969.

Except there was no discernible strategy, as some U.S. team members remembered. They simply went out and played golf. This was not meant as a knock on their captain. That's the way it often was in those earlier Ryder Cup days and, in particular, in 1969.

More than forty years later, Frank Beard could remember only one U.S. team meeting before the matches began. It might have lasted five minutes. Captain Snead wanted one bit of information from each of his twelve players. "He asked us to write down on a piece of paper who we didn't want to play with," Beard said. "So that was it. That was the whole meeting."

Presumably, Snead used the player input to form his pairings, but even those were a bit of a mystery. It was an era when the players were honored to make the team and usually willing to play with any of their teammates. It wasn't something players questioned or even thought about, although Beard was uncomfortable going out the first morning with Billy Casper, mostly because he was in awe of Casper.

With ten rookies on the squad, one might expect the veteran captain to offer some sage counsel on links golf, match play, and the Ryder Cup itself, but Beard struggled to recall Snead saying much of anything.

"I don't know. He may have said, 'Come on, boys, let's get out there and hit some balls and practice' and maybe 'if you've got any questions.' It was not a rah-rah meeting. It was not organized. We didn't talk about the old days and how we used to play the Ryder Cup. Nothing."

Tommy Aaron remembered Snead "as being a good captain, but not really too concerned about the matches, figuring we would win with ease." Aaron, who would play with Dave Hill in the first foursomes session, had no clue about Snead's lineup—or anything else the captain was doing, for that matter. "I don't think he got into it that much. I don't think he gave it much thought. He never talked to me about who I wanted to play with. I would have been okay playing with anyone."

Rookie Ken Still was of the same mind. "There was nobody on the team I wouldn't play with. We were a pretty close-knit team."

Sports Illustrated's Brown, while admiring Snead's greatness as a player who was still competitive at the age of fifty-seven, was critical of his captaincy, writing that Snead was "about as capable of leadership as Ebenezer Scrooge." He used adjectives such as "crude," "sullen," and "cantankerous" to describe the golf legend. The writer would say that a few of Captain Snead's lineups must have pleased Captain Brown. Thursday morning's didn't please Jack Nicklaus, though.

"Maybe in Sam's view I wasn't playing well," Nicklaus offered decades later.

Nonetheless, at least a handful of U.S. players held their captain in high esteem. "I thought he was top drawer," Still later said. "He was a player's captain. He knew what was going on. I don't think we had any problems with him at all. I didn't anyway, and I haven't heard any negatives from anyone else."

"Sam was good," agreed Casper, who also mentioned that Hogan, in 1967, was "the captain that really stood out. The other captains weren't as powerful or as strong, but yet each one brought something, too, that the others didn't bring."

"I played more golf with Sam than a guy my age probably ever deserved," Beard later said, chuckling. "He was a good guy. I didn't know what to do with him except just adore him. He was Sam Snead!"

Snead was known to dispense his own folksy brand of wisdom, even if little of it was forthcoming at Royal Birkdale that week. One of his most enduring quotes was three kernels of advice: 1. Keep close count of your nickels and dimes. 2. Stay away from whiskey. 3. Never concede a putt.

．　　　．　　　．

Hardly a breath of wind caressed the two flags as they slowly traveled up the flagpoles on Thursday morning. The Stars and Stripes was raised first during the playing of the "The Star-Spangled Banner." Then up went the Union Jack to "God Save the Queen." Many Ryder Cup players are unprepared for the strong emotions felt at the opening ceremony. Each man knows he is playing for his country long before he arrives on the scene, but as he watches his country's flag raised and hears his national anthem played, he knows it like never before. It can stir a heart, tighten a throat, and upset a stomach.

"You put the coat on, they play 'The Star-Spangled Banner,'" said Beard, who recalled unexpected tears at the opening ceremony. "The impact of this whole thing is beginning to hit you, playing for the country."

"All that is quite emotional," Tony Jacklin recalled, "and then you have to go straight to the first tee, as it were. It captures your attention, that's for sure."

"The flag goes up and there's a feeling in the pit of your stomach," Neil Coles said four decades later. "You are playing for your country. You are playing for your team. You are trying not to let your fellow team members down. So obviously that creates its own nerves, but personally I enjoyed that Ryder Cup feeling."

Billy Casper didn't just enjoy it; he loved everything about it. "I felt like it was the greatest experience I ever had playing professional golf. It was something I wanted to play in as many as I could possibly play."

Brian Huggett felt both pride and pressure when he heard "God Save the Queen." "Playing in the Ryder Cup was more pressure than playing for yourself and family. It was your toughest week for two years, despite being beaten most of the time. You had to play with a lot of self pride, not just national pride."

"You've got the pressure of representing your country and all your peers and there's going to be a different feeling," Floyd said. "That was my first one, and I always remember that feeling."

"It was an honor to be on the team and to represent the United States of America," Still said. "I'll cherish it to the day I die. In fact, I may be buried in the dark blue [Ryder Cup] jacket."

· · · ·

No matter what emotions were swirling around on the inside, the outward appearance of the twenty-four players and their captains was sharp thanks to their stylish uniforms. Both teams would wear cashmere sweaters and wool sports shirts designed by Pringle of Scotland. Over the three days, the Brits would wear power blue, Guardsman red, and, on that first morning, a light yellow shade called Corn. Underneath their sweaters they wore pumpkin-colored long-sleeved shirts. Their socks, courtesy of D. Byford Ltd., were noticeable because they matched the players' colorful tops rather than their dark slacks. The British players also wore brown-and-white Lotus golf shoes that complemented their outfits. British companies took pride in clothing and supplying the team: trousers and blazers by Daks, hats by Richards & Thirkell Ltd., golf gloves by George Jefferies, and rainwear by Morton Knight Ltd. Their handsome white golf bags were made by Ben Sayers.

The Yanks would look patriotic in their cardinal red, navy, and white combinations, with various shades of gray and blue to round out their uniforms. On that first day, azure blue slacks and white long-sleeved shirts were a prominent part of the American ensemble.

On the contrary, the twenty-four men who would carry the players' fancy leather Ryder Cup golf bags were unhappy about their caddie wear, coveralls made of nylon that were dubbed "boiler suits." "We look like house painters and milkmen," one complained. Their larger concern was sweating to death.

The caddies threatened to strike. The British PGA counterthreatened to recruit two dozen other caddies, if needed. Caddies spokesman Alf Fyles, on Peter Butler's bag, and Willie Aitchison, who worked for Lee Trevino, slipped on the suits for a trial run. They and the other caddies determined the suits were tolerable and chose to go along with the PGA. The men— none of whom was American, since caddies didn't typically travel with players, especially overseas—were on the job Thursday morning.

Stewart Logan was on young Gallacher's bag. Jimmy Cousins was Alliss's longtime caddie. Willie Hilton carried for Jacklin. They and the other caddies for the British players wore all-white suits. Casper's bag man was Jock Allen. "He always caddied for me when I went to England," Casper later said. Allen, Aitchison, and the other caddies for the Yanks wore royal blue suits. All twenty-four caddies wore white bibs over their coveralls with the Union Jack or the U.S. flag across their chest.

•   •   •

Speeches made, flags raised, and anthems played, the opening ceremony concluded. It was nearing 9:00 A.M., time to play golf. The men would have to gather themselves. This was not a simple matter for Miller Barber, called "X" by his teammates. One half of the pairing to lead off the matches for the favored Americans, Barber cried during the national anthem, but as he later told *Golf Digest*, "The song ends and now it's time to play."

"In that day," said Floyd, Barber's partner that morning, "we did the opening ceremony in the morning and the first match went to the first tee."

The two rookies had devised an alternate-shot strategy to take advantage of the strengths of their games. Barber would tee off on the odd-numbered holes. Floyd would hit first on the even-numbered holes, which included three of Royal Birkdale's four par-3 holes.

The moment had arrived; the two men were standing on the tee of the opening hole, a 493-yard par 5 with out-of-bounds on the right. The home-country gallery horseshoed itself around the teeing ground.

More than four decades later, Floyd recalled the opening moments of his Ryder Cup debut. "Representing the United States, Miller Barber and Raymond Floyd."

One of the American rookies has to hit the first shot of the Ryder Cup. As previously agreed, it's supposed to be Barber.

"But X had gotten so excited or upset that he couldn't tee," Floyd said.

After the anthems played, emotions were scrambled. Barber's had completely taken over.

"We go walking to the tee," Floyd said, "and X says to me, 'I can't hit it. I can't hit it.' I said, 'Pardon me?' He said, 'I can't hit it. I can't hit it. You gotta go. You gotta go.'"

The new PGA champion didn't want to abandon their strategy before the first golf ball was airborne.

"What do you mean, X?" Floyd asked. "You're playing the odd—"

"I can't do it. You gotta go. You gotta go."

Barber wanted no part of the first shot.

"He wouldn't go up there," Floyd added. "He said, 'I can't do it.'"

•   •   •

Captain Brown, who had five rookies on his squad, revealed an unmistakable pattern with his morning foursomes lineup. The Scot opened and anchored the first set of matches with experience. Coles and Huggett would face Floyd and Barber in the first game, while old guardsmen O'Connor and Alliss would take on Casper and Beard in the morning's final match.

"[Eric Brown] was very good in the team room," Coles later said. "He consulted you a lot, obviously—where you wanted to play, who you wanted to play with." Having played a lot with Bernard Hunt in past Ryder Cups,

Coles was happy to go out with Huggett. "I was quite comfortable with Brian. He was quite a little tiger, a terrier." Huggett enjoyed the international competition, later describing his strengths as "very good driver and short game with good temperament for the big occasion."

Four of Brown's talented youngsters—Gallacher, Bembridge, Jacklin, and Townsend—populated the middle two matches. It was a sound approach. Great Britain needed a strong start in foursomes to bolster their chances against the Americans, something they had often failed to do in previous Ryder Cups.

Captain Snead, meanwhile, was sending out his droves of first-timers on Thursday morning because, except for Casper and Littler, that was all he had. He sat down his most talented Ryder Cup rookie of all, Nicklaus, presumably to save him. Ward-Thomas wrote, "By leaving out Nicklaus, who will probably partner Sikes, Snead has shown that he wants them, in particular, for the fourball matches tomorrow." Still, benching the Golden Bear at the outset produced head scratching and invited criticism.

Snead apparently had his reasons, or maybe, as Aaron suggested, he didn't give too much thought to the draw. The United States had waltzed through most of these matches, and the current stockpile of talented rookies and two veterans had amassed more than 130 victories on the PGA Tour. Five of the twelve U.S. players had won major titles. In 1969 alone, the dozen Yanks had collected twenty wins and banked $1.25 million. On Great Britain's side, only Jacklin had experienced noteworthy success in the States and won a major, the recent British Open at Royal Lytham & St. Annes. Perhaps it made little difference how Snead sent out his men onto Royal Birkdale. If they were indeed better players, they would surely win.

If nothing else, the two captains resembled each other in one way: their physical appearance. Although Snead was thirteen years older than the forty-four-year-old Brown, they looked to be about the same age, both of them bald with the same amount of hair covering the sides of their heads. At some point before the battle began, wearing neckties and blazers, the captains sat down together for tea and coffee and pastries and smiled for a photographer. Being the fierce competitors they were, both men appeared to be smiling for the prematch photograph through clenched teeth—especially Brown. "There was no love lost between Eric and Sam Snead," Jacklin later said.

Paul Trevillion was on hand when the picture was snapped and knew something about the moment that others didn't.

"It was difficult to get Brown to smile," Trevillion later said. "He just bared his teeth, and the Snead smile was not one welcoming you to join them for a cup of coffee." The reason, according to Trevillion, was that "under the table was a can of fishing bait, which Brown had asked Snead to give to Jack. Nicklaus hadn't won a tournament since [February] of that year. This was vacation for Nicklaus, fishing and hunting."

The mind games had begun before the first shot was struck.

Brown brought fire and urgency to the opening matches. "We have got to give the needle to the Americans on the first tee," he said months earlier. "We have got to get off to a good start. They are great when they are up, but not that great when they're on the receiving end."

The veteran of four Ryder Cups felt he had learned from what he called "horrible mistakes" and would do everything in his power to prepare his players accordingly. One crucial element was attitude. "My contention," Brown said, "has always been that our fellows, or most of our fellows, have stepped on the first tee with an inferiority complex." The captain was determined not to let that happen on Thursday morning, or anytime thereafter.

"Eric was a hard man. Played in four Ryders, never lost a single. I never met a tougher competitor," Trevillion said.

"He didn't like being beaten," Townsend said.

Brown made a conscious effort to prepare Great Britain's players in a different manner than in the past. He wanted them to be relaxed, confident, and in "fighting form." He told them not to play safe but to go for broke, to go after birdies. "Never leave a putt short," he exhorted, "even if it means leaving your foursomes partner with 4-footers to putt back. Stay firm and play like hell in the crises."

"He was a fiery person," Gallacher recalled, "and we certainly didn't answer him back. He especially didn't take any nonsense during Ryder Cup time, and if you hit the ball into the rough or missed a putt, he'd let you know about it."

Barnes was different. The captain's exhortations "didn't work as far as I was concerned. It made no difference to me what anybody said. I had my own way of going about it."

Jacklin had a similar perspective, later recalling his captain gathering the players "in the corner of the locker room. 'C'mon boys, come around here and we'll go over here and strategy and all that.'"

Peter Willis detected something else that week. "By the time I arrived at Birkdale in time for the first [matches], I could see in the way that Brown walked and presented himself that he had succumbed to the Trevillion magic. Brown had joined the *Golf Illustrated*–Trevillion bandwagon, and he, too, was walking around telling people, 'We are going to win!'"

•   •   •

A lot was expected of the reigning British Open champion as he waited on the 1st tee with partner Townsend for the announcement of their match against Hill and Aaron. Tony Jacklin had ignited Great Britain with his thrilling Open victory. Now, thanks in large part to Jacklin, there was a fresh sense of hope for Great Britain's Ryder Cup chances. The captain sought to pump up Jacklin for the showdown with the Yanks.

"Eric Brown must have felt I could handle any amount of pressure," Jacklin later said, "because he said many times before and during the competition that he was expecting great things from me, and that I was essentially the team leader."

Townsend saw Jacklin in that light. "For me, that was a great boost to play with somebody as good as he was, and as confident as he was. He just didn't think like the other players, that the Americans were a very good team. I think he just thought they're there to be beaten."

The first two matches were under way as Jacklin looked north, the direction of the 1st green. Floyd, against design, had struck the first shot of the Ryder Cup. Partner Barber gave him no choice. Maybe it would make no difference in the end against Coles and Huggett.

"I was ready to go," Floyd later said, while also admitting he wasn't immune to Ryder Cup pressure. "There was no other like it. I was one of those that could kind of get myself together. [The Ryder Cup] was more difficult for me than playing in a major."

Gallacher and Bembridge were also on the golf course against Trevino and Still. The slender Still had the odd holes, while the squat Trevino would take the even holes, meaning Still hit first to begin their match. Four decades later he remembered hearing his name announced. "On the tee, Ken Still, USA. Play away, please." The Tacoma native wasn't scared, but he was "a little nervous. It got to me because here I am representing the great country of the United States of America. Twelve guys representing the country. I was part of the deal. Biggest honor ever in my career."

By 9:30 A.M., Jacklin and Townsend were off with Hill and Aaron, opposites in terms of temperament. Wearing horn-rimmed glasses and a billed cap, Aaron had the jitters. "When I drove off that first tee, I remember I was very nervous. I was very excited to be playing in the matches."

•　•　•

As if out of respect for the decorated golfers and the special occasion, Royal Birkdale was still. There was not a hint of wind, which was thought to benefit the U.S. team since it had less experience on blustery seaside links. Captain Brown didn't buy it. "That's a load of old rubbish," he said a week earlier. "Pebble Beach and Cypress Point have just as much wind as we get here."

Also uncharacteristic of Birkdale were the course conditions. Rain had recently fallen after weeks of dry weather, and the thirsty turf sprang to life. Anticipating sunshine and wind that would shrivel the grass, those in charge decided not to cut the fairways. As Ward-Thomas reported, the fairways "are not running fast, and the greens, even after their final cut, are hardly likely to be swift at first, and will hold."

While the home side could not control the weather, it did have charge of the tees (where the eighteen tee markers were placed each day) and the hole locations on the eighteen greens. Dai Rees and the Ryder Cup Committee had formulated a plan in recognition of their side's strengths and weaknesses. They drew on their experience from the 1965 Ryder Cup at Royal Birkdale, a pin-placement strategy that backfired. Holes had been placed in tricky spots such as near bunkers, but the Americans were more adept at hitting high, spinning approach shots to the tight pin positions. This time the general plan was to cut holes toward the back-center of the greens, allowing the Brits to play their trademark pitch-and-run shots. In addition, with flags centered on the greens, offline shots could still find the putting surface, which, although the same for both teams, was thought to be more of a confidence booster for the British players.

The Royal Birkdale course where the twenty-four players on the Great Britain and U.S. teams would meet had a par of 38 on the incoming 9, which was unusual in championship golf. There were four par 5s on the closing six holes, including the two finishing holes, 17 and 18.

HOLE	YARDS	PAR
1	493	5
2	427	4
3	416	4
4	212	3
5	358	4
6	533	5
7	158	3

(continued)

HOLE	YARDS	PAR
8	459	4
9	410	4
Out	3466	36
10	393	4
11	412	4
12	190	3
13	517	5
14	202	3
15	536	5
16	401	4
17	501	5
18	513	5
In	3674	38
Total	7140	74

• • •

With Jacklin, Townsend, Trevino, and Still departed, the four men comprising the final morning foursomes match—O'Connor, Alliss, Casper, and Beard—arrived at the 1st hole. The par-5 possessed a sandbank down the left side and out-of-bounds to the right, which caused players to favor the left side, especially if a cross wind blew from the player's left, the direction of the sea. Caddies suggested a particular Tudor-style house as a prudent target line in a freshening wind. As one story went, when Nicklaus was advised to aim his opening tee shot at the distant house, he dryly replied, "Which window?"

All of the last competitors except Beard were seasoned Ryder Cup veterans. O'Connor, who looked fatherly at forty-four, and the dark-haired Alliss had been paired on several occasions. "Christy O'Connor and I formed a very formidable partnership," Alliss said in 2012.

The two players were not strangers to Casper. "[Alliss] and I had many battles," Casper later said. "He really was a good player." The U.S. star also had considerable respect for O'Connor. More than forty years later, after visiting with O'Connor at Royal Dublin Golf Club in his native Ireland, Casper affirmed, "He and I are still great friends."

That genial attitude was typical of Casper. A fierce competitor, the two-time U.S. Open champion liked his British opponents. He was a member of the British PGA, unusual for a U.S. player, and he thoroughly enjoyed Great Britain and its people. "I love the conditions over there, love the way they play golf, and I possibly could have won a British Open early on in my career."

Off went the last match. All four groups had survived the 1st-tee terror experienced at Ryder Cups and were out on the golf course. Captain Brown rushed around the links in an electric golf cart to follow the progress of the matches and encourage his players. Tom Haliburton, captain of the British PGA, rode shotgun. Rees also seemed to be everywhere, on the scene if a golf ball landed in the rough or some matter required discussion.

After matching pars on the first three holes, Barber and Floyd went 1 up when Coles and Huggett bogeyed the par-3 4th hole. The next four holes were halved, including birdies for both sides at the par-4 8th hole, where Barber chipped in from off the green. The British pulled even after their opponents made their first bogey at the 9th, both teams shooting 36 on the outgoing 9. (Stroke scores are a measure of how the pairings were performing in relation to par; however, only holes won and lost and match scores matter at the Ryder Cup.)

Trevino and Still started red hot. The Merry Mex and his partner birdied the first three holes to take a 2-up lead against Gallacher and Bembridge, but the youthful Brits caught them at the long par-4 8th hole when the Yanks recorded a bogey. The second match was even at the turn, with both pairs carding 2-under-par 34s.

Another twosome sizzled through the opening holes—but it wasn't the Americans. Jacklin and Townsend birdied the first three holes to go 2 up on Hill and Aaron. Townsend sank a birdie putt at the 427-yard par-4 2nd hole after Jacklin hit an approach shot out of the rough to 2 feet. On the following hole, also a par 4, Townsend struck a 9-iron to within 4 feet of the hole, and Jacklin rolled in the putt. The Englishmen protected their lead with six straight pars to record a 33.

Aaron was fond of the course and his partner despite facing an early deficit in their foursomes match. "I liked playing Royal Birkdale. It was really good," he later said. "I did a pretty good job of adjusting, but I never thought my game was particularly suited for links golf." About his partner, Aaron commented, "He did everything well, and he could be very combative on the golf course."

"[Hill] had a terrible temper," Beard later said, "but it was always directed at himself. He was a wonderful player, very reliable, didn't hit very many bad shots. I wouldn't want to knock his edge off, but if he was just a little more accepting of an occasional bad shot he would have been a much better player."

In the fourth match, O'Connor and Alliss were engaged in a seesaw battle with Casper and Beard. Neither pair built more than a 1-hole lead, and all leads were short-lived. After a closing U.S. birdie, the four men walked off the 9th green deadlocked. Ryder Cup rookie Beard was uneasy from the start.

"It was a whole different pressure," he said in 2012. "This was kind of the first time I'd had the opportunity to get the feeling of a team thing. Man, it was hard."

Beard was considered one of the game's top players in 1969, but that gave him no comfort at Royal Birkdale. Playing with Casper on the morning of the first day only heightened his insecurities. "He was one of our idols," Beard said about Casper, who at the time had collected forty-three titles on the PGA Tour. "I didn't know what to do with him. He was ten years older than I was and . . . I just kind of stood in awe of him."

Beard's partner thrived on Ryder Cup competition. "I loved the pressure.

I was the type of individual, the more pressure I had, the better I liked it. I loved to be where I could win," Casper later said.

At some hole early on, Beard confronted one of his worst fears. He put his partner in a bad spot—"under a bush"—the result of a wayward tee shot. "I'm thinking, 'Oh, man. This is not good.'"

Upon arrival at the jailed golf ball, Casper didn't say a word. He surveyed the predicament and considered the options. Then, as Beard recalled decades later, Casper turned to him.

"If I chip this out in the middle of the fairway, can you put it about 15 feet?" Casper asked. "If you can, I'm going to make the putt for a par and we're going to go on from here."

"Okay," Beard replied.

Casper chipped the golf ball out into the fairway, and then Beard hit the ball on the green about 12 feet from the hole.

"He made it," Beard said about Casper's putt, "and off we went. I don't remember us having any more discussion at all. I was just so relieved that that turned out so well."

· · ·

As the matches headed out on the second 9, Barber and Floyd were holding their own against Coles and Huggett until the match reached the 517-yard par-5 13th. The Yanks were bunkered, and their opponents made birdie to break the tie, the beginning of a British spurt and an American slide. Barber's tee shot missed the green at the par-3 14th hole, resulting in a bogey that put his side 2 down with 4 holes to play. "Coles rarely can have played better," noted Ward-Thomas. The balding Englishman had struck "perfect" tees shots at the two par 3s, 12 and 14, while his opponent Barber had missed the greens, "to the irritation of Snead." As Ward-Thomas observed, Barber's unorthodox swing was hitting "everything straight right." It happened again at 15, where Barber's second shot flew into the willow scrub. He and Floyd conceded the hole, their third straight loss. Unless there was a dramatic turnaround, the first point of the eighteenth Ryder Cup would go into Great Britain's column.

After winning the par-4 10th hole, where Gallacher dropped a 12-foot birdie putt, and matching their opponents with pars at 11 and 12, the Gallacher-Bembridge duo arrived on the 13th tee with a 1-up lead on Trevino and Still. The Brits had the honors on the par 5, meaning the boyish, fair-haired Bembridge would hit first, followed by Still. Then came the first of several incidents that would cast Still as a poor sport in the eyes of British spectators and some in the press. As Bembridge prepared to hit his tee shot, he determined that his opponent was standing too close and in his line of sight, a distracting presence. The Englishman asked Still to move, a reasonable request. Still complied, but he did more than that—he moved players, caddies, and officials away from Bembridge, to the other side of the tee, in a dramatic fashion. Still was an excitable player and, as one writer observed, had "overreacted." When asked about it decades later, Still could not recall the episode with Bembridge in the opening foursomes match, but he vividly remembered what happened the following day.

The exchange seemed to have a disquieting effect on the American. Still hooked his drive into the rough. Trevino's next shot plugged in a bunker, under the lip. Still was faced with the difficult task of excavating the golf ball from a buried lie. He blasted away, but the ball caromed off the upslope and appeared to strike him on the shoulder. Trevino asked for confirmation. "It hit you, didn't it?" Still didn't answer, so Trevino decided. "Pick it up," he told Still, conceding the hole to Bembridge and Gallacher. The unnerving occurrences at 13 turned a small U.S. deficit into a bigger hole. The Yanks were 2 down to the Brits with 5 holes to play.

At the par-4 10th, a relatively short dogleg to the left, Hill and Aaron birdied to cut the Jacklin and Townsend lead to 1 up. Photographs later showed an animated Hill reacting when putts dropped into the hole. At one juncture he tossed his putter in the air in celebration while Aaron stood off to the side, arms crossed, looking deep in thought.

"[Hill] really got into the Ryder Cup," Casper later said. "He had a strong demeanor about him, and he wanted to win—that's all there was to it. He was probably more expressive than any of the other players that were on the team."

The British and U.S. pairs traded pars on 11, where Townsend cooly sank a 6-footer, and also on 12.

Behind them, O'Connor and Alliss and Casper and Beard were still deadlocked after recording pars at 10, 11, and 12. Up ahead, Trevino and Still fought back. After a tying par at the long par-3 14th, they birdied the par-5 15th hole to climb to 1 down against the British upstarts. They hoped to avoid the fate of Barber and Floyd, whose match had ended on the 16th green with a 3 and 2 defeat at the hands of Coles and Huggett. Great Britain had snatched the first point.

Jacklin and Townsend again widened their lead when Hill and Aaron visited the rough on 13 and made a bogey 6. They were still 2 up when they arrived on the 17th tee. Victory was in sight—in more ways than one. Ahead at the green, Gallacher and Bembridge could finish off Trevino and Still. After driving into the sand dunes, forcing a recovery shot by his partner, Bembridge had swatted a 6-iron to within 7 feet of the cup. "Come on, my little darling," Captain Brown said as he watched Gallacher crouch over the clinching putt. "Put it in." The twenty-year-old stroked it home for a 2-and-1 win over the Americans. Moments later a smiling Bembridge and Gallacher gave the thumbs-up sign to a press photographer. The Brits had claimed the first two matches and were guaranteed at least a halve, or tie, in the third match. It was still early, but this was exactly the start Brown had hoped for.

At the straightaway par-5 17th measuring 501 yards, Jacklin and Hill lashed drives for their respective teams. Their partners followed with 3-wood shots that made the green in 2, although Townsend's was the superior stroke, finishing 6 feet from the hole. Hill faced a long eagle putt from the front of the green that had to go in for a chance to stay alive in the match. His aggressive stroke ran the golf ball 9 feet past the hole. Aaron missed the next one, and it was all but over. As if to put an exclamation point on their brilliant foursomes display, Jacklin rolled home the eagle putt for a 3-and-1 victory. He and Townsend looked unbeatable, shooting 7 under through 17 holes.

"The thing that stood out," Aaron said decades later, "was how well Jacklin and Townsend played together. They shot a very low score."

Townsend, too, could remember that first game some forty years later. "We had an unbelievably good match. I guess it was a wonderful way to finish off, to make an eagle at the 17th."

Three matches, 3 points for Great Britain. Captain Brown was thrilled. Captain Snead, on the other hand, was coming to a slow boil. Excited spectators were walking briskly across the sand dunes to get a look at the morning's final match. Thursday's attendance was an estimated 9,000.

"You can always tell the state of the matches by the speed of the crowd walk," a course steward said later that day. "When we are doing well, they fairly charge along."

Could the British make it a clean sweep?

Casper and Beard had slipped ahead of O'Connor and Alliss with a birdie at the par-5 13th hole but relinquished the lead on the next hole when the Brits carded the only birdie of the morning at the difficult 202-yard par 3. At one point as O'Connor stood over a lengthy putt, a fan commented, "If he holes this, the roar will bring the TV tower down." Fortunately for BBC announcer Henry Longhurst, O'Connor missed, quipped Peter Willis.

With both teams recording pars at 15, 16, and 17, the morning's culminating match arrived at 18 tied, the only match to reach the final hole. The Americans got into trouble when Beard fluffed a short pitch shot into a greenside bunker, but Casper blasted their fourth shot out of the sand to 5 feet from the hole. All they could do was watch as Alliss took measure of an 18-foot birdie putt to win the match and stake Great Britain to a 4–0 lead. It would have been an easier assignment for Alliss had O'Connor not hit an indifferent chip shot.

Allis, who was using a George Low–model putter, later said that by this stage in his career "my putting was decidedly creaky." Alliss's collaborator on *Easier Golf* knew it. "I was well aware of his one weakness," Trevillion later said. "Alliss at that time treated his putting as a joke. The number plate on his car was 3 PUTT. Personally, I never thought that funny. He was by far the best golfer in the Great Britain team, but his putting was his Achilles' heel."

This time, on Birkdale's 18th green, Alliss hit a good one. "I thought I had it," he said.

Trevillion couldn't watch. "I turned away. The loud groan from the crowd told me what I already knew. Alliss had missed."

The birdie effort had agonizingly rimmed the hole, a small opening for the Yanks. Beard sank the 5-footer to secure a half point for his team and, at last, wipe the U.S. goose egg off the scoreboard. The unusually calm morning at Royal Birkdale had belonged to Great Britain.

MORNING FOURSOMES RESULTS

Coles-Huggett (GB) defeated Barber-Floyd (USA) 3 and 2
Gallacher-Bembridge (GB) defeated Trevino-Still (USA) 2 and 1
Jacklin-Townsend (GB) defeated Hill-Aaron (USA) 3 and 1
O'Connor-Alliss (GB) halved with Casper-Beard (USA)
Session total: Great Britain 3½, United States ½

"When I talked to Eric Brown, he was delighted," Trevillion later said. "A 3½–½ lead was beyond his wildest dreams. He asked why I was so disappointed. I pointed out that if it had been 4–0, there was no way, no matter how well the USA team played in the afternoon, the Great Britain team would be behind at the end of the day. Eric tried to cheer me up by saying, 'Half a loaf is better than none. The O'Connor and Alliss half point could win us the Ryder Cup.'"

"My first vivid memory," Willis said decades later, "was probably standing behind the 17th green on the first morning and realizing that it was Great Britain 3, United States 0, with one match halved after the

The 1969 British tour offered a variety of tournaments but was far from lucrative for the golfers.

Paul Trevillion

The 1969 Ryder Cup press badge and materials of *Golf Illustrated's* Paul Trevillion.

Paul Trevillion

The Official Souvenir Programme of the 18th Ryder Cup and other event materials.

Paul Trevillion

The 1969 Great Britain Ryder Cup team at Royal Birkdale. From left to right: Brian Huggett, Maurice Bembridge, Alex Caygill, Christy O'Connor, Brian Barnes, Bernard Hunt, Captain Eric Brown, Peter Alliss, Peter Butler, Tony Jacklin, Neil Coles, Peter Townsend, Bernard Gallacher.

Evening Standard/Hulton Archive/Getty Images

The 1969 U.S. Ryder Cup team at Royal Birkdale. From left to right: Captain Sam Snead, Lee Trevino, Raymond Floyd, Gene Littler, Ken Still, Frank Beard, Dave Hill, Dan Sikes, Miller Barber, Billy Casper, Dale Douglass, Tommy Aaron, Jack Nicklaus.

Bob Thomas/Bob Thomas Sports Photography/Getty Images

Tony Jacklin (right) and Peter Townsend led the early British charge at Royal Birkdale.

Bob Thomas/Bob Thomas Sports Photography/Getty Images

One of ten rookies on the U.S. team, Frank Beard was uncomfortable playing in his first Ryder Cup.

Bob Thomas/Bob Thomas Sports Photography/Getty Images

Great Britain's Brian Huggett (second from left) wept after holing a putt on the final green that he and others thought clinched a rare victory.

Bob Thomas/Bob Thomas Sports Photography/Getty Images

Jack Nicklaus and Tony Jacklin walk off the final green after the stunning conclusion of the 1969 Ryder Cup.

Bob Thomas/Bob Thomas Sports Photography/Getty Images

For the first time, two opposing teams and their captains, Sam Snead and Eric Brown, shared the Ryder Cup.

Bob Thomas/Bob Thomas Sports Photography/Getty Images

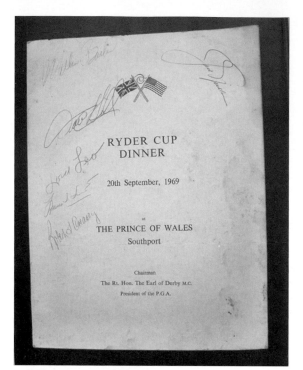

A 1969 Ryder Cup Dinner Menu with player autographs, including Jack Nicklaus's at upper right.

Paul Trevillion

The entrance to The Concession Golf Club in Bradenton, Florida, which opened in 2006.

Neil Sagebiel

A player station at The Concession Golf Club displaying the emblem of the famous
moment. *Neil Sagebiel*

A view of the 18th hole at The Concession Golf Club.

Neil Sagebiel

Tony Jacklin inside The Concession Golf Club in 2013. Paintings of him and Jack Nicklaus hang in the background.

Neil Sagebiel

Jack Nicklaus at Golden Bear Plaza in North Palm Beach, Florida, in 2013.

Neil Sagebiel

In 2013, sports artist Paul Trevillion, 79, drew this sketch of Jack Nicklaus during breakfast.

Paul Trevillion

morning session. I can still feel the tingle of excitement of that moment and the realization that the campaign was working in front of my eyes. It was hard to take in."

The Guardian's Ward-Thomas lauded the surprising start. "Nothing can diminish the morning glory," he reported, "no matter what the coming days may bring. Never has a British team begun more impressively, not only in the winning but in the manner of the winning."

It was true. Even at Lindrick, the site of a rare win, Great Britain trailed after foursomes. It was only the fourth time the United States had lost the opening session of the Ryder Cup—and the first time since 1949. In fact, as both teams headed off to lunch between foursomes sessions, the 3-point lead was Great Britain's best start since Samuel Ryder donated the gold chalice for the first biennial matches in 1927.

—10—

THURSDAY: AFTERNOON FOURSOMES

A short distance from the excitement at Royal Birkdale was the city of Southport, a seaside resort and holiday destination with a residential population of 80,000 that could lodge and entertain thousands of visitors during the Ryder Cup and other special occasions. A little more than a century earlier Southport was a small hamlet with one hotel and a few cottages used by fishermen. In recent years it had become a recreational, shopping, and cultural paradise and was now hosting the Ryder Cup for the third time. A wide, bustling promenade stretched along the city's western edge a short distance from the Irish Sea. An array of family-oriented attractions were within steps of each other, including Pleasureland, an amusement park that boasted a wooden roller coaster named Cyclone that opened on Good Friday in 1937. Southport was filled with cafés, gardens, parks, museums, dance halls, and cinemas, like other English cities, but it also had beaches, swimming pools, an aquarium, rides (including a new go-kart track), and Peter Pan's Playground, which featured a boating lake and catering establishment. Lord Street was the central thoroughfare for Southport's fashionable shopping district and fine restaurants, with fountains, gardens, and an open-air café intermingled for aesthetic appeal.

With five 18-hole golf courses—two of them Ryder Cup venues—Southport had become a popular golf destination on England's northwest coast, a primary goal of Brian Park's when he financed the 1965 Ryder Cup and brought it to Royal Birkdale. One could even knock the small white ball around within the city limits at the Southport and Birkdale Cricket Grounds, where there were putting greens and the Arnold Palmer Putting Course.

Southport seemed to have it all, but it was a foreign experience for American players such as Frank Beard.

"Birkdale," Beard said decades later, "in Southport there, it was sort of one of their resorts. They tried to explain to us that it was kind of like Miami Beach, or something. Well, it wasn't like Miami Beach at all, but it might have taken some characteristics of better weather there than some other places in Great Britain."

That week's weather was not bad, as Beard recalled, but it was definitely on the cool side. "It was not warm at all." As for adapting to the British way of life, he admitted, "I was a typically spoiled American," which, among other things, meant he was partial to his mother's cooking. "I don't remember enjoying the food real well. The accommodations had one or two beds on each floor. I had my wife with me, and we share these bathrooms, shower, the whole thing. That was a little odd, a little difficult to do."

Henry Longhurst anticipated some level of discomfort for U.S. players. A week earlier in *Golf Illustrated*, Longhurst opined that, in addition to "a courage and spirit which was beyond praise," something else aided Great Britain's most recent Ryder Cup victory at Lindrick in 1957. "Their main ally," Longhurst wrote, "was the primitive nature of the Americans' accommodation both in their Sheffield hotel (since modernised), which was unable to serve them breakfast at all and sent them out early in a coach [a bus, to Americans] complete with wives to get it at the clubhouse." Things did not dramatically improve once they got there. The Lindrick clubhouse was far from modern. The large American golf bags would not fit in the lockers. There were only two lavatories. One of them had a faulty bolt.

It was twelve years later, and Southport and Royal Birkdale had more to offer in terms of creature comforts. Longhurst pointed out that it was still a long way from America—and he wasn't talking about distance. "They will be lucky if all of them get a private bathroom and very lucky indeed if they have anywhere comfortable in their room at which to write the duty postcards to the folks back home, or if they can get their trousers pressed or their shirts washed and returned the same day."

In addition, the locker rooms were still somewhat primitive, but during the lunch break on Thursday the twelve players on the U.S. team probably didn't take much notice of their surroundings because they were 3 points down to Great Britain and getting a righteous earful from Captain Snead. By all reports, whatever old Sam said during the break was laced with colorful language. He was hot, and apparently so were others. Peter Willis reported "frayed tempers in U.S. dressing room at lunch."

When the twelve men emerged after enduring the fury of their captain, three players who sat out the morning session were in the afternoon lineup: Gene Littler, Dan Sikes, and Jack Nicklaus. The draw was set as follows:

AFTERNOON FOURSOMES

Neil Coles–Brian Huggett (GB) vs. Dave Hill–Tommy Aaron (USA)
Bernard Gallacher–Maurice Bembridge (GB) vs.
Lee Trevino–Gene Littler (USA)
Tony Jacklin–Peter Townsend (GB) vs. Billy Casper–Frank Beard (USA)
Bernard Hunt–Peter Butler (GB) vs. Jack Nicklaus–Dan Sikes (USA)

Morning players Barber, Floyd, and Still would rest. So would Dale Douglass, the one U.S. player still waiting to make his debut. Hill and

Aaron were together again, as were Casper and Beard. Trevino was with Littler, and first-timers Nicklaus and Sikes were in the anchor match.

For the British squad, Captain Eric Brown kept all but one of his morning foursomes pairings intact. With a near-perfect opening session and an unprecedented 3-point lead, why change things up? In three of the afternoon matches, Brown would send out the same six players in the same order. Hunt and Butler would go out for the first time in the final match against Nicklaus and Sikes.

Beard and his U.S. teammates were still learning the names of their opponents. "Almost none of them, except for Jacklin and one or two of the older guys, had ever come to America," he later said. "So we were just kind of getting a look at them."

The British reserves that afternoon were Brian Barnes, Alex Caygill, Christy O'Connor, and Peter Alliss, which was by prior arrangement with Brown.

"I was getting into television and the captain allowed me to play in the mornings and then I went and did television in the afternoon," Alliss said.

Alliss would serve as a commentator alongside Longhurst and announcer Harry Carpenter for BBC Television, a rare double role in the Ryder Cup. "I didn't think much about the change from being a competitor in the morning and a TV commentator in the afternoon. You had your job to do and you did it constructively and without too much patriotism."

Although Alliss had won more Ryder Cup points than any other man on the current team and any other Brit of his generation, he later said that Captain Brown kept to their agreement and never asked him to play afternoon matches over the three days. When he was not fighting for points against Casper, Beard, and others, there was perhaps no better place to be than in his broadcast position for the BBC.

•   •   •

BBC-1 and BBC-2 would provide extensive coverage of the Ryder Cup matches all three days throughout Great Britain. Cameras were set up on the final seven holes, the 12th through the 18th, and a roving "radio" camera strapped on a BBC man aided by a technical assistant captured the action elsewhere on the championship layout.

The Ryder Cup coverage would receive high marks. "Much credit," wrote one fan, "is due to the two Peters, Thomson and Alliss, who, with their intimate knowledge of the players and courses have added an extra, most interesting, ingredient to the overall pattern of the commentary team." On Thursday BBC-1 began its television coverage at noon, not long before Alliss nearly holed a match-winning putt on the final green.

For those who couldn't be near a TV screen or when other programming interrupted televised Ryder Cup coverage, BBC Radio brought the excitement at Royal Birkdale to eager listeners. Starting on Thursday morning at 10:31, there were one-minute reports on BBC Radio 2 every hour until suppertime, or 6:32 P.M.

The man behind the microphone for BBC Radio was *Golf Illustrated* editor Tom Scott, a veteran of nearly two thousand broadcasts dating back to 1951 when Longhurst invited Scott to join a small radio team at Royal Portrush in Northern Ireland. In an article he wrote for the Ryder Cup program, Scott marveled at how far radio had come since his early days when places such as a shed, a chicken house, and a space beside a ladies' changing room had served as makeshift broadcast studios.

"I hope what we will have to tell you from this year's Ryder Cup match will be to your liking," Scott wrote.

At midday Thursday, there was a lot for the home team and home nation to like.

• • •

The afternoon foursomes matches were on the golf course. Captain Snead would find out in a few hours if his ripe words had motivated his players.

The United States had a lot of work to do on Thursday afternoon to climb back into the Ryder Cup.

Hill and Aaron fell behind early in the first match. With a bogey at the 1st hole and an early Coles-Huggett birdie, the U.S. duo was 2 down after 3 holes. Then, beginning at the short par-4 5th hole with a birdie, the match turned the Americans' way. They were still 1 down to Coles and Huggett when they arrived at the 158-yard par-3 7th hole. Another U.S. birdie, followed by a par-birdie finish to win three consecutive holes, and Hill and Aaron were 2 up at the turn.

Two of the young British heroes from the morning followed close behind. After halving the first four holes with Trevino and Littler, Gallacher and Bembridge went 1 up with a birdie at the 358-yard 5th hole. The lead was momentary, as Trevino and Littler went on a three-hole win streak to go 2 up, which included a Littler chip-in for a birdie at the 7th. Trevino and Littler were a contrast in styles. Gene was quiet and possessed a textbook golf swing. If he felt added pressure at Royal Birkdale, no one would know from his outward appearance. "It was kind of fun," he later said in his typical low-key fashion about playing in the Ryder Cup. Conversely, Trevino was lively, a jokester who carved shots from left to right with a short, quick swing action. They played well together, though, the ultimate measure of a partnership. After the two pairs halved the 9th with pars, the Yanks were ahead at the midpoint of the first two matches.

Playing in the third match, Jacklin was unable to ignore a foot problem as he walked down the 1st fairway. His captain hurried to the clubhouse to locate a Band-Aid and soon returned. Amused men and women in the gallery watched intently as the Open champion removed his Lotus golf shoe and sock to apply the Band-Aid to the tender spot on his left foot.

Jacklin and Townsend matched pars with Casper and Beard on the first three holes, fell behind with a bogey at the long par-3 4th hole, and leveled the match with a birdie at the 533-yard par-5 6th. Another bogey at the short 7th put Jacklin and Townsend 1 down, but they rebounded with a birdie at the 9th hole to square the match at the turn.

Elsewhere on the course, Captain Snead was crisscrossing fairways in his golf cart to monitor the matches, which annoyed at least one of his players—Billy Casper. "Get out of the way," yelled Casper as his captain drove in front of the 8th green.

"He was out there," Beard later said about Snead. "It wasn't like he disappeared. He was around. He'd show up at your match."

•   •   •

The ebb and flow of the matches was compelling, but that wasn't all that attracted the notice of golf journalists. Four players' wives were following the matches. Wearing a miniskirt, red tights, and black boots, Patti Beard looked "delightful," reported Paul Trevillion, who habitually roamed the golf course. Willis agreed. "Hard to watch the golf with Frank Beard's wife, Patti, around."

Meanwhile, Patti's husband agonized about missed putts, at one point bowing his head and pulling down the bill of his golf cap over his eyes. His often trusty Bulls Eye putter extended from his left hand. Beard was one of the best putters on tour, but everyone missed putts, especially in the Ryder Cup.

The other three ladies were also a pleasant sight. Peter Townsend's wife, Lorna, was a "dazzling picture" with her long blond hair. Vivien Jacklin was "equally charming," clad in her finely tailored cape coat. (Because she was expecting, Mrs. Jacklin would not do as much walking during the matches as the other wives. She had been busy preparing for the baby and furnishing the Jacklins' new home at Scunthorpe.) Shirley Casper rounded out the attractive quartet, donning a stylish plaid suit and calf-high white boots.

The British and American women stood side by side in the long grass—Lorna, Patti, Vivien, and Shirley—watching their husbands battle each other on the nearby fairways. They looked like fashionable friends on an afternoon stroll through the English countryside.

. . . .

The last match of the day featured two Ryder Cup veterans, Great Britain's Hunt and Butler, and two rookies, Nicklaus and Sikes of the United States. The two Americans had drawn a sizable crowd on the practice tee. Alan Dunn of *The Guardian* reported that Sikes was the more impressive ball striker of the two players, hitting practice shots with a draw (a slight right-to-left curve for a right-handed player) directly to the caddie's shag bag from 200 yards away. Onlookers watched Nicklaus curve his golf ball the opposite way, a fade. After witnessing Sikes hit six splendid 4-iron shots, an elderly man, with a tinge of apprehension, asked, "Are you going to play this afternoon, Mr. Sikes?" Sikes replied, "I sure am, I'm sorry to say."

After tying birdies at the 1st hole, the opposing pairs took turns winning the next three holes. Nicklaus and Sikes held a 1-up lead when the match reached the 5th tee and maintained their slim advantage to the clubhouse. Through the first nine holes, America was ahead in three matches and tied in the other, but its leads were not large and could quickly disappear. The next two hours would tell a lot about Thursday and the overall tenor of the matches.

. . . .

The Ryder Cup was a spectacle that attracted, among others, several sports celebrities who were spotted in the sizable Thursday gallery. Famed footballers (soccer players to Americans) Bobby Charlton, Denis Law, Roger Hunt, and Sir Matt Busby roamed Royal Birkdale during the afternoon matches. It was the first Ryder Cup sponsored by a commercial company, and the four stars and other spectators—at some points a half-dozen deep along the temporary chestnut fencing set back a cautious distance from the fairways—could not have missed the sprawling sponsor sign near the 18th green. The sign featured a gigantic golf ball with SENIOR SERVICE LIMITED printed on it in large letters. On the sign's right-hand side 18TH RYDER CUP appeared in light-colored letters set against a dark background.

Owned by the Gallaher Group, a large tobacco concern that originated in Belfast, Ireland, Senior Service was a brand of cigarette named to coincide with the popular name of the Royal Navy. The product packaging displayed a sailing ship and two sea gulls and included the verbiage "The Perfection of Cigarette Luxury."

The company's involvement in the Ryder Cup had begun in 1965 when it acquired concession rights from Brian Park. In 1969, the cigarette maker was returning to golf in a big way. "Senior Service have become sponsors to raise the standard of organization and presentation of such an important event," said British PGA secretary John Bywaters in April. Senior Service Limited was contributing a large but undisclosed sum of money to the eighteenth Ryder Cup, which must have been evident to the thousands of people who flocked to Royal Birkdale that week. This was not merely a golf tournament; it was a golf extravaganza and a vast golf village. Senior Service had a hand in much of it.

The many administrative aspects of the event—what today would be called a hospitality area—were mostly housed under one huge canvas roof. Beneath the roof were partitioned areas with transparent walls that provided virtually everything a spectator might require at a tournament outing. There was a Senior Service information area and rest lounge that included air and rail travel lines and local information. There was also a mobile post office, a first aid station, at least one trade exhibition, telephones, six banks, and, importantly, "comfortable toilet facilities." In addition, the cafeterias, dining areas, and bars offered ample food and drink for the masses.

First, golf fans had to get there and get in. The cost for car parking and admission increased as the week wore on. Both were free on Monday, the first practice day. Once the matches began on Thursday, parking was £1. A three-day ticket purchased at the gate was £2 10s. A Patron's Ticket cost £10, which gave a person the full run of Royal Birkdale for the week, including the car park, the golf course, and the clubhouse.

Once on the grounds, spectators could procure the Official Souvenir Programme and the Daily Draw Sheet that listed the morning and afternoon matches. Out on the golf course fans could follow the progress of the matches in a number of ways. The *Daily Express* erected a hole-by-hole scoreboard and leaderboards in key positions on the course. Driven by female amateur golfers, Harbilt buggies (motorized golf carts) with four-sided scoreboards mounted on them trailed each match. Portable scoreboards manually carried by volunteers also accompanied each group. PGA members transmitted hole scores throughout a wired network, and a massive map of Royal Birkdale in the tented administrative area continually updated the status of all matches.

If one somehow failed to keep abreast of the matches through the various forms of modern communications, then the nuanced sounds of the British galleries—the murmurs, the polite applause, the roars, the occasional comment, all separated by well-timed silence—surely transmitted much of what a casual onlooker needed to know about the Ryder Cup matches.

Corporate hospitality, a growing presence in tournament golf, was also in full bloom at Birkdale. "Prestige Pavilions," wooden hutlike structures with roofs, awnings, and business signage, served as Ryder Cup headquarters for about a dozen companies that entertained their clients, top brass, guests, and others. Each pavilion was outfitted with closed-circuit television so the invitees could sip drinks and watch the golf action without tromping around the sand dunes.

Apparently nothing had been overlooked in the preparations for this Ryder Cup. There was even insurance in place should a disaster of some kind disrupt the event. It included such things as the U.S team failing to arrive in Great Britain due to an airplane accident, war, or other calamities. In fact, the insurance policy remained in force until the first ball was struck from the 1st tee.

· · ·

A 2-up lead at the turn wasn't safe for Hill and Aaron. Coles and Huggett caught them at the par-5 15th with a bogey, of all things. The Yanks had hacked their way to the green, finding themselves bunkered three times on their way to a double-bogey 7. The Brits had cut the lead to 1 down at the par-4 10th hole when Coles sank a 30-foot birdie putt. With 3 holes left to play, it was anybody's match.

Directly behind them Trevino and Littler were hanging on to their lead on the inward 9, alternating between 2 up and 1 up as they surrendered the 11th and 13th holes but offset the losses with wins at the 12th and 14th. Ahead, Coles-Huggett and Hill-Aaron looked sharper at the par-4 16th hole, both sides making birdies. After pars at the 17th, the first afternoon match, all square, proceeded to the 18th hole.

Two up with 2 holes to play, Trevino and Littler could close out their match at the 17th by tying Gallacher and Bembridge on the par 5, but the Brits made a birdie to extend the match to the home hole. Captain Snead might have been losing a few more hairs from his mostly bald head.

The Jacklin-Townsend pair fell behind for the first time on Thursday when Jacklin drove into the rough at the 11th, resulting in a bogey. Casper missed a makeable birdie putt at 12 that would have put him and Beard 2 up. Failing to seize momentum, the Americans instead slammed into reverse at the par-5 13th. Beard hit his tee shot into the rough, and Casper sprained his right hand while hitting the recovery shot. "The ball was in half an old divot hole," he said about the swing that tweaked his hand. They made a bogey, while Jacklin and Townsend recorded a routine par that evened the match.

The drama in the final match centered around which side would crack first. After Nicklaus and Sikes took a 1-up lead at the 4th hole, they tied with Hunt and Butler on each of the next eleven holes, making ten pars and a lone birdie. They were hanging on as each tied hole brought them closer to a precious point.

Teammates Casper and Beard were also trying to hang in their match, but it was made harder by wayward drives such as the ugly hook Casper hit at the reachable par-5 15th. He and Beard caught a break when Jacklin deposited his approach shot into a greenside bunker. The Americans scrambled to a tying par and went on to the 16th still even in the match. They again tied Jacklin and Townsend with a par, but their trailing teammates stumbled when they arrived at the 16th green. The Golden Bear left his first putt 5 feet short of the hole, and Sikes was unable to sink the next one. The last two matches were deadlocked with 2 holes to play.

•   •   •

While his teammates were in a desperate fight on Royal Birkdale's final 9, Miller Barber was trying to settle a disagreement with his hickory-shafted, mallet-head putter on the practice green. Barber had hooked putts (stroking the ball with a slight right-to-left spin) in his morning match that he and Floyd lost to Coles and Huggett. Under the watchful eye of his caddie, with three golf balls at his feet, Mr. X was experimenting with his putting technique in an effort to roll the ball straight and true. Except for a spectator or two, player and caddie were alone as they attempted to solve the putting mystery.

Barber tried everything: He adjusted the ball position in his stance, he adjusted his hands, and he worked at squaring the putter's clubface after his caddie advised it was in a closed position. At one point during the practice session, he stroked 3-footers while looking at the hole instead of the ball. That worked, he decided, saying, "I've got it."

Barber told his caddie to remind him to keep his head positioned behind the golf ball. He then sank two putts from 10 feet but hooked the third and still looked somewhat perplexed when he walked off the practice green.

•   •   •

On the 18th green a short distance from the white clubhouse, Coles and Huggett watched as Hill hunched over a birdie putt to win their hard-fought match. A few minutes earlier, Hill had laced a 3-wood that hopped over a greenside bunker and stopped on the fringe at the back of the green. Using his putter, Aaron coaxed their third shot to an awkward distance from the cup, close but not automatic. After Coles had driven into the rough and his side could do no better than a par, the outcome of the match depended on Hill.

The putt was not a long one, in the 4-foot range, but so much depended on it. The dark-haired, intense player tapped the putt and watched the ball catch the cup, half circle it, hesitate on the far edge, and tumble in for a 1-up victory and the first point of the afternoon. "A shaky putt but a solid point to the Americans," reported Peter Ryde of *The Times*.

Directly behind them, 1 down to Trevino and Littler, the best Gallacher and Bembridge could hope for was a halved match that would earn the British side a half point—if they could win the 18th hole. It began badly, with Gallacher knocking his drive into the rough. The Americans took care of business. Trevino knocked their second shot inches short of a bunker alongside the 18th green. When Littler deftly struck a chip shot within a yard of the hole for a birdie, it was over, a 1-up victory for the Yanks. By winning the first two afternoon matches, the United States had cut Great Britain's lead to 1, 3½–2½.

At the 17th, the first of the two finishing par 5s, Casper again hooked a drive that put him and Beard in trouble on a hole that players expected to birdie much of the time. Perhaps Billy's sore hand had contributed to his poor tee shots at 15 and 17, but he would not use the injury as an excuse. On his side's second shot, Townsend walloped a 3-wood into a breeze that ended close to the green. Jacklin's chip scooted up beside the hole for a certain birdie. After a strong recovery by Beard and a superb chip by Casper, Beard's putt for a birdie to halve the hole came up short. The U.S. tandem was behind in the match for the first time, 1 down with 1 hole to play. The British pair was destined to be heroes once more. Beard struck a beautiful approach shot that stopped 15 feet shy of the flagstick on the final green. An American birdie was a near certainty. Jacklin missed the putting surface to the right with his second, but his partner came through. Townsend floated a delicate pitch over the edge of the bunker that rolled to within 6 inches of the cup for a match-clinching birdie. "At the time, my ability to get up and down was excellent," Townsend later said. "I was good around the greens from awkward spots."

Jacklin later said that he got a little tired during afternoon play but that he and Townsend "pulled ourselves together" at the end. They had 2 points to show for it. Dai Rees had noticed the Jacklin-Townsend demeanor from the day's start. The pair exuded confidence, which portended good things for the British side.

Great Britain again led by 2 points, with Hunt and Butler still fighting to the end in their duel against Nicklaus and Sikes. The afternoon's final match had reached the final hole. It was tied.

The 17th hole had not been pretty for either set of partners. Nicklaus sprayed his second shot into the gorse, a native evergreen shrub, which led to a fat 6, his side's second consecutive bogey. Their British opponents were also bad: a pushed drive, a mediocre pitch, and then a gift—Hunt missed a 6-foot par putt. The day's only two 6s at 17 had come from the same match. After going bogey-bogey, Nicklaus and Sikes were fortunate to be tied as they stepped onto the 18th tee.

Nicklaus had the honors and hooked his tee shot into the rough. Sikes came to the rescue. He slashed their second shot 250 yards into the open fairway, just short of the green. Nicklaus answered with a fine pitch that cozied up to within 2 feet of the hole for a certain birdie. Hunt had a putt to tie from 25 feet, but it stopped 2 inches wide of the cup. The United States had earned the afternoon's last point.

AFTERNOON FOURSOMES RESULTS

Hill-Aaron (USA) defeated Coles-Huggett (GB) 1 up

Trevino-Littler (USA) defeated Gallacher-Bembridge (GB) 1 up

Jacklin-Townsend (GB) defeated Casper-Beard (USA) 1 up
Nicklaus-Sikes (USA) defeated Butler-Hunt (GB) 1 up
Session total: United States 3, Great Britain 1
Overall score: Great Britain 4½, United States 3½

All four afternoon matches had gone to the last hole. The Americans had escaped with three of them to win the session, 3–1. Nonetheless, at the end of the first day, Great Britain led. It was a slim advantage after the morning ecstasy, but it didn't dim the spirit of Captain Brown.

"We went in as the underdogs and we finished ahead," he said with a wide grin. "If we can get another good start tomorrow we'll be in with a chance."

Captain Snead, forcing a smile, was relieved that his team had fought back in the afternoon and was only 1 point behind. He felt luck had not been on his team's side at times on Thursday but also expressed confidence that his boys would play better, "especially in the mornings."

Maybe so. If the celebrated U.S. team hadn't awakened to the competitive challenge presented by the British squad when the flags were raised on Thursday morning, they certainly had by now. Great Britain was ahead after the first day of the Ryder Cup for the first time in twenty years.

—11—

FRIDAY: MORNING FOURBALLS

With two foursomes sessions completed on the opening day and Great Britain holding a slim lead, the eighteenth Ryder Cup shifted to fourball matches on Friday, "a more familiar style of play to the Americans," reported *The New York Times*'s Fred Tupper. Fourballs got its name because each match pitted two teams of two players, or four balls. Each golfer played his own ball—no alternating shots as in foursomes matches—until the ball was holed or picked up. Only the lowest score on each two-man team was recorded for each hole. This match-play format is also known as better ball or best ball. The Brits played fourball events somewhat regularly on the amateur and professional circuit, the Yanks only occasionally, although there were those who felt better-ball matches favored the Americans—and for good reason if considering recent history.

The British had lost seven of eight fourball matches at Champions in the 1967 Ryder Cup. Two years had passed, and in familiar surroundings at Royal Birkdale, Great Britain's twelve were a long way from Houston. Still, *The Daily Telegraph*'s Leonard Crawley recalled the last time the Ryder Cup had visited Southport. "The Americans . . . are never more dangerous than when their backs are to the walls, and it was in these pestilential four-ball matches that they went into the lead in the match four years ago at Birkdale. Britain never saw them for dust, after that."

On another relatively calm morning, the sun warm for northern England in September, the fourball matches began at 8:45 A.M. The draw was set as follows:

MORNING FOURBALLS

Christy O'Connor–Peter Townsend (GB) vs.
Dave Hill–Dale Douglass (USA)
Brian Huggett–Alex Caygill (GB) vs.
Raymond Floyd–Miller Barber (USA)
Brian Barnes–Peter Alliss (GB) vs. Lee Trevino–Gene Littler (USA)
Tony Jacklin–Neil Coles (GB) vs. Jack Nicklaus–Dan Sikes (USA)

Captain Brown changed his lineup on Friday morning. He split up Thursday's star pairing—Townsend and Jacklin—putting them with veterans O'Connor and Coles, respectively, in the session's opening and closing matches. "I played with Coles, whose aggression I have always admired, and we certainly needed that sort of thing against Nicklaus and Sikes," Jacklin later said. "Neil Coles would remind me a little bit of Hogan," Casper said decades later. "He was a very straight player, a very sound player, a very dedicated player." Townsend had no qualms about partnering with elder statesman O'Connor. "He was a superb player," Townsend later said.

Brown also brought two of his five rookies off the sidelines for their first Ryder Cup matches. Caygill, twice a winner in 1969, would debut with Huggett in the second game; Barnes would go out with Alliss in the third match.

"Every time you went out," Barnes later said about Ryder Cup competition, "whether you won or lost, your points went up on the board for the team and for your country. So it was a different feeling entirely, far more pressure. You felt that everyone was relying on you to be able to do well."

Captain Brown explained the new pairings by saying, "I wanted the best possible linking of youth and experience in the fourball matches." Then he expressed confidence in his strategy. "It should work well."

Maurice Bembridge, Peter Butler, Bernard Gallacher, and Bernard Hunt would sit out the morning fourballs session. The captain was saving young horses Gallacher and Bembridge, who paired successfully on Thursday, for Friday's afternoon play.

Captain Snead's lineup featured three of Thursday's pairings. One exception was Hill and Douglass, the tall, slender Oklahoman who would be playing in his first Ryder Cup match. Tommy Aaron and Ken Still would watch, as would Frank Beard and Billy Casper, two of America's most feared players.

Playing or not playing, Beard was not in his element. "I just didn't like it. I just was uncomfortable the whole time. And I don't know whether it was the match-play aspect of it, or just being nervous, or playing for my country, or all of the above."

Casper thrived on this competition, so his injury was bad news for Snead. The longtime standout was getting treatment for his jarred right hand, and it was uncertain whether he would tee it up on Friday. Perhaps Snead would have to save him for singles on the final day.

·　　·　　·

Sam Snead, as Paul Trevillion wrote in *Golf Illustrated*, knew how to size up a match-play opponent. From his three-plus decades of experience, Snead could detect telltale signs of nerves on the golf course. On the eve of the Ryder Cup, Trevillion revealed Snead's "gospel." It included enlarged pupils, white lips, complexion changes, nervous twitches, increased smoking, and a short temper, among other tip-offs. "The moment he starts to get white around the lips or his complexion fades, the warning lights are on—his nervous system has rebelled."

Snead watched for nervous habits that heightened on the golf course—squirming, scratching, you name it. If two waggles was the normal preshot routine for an opponent and he waggled three or more times, "he's crying inside." If he smoked more cigarettes than usual, he was probably jumpy. Longtime student of the game Snead pointed out that Harry Vardon, winner of a record six British Opens, refused to smoke on the golf course because he knew it might reveal clues about his state of mind to competitors. Some golfers had trouble with the small task of lighting up in pressure situations, a sign their hands were trembling. Faster walking and jerky swings were also evidence of the jitters.

Trevillion called his short column of tip-offs Snead's "psychological warfare," available for all of the British team to read. It's unclear whether the U.S. captain shared any of the wisdom with his own twelve players. The handful of U.S. players who looked back four decades later could not recall specific pearls of advice from Snead, mostly just lineups and his presence in the locker room and on the golf course.

· · ·

With Great Britain leading after Day 1 of the Ryder Cup for the first time in two decades, another large crowd streamed onto the grounds throughout the morning hours. The galleries assembled behind the chestnut fencing near Birkdale's fairways. The mass of spectators was well dressed for the international occasion. Men wore suits and ties, sport coats, jackets, and sweaters. Some carried binoculars around their necks. Most women were clad in dresses and skirts; only a few had on slacks. Overcoats were also in abundance since the weather, warm at times, could also turn cool during the three days. All types of headwear were evident: scarves for the ladies and caps and hats for both men and women.

As if to match their bright and bold mood after Thursday's play, Great Britain's team was outfitted in Guardsman red sweaters and black trousers, with in at least one case—Jacklin—matching red socks. O'Connor (and perhaps other teammates) slipped on a red golf glove that matched his sweater. Off-white long-sleeved shirts and black leather golf shoes completed the British uniform.

The dominant color for the U.S. team on Friday was the solid navy blue in their V-neck sweaters. Their combinations varied. Nicklaus wore light blue pants and a matching turtleneck underneath his sweater. Sikes wore a white polo shirt and was hatless, as was his partner, Nicklaus. Barber, going out again with Floyd, looked conservative in his gray trousers, a white golf cap atop his head and aviator sunglasses shielding his eyes. The Americans wore solid black golf shoes, although the Golden Bear and Floyd were exceptions with their black-and-white Oxfords.

The Brits and the Yanks looked immaculate on the outside. One could only guess what each player felt on the inside as he stepped onto Royal Birkdale, lined with thousands of excited spectators.

* * * *

Great Britain got off to a fast start when Townsend sank a birdie putt on the 1st green to take the lead in the first match. After halving with pars at the 2nd hole, the match was squared at the par-4 3rd when the British pair stumbled to their first bogey. O'Connor made up for it at Royal Birkdale's first par 3, the 212-yard 4th hole. The Irishman rolled in a 20-footer with his Bulls Eye putter for a birdie. The gallery roared, and O'Connor pumped his fist. He and Townsend once again had a 1-up lead. After another par, they still held the slim advantage as they stepped onto the 6th tee box.

In the second match, Floyd and Barber struck first with a birdie at the opening hole but relinquished their lead when Huggett and Caygill made a birdie at 3. "At first Caygill was swinging far too fast," observed Pat Ward-Thomas, "but Huggett was solid as ever." Huggett and Caygill inched ahead when Caygill chipped in for an eagle at the par-5 6th hole. Directly behind them, teammates Barnes and Alliss were locked in battle with Trevino and Littler. The American pair raced to a 3-up lead with

165

birdies at holes 3, 6, and 7. It was a rude introduction to the Ryder Cup for rookie Barnes.

"To stand on the first tee, it was very thrilling," Barnes recalled, "but it was also—I was actually bloody petrified. It didn't improve in any of the Ryder Cups that I played. Every time you stood up on the tee, it was always the same feeling. The first shot, I was quite convinced I was going to miss it completely."

The morning's final game was a shootout. Nicklaus and Sikes birdied the opening hole to take the lead. Jacklin and Coles birdied the second to square the match. Both sides parred the 3rd hole, and then the Americans recorded another birdie at the long par-3 4th hole after Sikes struck his tee shot to within 18 inches of the cup. Nicklaus got into the act on the next hole, the short par-4 5th, canning a 2-foot birdie putt. The Americans were 2 up in the anchor match, but, as Coles explained in 2012, he would not shrink when a hole or match started slipping away.

"I played with Bernard Hunt quite a lot, and our agreement was, however much trouble we were in in fourball, we'd try to be in a position to support each other. If we hit a bad shot, we'd try to recover as well as we could so we'd support each other, and that worked well for us."

The veteran Coles, with Jacklin alongside, could be expected to hang in the match.

Douglass made his partnership's first birdie of the morning by sinking a 5-foot putt at the 6th hole to even the match with O'Connor and Townsend. Both pairs notched pars on the next three holes, and the match was deadlocked after the opening 9, 1-under 35s on the scoreboard.

With a par at the 7th and a birdie at the 8th, Huggett and Caygill still held their 1-up lead as they reached the 410-yard par-4 9th hole, but Floyd struck back for the United States. The PGA champion sank a 20-foot birdie putt to even the match at the halfway point. Carding several birdies and an eagle, both pairs posted 4-under 32.

Three down after 7 holes to Trevino and Littler, Barnes and Alliss were looking for any way out of a deep hole. The British duo managed a tying par at the long par-4 8th, and then the twenty-four-year-old rookie broke through at the 9th hole. Like Floyd ahead of him, Barnes rolled in a 20-foot birdie putt to help his side creep back into their match, 2 down at the turn to the Yanks, who carded a 32.

Barnes later explained the partnering dilemma. "It was always good to play with somebody who had played in [the Ryder Cup] in the past. You just felt like you had that steadying influence there, but you were still nervous kittens, let's face it. So to have the opportunity of playing with [Alliss] in the Ryder Cup probably put extra pressure on as well because I was scared to death of not playing well enough to help him to win the match."

Jacklin and Coles did not stay down long. Still 2 holes down after matching the birdie of Nicklaus and Sikes at the par-5 6th hole (Nicklaus missed a 5-foot eagle putt to go 3 up), the Brits sank two more birdies at 7 and 8 to draw even. First it was Coles with an 8-footer at the 7th, followed by Jacklin, who dropped a putt of similar length at the 8th, Birkdale's longest par 4 at 459 yards. Pars at the last and the final match was all square, another pair of 32s on the large scoreboard.

Five of the eight pairs had carded 32 on the opening 9, reliable evidence that the intense competition was producing great golf on a favorable weather day. Approach shots were finding the flagsticks. Putts were falling into the cups. The 4 points available in the morning fourball matches were still very much up for grabs.

Reports on the progress of the Friday matches were reaching listeners throughout the British Isles. Again beginning at 10:31 A.M., BBC Radio 2 would broadcast one-minute updates every hour from late morning until early evening. BBC Television coverage would begin at noon.

•　　•　　•

The fight for the day's first point ensued on the par-4 10th hole, where O'Connor sank an 8-foot birdie to put him and Townsend 1 up. Hill answered at 12, a 190-yard par 3, with a long putt for a birdie 2 that squared the match. Now it was Great Britain's turn. Townsend, with two mighty woods, made the green on the 517-yard par-5 13th in 2 shots. O'Connor, who later called his partner's display two of the best long shots he had ever witnessed, swatted at a wasp—with his putter. An amused gallery soon focused its attention on the young Englishman. When Townsend's eagle putt of a dozen feet fell into the hole, the large crowd erupted, later reported as the loudest roar of the day.

Hill and Douglass won the tough par-3 14th with a par. Mrs. Hill offered her husband and Townsend cold drinks as they made their way to the 15th tee. Both men were grateful for the refreshments. The nearby ice cream and beer tents were serving many spectators on the sunny day. Thanks to a gorgeous pitch and putt by O'Connor, the British pair regained a 1-up lead with a birdie at the 15th, the first of three par-5s in the closing four holes. Could they hold on against the dogged Americans?

The second match was anything but a seesaw battle. Huggett-Caygill and Floyd-Barber were stuck in a long march of pars to the white clubhouse, neither side able to edge ahead, not even on the birdieable par-5 13th and 15th holes. It looked like the Americans might win the par-4 16th when both of their opponents missed the green with their second shots, but the Brits scrambled for a par, running the streak of tied holes to seven. The four men walked to the 17th tee knowing they had missed opportunities to seize control of the match, but two birdie opportunities and an all-important point still lay ahead for the pair who could summon a timely shot and sink a pressure putt.

In the third match, Barnes made it two long putts in a row with a birdie at 10 to pull him and Alliss within 1 hole of Trevino and Littler. Trevino followed with a birdie from 20 feet at the 11th to again go 2 up. The former marine was a tough competitor. Back on the 5th hole, he had even opened a Coke bottle with his teeth.

The inspired Barnes birdied 13 and 15, and with 3 holes to play the match was tied for the first time since the 2nd hole. With four birdies in a seven-hole stretch, it was an auspicious debut for Barnes, but it wasn't over; the point still hung in the balance.

·   ·   ·

At some point during their morning fourball match, O'Connor, Townsend, Hill, and Hill's caddie searched for a golf ball in the intermediate rough. A press photograph offered two proofs: one, that the opposing sides would join in a ball search—an open question earlier in the week after Captain Brown's decree—and two, that American Hill and Englishman Townsend bore an uncanny resemblance.

"There was a picture in one of our newspapers of [Hill] and I looking for his ball," Townsend later said. "It was very hard to tell who was who." ("No they are not brothers!" read a caption in one golf publication.)

Hill and Townsend certainly could have passed for brothers as, in tandem, they stepped carefully through the rough in search of Hill's golf ball, a sibling rivalry of sorts during their tight morning fourball match.

·   ·   ·

O'Connor had strained his right shoulder hitting out of the rough on the 3rd hole but gamely played on, the able Townsend at his side. At 16, the Irishman's birdie putt to win the hole stopped on the lip of the cup. On the scene and glued to the action, Captain Brown jumped, twisted, and groaned. O'Connor and Townsend halved the hole to maintain their 1-up advantage on Hill and Douglass. The Americans fought to the finish, making birdies at the par-5 17th and 18th holes, but so did their opponents to close out the match, a 1-up victory. A fan yelled at a referee who inadvertently walked on Townsend's putting line, but it made no difference. Friday's first point was on the board for Great Britain. The cheering gallery heartily approved.

Floyd and Barber were in trouble at 17. Both players had sent their tee shots into the rough on the 510-yard par 5. Barber didn't find his golf ball, so it all depended on his partner. Floyd hacked out of the rough and struck his third shot onto the green about 8 feet from the hole. Caygill was also close to the hole in 3, and when he made his birdie putt and Floyd missed, he and Huggett snatched the lead heading to the last hole. Perhaps the untimely miss ignited the playboy bachelor, because Floyd walloped a drive and second shot to get home in 2 on the 513-yard 18th. Caygill blasted from a greenside bunker, and the demonstrative Huggett nearly sank his long putt. The Brits got their birdie, but it wasn't enough to hold off the Americans. Floyd rapped home his 18-foot putt for an eagle 3 to win the hole and halve the match, a half point going to each team.

With the last two morning matches in the stretch run, Great Britain had widened its lead on the United States to 2 points, 6–4.

The third match had turned into a two-man duel between Barnes and Trevino. After pars at the 16th, the match deadlocked, Trevino rolled in a long birdie putt at 17 to put the United States back in the lead. "All [Trevino's] banter and gestures concealed tough resolution," reported Ward-Thomas.

Thus far making up no ground on Friday—actually losing some— the Americans could certainly use a point. Captain Snead may have wondered, "What's going on here?" At one point during the morning session, Snead turned to the idle Beard at the 12th green. "If our man sinks this they'll crumble," he told Beard. After the player missed the makeable putt, his captain wore a look of disbelief.

Captain Snead would soon want to slap the back of one of his rookies— Trevino. The 1968 U.S. Open champion rescued the third match by making a birdie at the 18th hole to hold off Barnes and Alliss, 1 up. Trevino had bagged seven birdies on his trip around Royal Birkdale. "Trevino practically carried Littler around the course to defeat Barnes and Alliss," reported Leonard Crawley. "In spite of strong opposition," Alliss later observed, "it was a match we should certainly have won."

The anchor match would decide Friday's opening session and also whether Great Britain would maintain its overall lead or if the United States would pull even. The game between Jacklin-Coles and Nicklaus-Sikes—called "four precious eggs in the same basket" by Crawley—was tight, neither side able to build more than a 1-up lead. The Brits took control with a Jacklin birdie from 8 feet at the 393-yard par-4 10th. The next four holes were halved with pars. Sikes squared the match with a birdie at the par-5 15th hole. The par-4 16th was halved with birdies. (After Sikes holed his 3, Jacklin bravely sank a 15-footer to keep his side from going 1 down with 2 holes to play.)

Long hitters Nicklaus and Sikes might be considered the favorites with reachable par 5s as the two closing holes, but Sikes found trouble, and the Golden Bear bunkered his second shot at 17. Neither Yank birdied, a critical missed opportunity.

Coles recalled the 17th hole of that match decades later. "I used to use an old 2-wood in those days, which I could make this thing talk. Anyway, I hit a 2-wood on the right-hand corner of the green. They had long irons into the green. They all, Jacklin included, hit them out into the sand dune. So that left me to get down in 2 putts to win the hole, with a back-left pin, and I was on the right-front corner. Jacklin came up to me and said, 'Don't be short.' Just what you needed at that point in time. I rolled it up to about 2 feet and got a 4."

The 2-footer wasn't conceded. "They made me putt it," Coles added.

Jacklin and Coles were 1 up with 1 hole to play. The lead held, each side making birdie at the last. Great Britain claimed another point, which meant it had also prevailed in the morning fourball session.

Jacklin and Coles had toured Royal Birkdale in 9-under 65. Nicklaus and Sikes had posted the morning's second-best score, a fine 66, but had nothing to show for it. Their opponents had finished birdie-birdie-birdie to nip them. Asked years later about beating an American duo that included Nicklaus, Coles, chuckling, said, "You've done your job."

At the conclusion of the match, Nicklaus and Jacklin shared a light-hearted moment as Sikes and Coles also converged at the back of the green to exchange congratulations. The September sun was bright, and the four golfers cast large shadows. Nicklaus placed his left hand on Jacklin's upper right arm and moved in close. The personal exchange between the two men produced wide smiles. Despite being fierce competitors, Jacklin and Nicklaus obviously liked each other. Nicklaus's demeanor, however, would not have been surprising even had it been a different opponent on the 18th green. He was known for being as gracious in defeat as in victory.

Captain Brown was also in a cheerful mood. The scoreboard told why.

MORNING FOURBALL RESULTS

O'Connor-Townsend (GB) defeated Hill-Douglass (USA) 1 up

Huggett-Caygill (GB) halved with Floyd-Barber (USA)

Trevino-Littler (USA) defeated Barnes-Alliss (GB) 1 up

Jacklin-Coles (GB) defeated Nicklaus-Sikes (USA) 1 up

Session total: Great Britain 2½, United States 1½

Overall score: Great Britain 7, United States 5

Whether because of skill, luck, or a bit of both, Brown was looking like a genius with his pairings. Splitting up Jacklin and Townsend had worked beautifully in the opening fourball sessions. They had both won a point with new partners Coles and O'Connor. In addition, Huggett and his new partner, Caygill, had halved their match, and Alliss and Barnes had fought valiantly in a losing effort.

The players headed off to lunch. The captains considered the afternoon draw. What would the clever Brown do next? Short of inserting himself into the lineup, what could Snead try to get his boys to close the gap?

Alliss was done playing for the day and would soon be at the microphone fulfilling his broadcast duties. There would be plenty of excitement to report about on a radiant September day at Royal Birkdale. The most surprising thing of all was that Great Britain had taken a 2-point lead into Friday afternoon.

—12—

FRIDAY: AFTERNOON FOURBALLS

The eighteenth Ryder Cup was behind schedule. The morning matches "were such long tedious affairs . . . they completely disrupted the day's match planning," reported Paul Trevillion. The rounds lasted nearly five hours, which was just shy of an eternity for tournament golf in those days.

The lunch break was cut to a minimum. The afternoon matches would still begin late—so late that completing play before dark was a genuine concern for Ryder Cup officials and others. If players repeated the morning's snail's pace, some of the sixteen men would be wandering around Royal Birkdale in darkness.

The Friday afternoon draw was set as follows:

AFTERNOON FOURBALLS

Peter Butler–Peter Townsend (GB) vs. Billy Casper–Frank Beard (USA)

Brian Huggett–Bernard Gallacher (GB) vs. Dave Hill–Ken Still (USA)

Maurice Bembridge–Bernard Hunt (GB) vs.
Tommy Aaron–Raymond Floyd (USA)

Tony Jacklin–Neil Coles (GB) vs. Lee Trevino–Miller Barber (USA)

Captain Brown hoped he had again worked his pairings magic. Two of the Peters would lead off. O'Connor, Townsend's morning partner, would rest his ailing right shoulder. "Butler," Townsend later said, "was a bit like Christy—maybe not quite as good a player as Christy, but a very experienced player who had been around a long time."

After struggling through the morning match, O'Connor asked to sit out the afternoon session. The captain fulfilled the request knowing he would need O'Connor for singles on Saturday.

"I've had trouble since 1955," O'Connor told reporters about his shoulder. "It plays up now and again, but if I rest it today, I should be okay for tomorrow."

In the second spot, Huggett and Gallacher were together for the first time, and so were Bembridge and Hunt in the third match. The morning's winning duo of Jacklin and Coles was back in the anchor position for what Brown hoped was an encore.

Captain Snead again mixed it up. Perhaps he was still trying to hit on pairings that produced new or better chemistry, or maybe there was some sense of desperation after the morning only netted $1\frac{1}{2}$ points for the United States. Whatever his method, like his rival Brown's, three of Snead's afternoon pairings were new combinations. Maybe this was good. After all, Captain Brown seemed to be making all the right moves.

Snead's pairings were also notable for who wasn't playing—Jack Nicklaus. Dan Sikes, too. Despite narrowly losing in the morning to Jacklin and Coles, Nicklaus and Sikes had fired a 66, the lowest U.S. score of the session.

"Everyone's trying damned hard," *Sports Ilustrated*'s Gwilym Brown quoted one unnamed member of the U.S. delegation as saying, "but you could say that team morale is just about zero."

Nicklaus and Sikes had played two of three matches. Snead's rationale, in all likelihood, was to rest them for the singles sessions on the final day. Also sitting out on Friday afternoon were Gene Littler and Dale Douglass.

Snead's one recognizable duo from Thursday's foursomes matches was Casper and Beard, both rested after watching in the morning. Billy's sprained right hand had apparently responded well to treatment and a half day's rest. Beard would have been more comfortable pairing with someone else, such as Ken Still, for instance, one of Beard's pals on tour.

"I played with Casper a couple of times," Beard said long after about his first Ryder Cup. "He never said a word. We weren't enemies or anything. That was Billy Casper. You didn't have to ignore him or kiss his butt or anything. He was Billy."

For the third time in two days, Beard would head out with the future Hall of Famer. "I didn't have any plan," he said. "Nobody gave me one, whether it was Snead or anybody else."

Hill, one of two U.S. players who had played in every match (the other being Trevino), would play with his third different partner, Still, on Friday afternoon. Hill's new partner was in the midst of his best season. "I was a straight driver," Still later said about his game. "Not a great putter, but a good putter. And I loved irons."

The American skipper also split up Floyd and Barber for the first time. Aaron would join Floyd; Barber was penciled into the last match with Trevino.

"Fortunately," wrote Gwilym Brown, "the U.S. had two players, Lee Trevino and Dave Hill, who couldn't care if they were being led by Sam Snead or Shirley Temple. They infected their teammates with new serve just by the way they hurled themselves into each shot."

Arriving on Sunday surely expecting another Ryder Cup victory, Captain Snead could only hope that Trevino, Hill, and the other six men he sent out on the golf course on Friday afternoon would come back with points. They needed to turn these matches back in America's favor. No one even wanted to think about going home a loser.

•   •   •

Casper and Beard, with a birdie at the par-5 1st hole, took the lead in the first match, but Butler and Townsend evened the contest with their birdie at the par-3 4th hole. The Brits won the 5th with another birdie to go 1 up, but their lead was short-lived. Beard's Bulls Eye putter was heating up. At the par-5 6th hole, the PGA Tour money leader ran in an eagle putt from the green's fringe. Wearing a white golf cap, Beard pumped his right fist as the golf ball dropped into the cup and squared the match. His opponents answered with a birdie at the 158-yard par-3 7th. The 8th hole was halved with pars, the first time in four holes either side hadn't made a birdie or an eagle. A U.S. birdie at 9 again leveled the match. Butler and Townsend were out in 33. Casper and Beard had fashioned an opening 32. If the first match was any indication, the afternoon competition was going to be another nail biter.

Seeing action for the first time since Thursday morning, Still teamed with Hill to win the 1st hole against Huggett and Gallacher. It was a routine beginning to a long match, except for an unpleasant tone that arose on the 1st green. Preparing to putt, Huggett asked Hill to stop moving.

"Dave Hill was a very jumpy sort of guy," Gallacher later said, "a nervous sort of guy, chain-smoker, that type of thing. He couldn't stand still on the green. He couldn't stand still on the tee."

Hill's hyperactivity wasn't all Huggett had to sort out at the beginning of his fourball match. There was also Still, who was standing too close for comfort. (Bembridge had the same problem with Still on Thursday.) The assertive Huggett addressed the situation. "I want you behind me from now on," he told Still, to which Still made a disapproving sound.

The next hole was halved with pars, but another small drama played out on Birkdale's 3rd green. Still's caddie tended the flag for opponent Gallacher. As Gallacher later pointed out, this was a common practice during that era.

"It's not like today where you have your own [traveling] caddie, and [your] caddie holds the flag," Gallacher said. "Whichever caddie was closest to the flag, in those days, holds the flag."

On this occasion, however, Still objected. Gallacher's putting routine included excessive looks from the ball to the hole, numbering fifteen to twenty, according to Huggett. Gallacher went through his routine and was finally ready to stroke his putt on the 3rd green while Still's caddie held the flagstick.

"I was in the front of the green and just as I was about to putt, Ken Still runs onto the green and says, 'Get your own caddie to hold the flag,'" Gallacher later said. "He was waiting until I was just about to putt before he did it. To me, that was gamesmanship."

Gallacher lagged the putt to within inches of the cup but, as Leonard Crawley reported, was made to hole "the tiddler." "There was plenty of friction there," Huggett later said.

The match moved on to the 212-yard par-3 4th hole, where the Huggett-Gallacher pairing stumbled to a bogey and went 2 down to the Americans. The Yanks tied their British opponents with a par and a birdie at holes 5 and 6, but a storm was brewing.

. . .

In the third game, Aaron and Floyd took a 1-up lead when Floyd dropped an 8-foot birdie putt on the 3rd hole. Then, as if someone placed an invisible lid on the hole, birdies dried up for both sides. The two pairings matched pars all the way to the clubhouse. Out in 34, Aaron and Floyd clung to their 1-hole lead, while Bembridge and Hunt, authors of an uninspired 35, could draw solace from not being in a deeper hole.

Jacklin and Coles, together again, might not have relished the prospect of facing Trevino, whose shotmaking and talking skills were on display. Trevino's incessant chatter could get in opponents' heads as much as birdies. It was simply his nature on the golf course, a tension reliever. One story that later circulated had Trevino and Jacklin playing a match in England. Before they teed off, Jacklin made a special point of telling Trevino that he didn't want to talk. He wanted to focus solely on his golf.

"You don't have to talk," Trevino replied, "just listen. I'll talk enough for both of us. If I keep my mouth shut for four hours out here, I'll have bad breath."

Partner Barber was still in search of his first Ryder Cup win. His chances looked good with Trevino alongside. Barber hoped to contribute to the cause.

"Take it from me, boy, we'll be trying," Barber told Trevillion in July. "When you're playing for your country you get a real feeling of national pride—and you make goddam sure you win."

Jacklin and Coles got out fast with two birdies in the first three holes to grab a 2-up lead. The Americans cut into the lead with a birdie at the 5th, Birkdale's shortest par 4. Both sides birdied the par-5 6th hole. At the 7th, Trevino canned a 25-foot birdie putt to win one for the Stars and Stripes. The Brits' 2-up lead had evaporated in three holes, all birdied by the Americans. The match was all square at the halfway point, each side posting 3-under 33s.

•   •   •

Willie Aitchison, the popular Scottish caddie carrying for Trevino in his first Ryder Cup, retrieved his employer's putter as he walked off the 9th green. Trevino had inherited the services of Aitchison at a tournament in which the caddie's player, Roberto De Vicenzo, didn't compete. The two men began a long partnership. Whenever Lee ventured overseas, Willie was on his bag.

Trevino gave Aitchison pointers on how to diagram holes and chart yardages in a notebook, but early on there was a problem that had nothing to do with course knowledge. The caddie talked too much, even more than his boss, which was hard to imagine. Trevino straightened that out in a hurry.

"Willie, you've got to be the listener. We can sing together, but we can't talk together."

•   •   •

Dave Hill was an impatient golfer, which may explain why he putted out of turn on the 7th green in his match with Huggett and Gallacher. Another and perhaps better explanation is that Hill simply lost track of the situation at the par 3, as can happen in the heat of competition. Whatever the reason for Hill's error, it set off an explosion that reverberated across the sand dunes.

Hill had putted up to within 2 feet of the hole, according to at least two British press reports. He had then finished out, tapping the short putt into the cup. There was a problem, though. Hill wasn't away; Huggett was, his mark resting 3 feet from the hole. It was Huggett's turn to play, but Hill had gone ahead and played his next stroke. Accounts vary about the verbal exchange that followed but are unanimous about the rancor. Huggett spoke, and the short fuse was lit.

"You've putted out of turn," said the Welshman, as quoted by *The New York Times*'s Fred Tupper. Huggett called in the referee, David Melville, a professional at La Moye on the Isle of Jersey.

Then Still got into the act. Tupper reported the following Still-Gallacher exchange concerning Hill's golf ball, played out of turn and already holed.

"We'll put it back," Still said.

"No you won't," Gallacher replied.

(As Still recalled decades later, his own tee shot stopped on the back fringe of the green and he chipped to within 3 feet of the hole. Hill tapped in and picked up Still's coin since Still could do no better than a 3. Both Hill and Still would later contend that Hill's golf ball was less than a foot from the hole. "In international golf, a 6-inch putt should be given," Still said. In 2013 Gallacher said he distinctly remembered the incident. "It wasn't a gimme putt," he emphasized. Gallacher remembered the distance as at least 2 feet.)

Still had it right. Hill could have put his golf ball back. According to the Rules of Golf, there was no penalty for playing out of order in match play, but a player could be asked to replay the shot. (At the time, *The Daily Telegraph*'s Leonard Crawley cited Rule 40 in his reporting.)

Reason, however, had ducked out of the second match. Anger and confusion took over on the 7th green. One report said that referee Melville called for help to deal with the heated dispute. According to multiple accounts, Still came unhinged and blurted out what amounted to a concession of the hole, although he later claimed the referee had already ruled "loss of hole" for the Americans.

"Ken Still sort of blew up," Gallacher said in recent years. "He took this very personally. He wouldn't allow the referee to read the book properly. The referee couldn't find the rule right away for putting out of turn in a fourball match. While the referee is looking in the rule book, he's ranting and raving."

Two decades later Hill would say he asked Melville for a ruling but the referee was constantly interrupted. Hill also said that his opponent wouldn't accept that he could respot his golf ball. *The Guardian*'s Ward-Thomas appeared to corroborate Hill's version, reporting that Huggett was told by the referee that Hill could replace his golf ball. "The referee said later that Huggett would not accept this ruling," Ward-Thomas wrote on the day following the incident. The British players countered that their U.S. opponents conceded the hole and walked off the green before an official ruling.

"We weren't claiming the hole," Gallacher insisted in 2013. "He putted out of turn, and we wanted to know what the rule was, but he never allowed the time to find the correct ruling in the book."

"Pick 'em up fellas, and let's go," Hill, in 1989, recalled saying on the 7th green that day.

"What the hell," Still was quoted as saying by two press sources at the time, "if you want to win this badly, you can have the hole." Another reported Still saying, "You can have the hole and the goddam Cup."

Forty-three years later, Still did not attempt to reconstruct the dialogue from the dispute on the 7th green, but he did feel that he and Hill were victims of gamesmanship and a bad ruling. "Sam Snead said don't argue with the referee. Whatever [the referee] says goes. He said, 'Loss of hole.'"

As Gallacher later pointed out, it didn't help that referees were weak in those days, a group of club professionals content to shadow famed tour players during the competition but in over their heads when a situation like the one on Birkdale's 7th green threatened to become an international incident.

"They were given the rule book and sent—off you go," Gallacher said. "That wouldn't happen today with the professional referees that we have. They would probably have a word if they thought it was overheating, and they would probably handle it different."

Tupper was unsure about how the Americans lost the 7th, reporting that the hole was "conceded" or "taken away," while the British press called it a concession. "The men didn't seem to get along," Tupper added. That might have qualified as the understatement of the year.

Up by 1 hole in the match, Still and Hill stomped to the tee box of the 8th hole, which, at 459 yards, was the longest par 4 at Royal Birkdale. Hill was fuming. The crowd was becoming more unruly by the second. "All of a sudden all hell breaks loose," Still later said. "[People] are swearing at us, they're throwing garbage at us, everything."

"It is a pity that the crowd got so worked up as to voice their disapproval of Still during the incident and afterwards," Tom Scott later wrote. "It will be a sad day for golf if galleries start to ape those at football grounds." It seemed that sad day had already arrived.

The four men struck their drives at the 8th and started down the fairway. Hill overheard referee Melville tell his partner that Hill could have replaced his golf ball on the 7th green after putting out of turn. In his words, Hill went "totally bonkers. I called the referee every four-lettered word I'd learned since I was a kid and was in a terrible frame of mind after that because I felt we had been cheated out of a hole."

"It was a highly tense situation," Gallacher said. "I think we probably realized when we walked up the 8th fairway that [Hill] would only be asked to replace the ball."

Still was also unhappy with the referee and let him know about it, loudly enough for the worked-up gallery to overhear. The crowd booed and shouted at the American. Then Huggett had words for Still, and the two men began yelling at each other in the 8th fairway.

"It really looked now as if the argument was going to be settled by fists," reported Trevillion. Dai Rees and Lord Derby, the British PGA president, came out onto the fairway to calm down the two golfers before a first punch was thrown. "[Rees] was the one who bravely stopped [them] from coming to blows," Trevillion later said.

"It was the closest I ever saw to an actual fistfight on a golf course," Ben Wright later wrote. "Samuel Ryder . . . must have been spinning in his grave."

The crowd was teetering on a ragged edge. The boos were thunderous. "I had never heard booing at a golf tournament before," Peter Willis said about the match. "It was like a football-match atmosphere at one point."

A couple of people in the gallery tried to climb over the chestnut fencing, apparently to rush onto the field of battle. They were restrained, as was a man who wound up to throw a bottle. Fisticuffs averted, the match moved toward the 8th green.

An enraged Hill proved to be dangerous with his golf sticks. The U.S. player struck his long approach shot to the 8th to within 4 feet of the hole. His focused anger gave him an edge, which probably would not have surprised any of his teammates.

"Dave Hill was someone who would take exception to something and blow it out of proportion," Aaron later said. "I just remember Dave as being a very good player."

Still also made the green and took a run at his birdie. The effort was too strong, rolling past the hole and beyond Hill's mark. Still was farther from the hole and intended to putt next. Moreover, he was anxious to hit a putt that would show his partner the line—that is, how the contour of the green would influence the roll of the golf ball. A birdie 3 would win the hole—if Hill sank the 4-footer.

Gallacher spoiled Still's plan. The clever Scot conceded the par putt for the same reason that Still wanted to putt it. Gallacher also picked up his opponent's ball in the process. Still was incensed.

"[Still] wouldn't accept it," Gallacher later said. "He said, 'No, I'm not accepting this. I want to putt it.' I said, 'I'm giving you it. These are the rules of match play. I can give you this putt.' And then we had a real hoo-ha on the 8th green as well because he wanted to putt this 5-foot putt on the same line to help Dave Hill and we didn't want him to do that."

Still wouldn't let it go. He said that Great Britain had forfeited the hole because Gallacher had touched his golf ball, but he was incorrect. Gallacher had not violated a rule, nor had he resorted to gamesmanship.

"He just completely blew his top on the 8th," Gallacher added, "and that's why the crowd started to get on top of the Americans, because British crowds are quite knowledgeable, especially in match play, and they could see that I was entitled to give him that putt. It just came at the wrong time, that putt. [We] had just gone through that controversy on the 7th green. I wasn't trying to upset him. I was just not trying to help Dave Hill with his putt."

Still more or less acknowledged Gallacher's point decades later. "They know match-play rules better than we do," he said while discussing the 1969 matches. "We don't play that stuff here in the United States."

"I must say I just got on with the game," Gallacher said. "Dave Hill played absolutely out of his skin. Ken Still couldn't hit a ball after that. It inspired Dave Hill, and it had the opposite effect on Ken Still."

The gallery was nearly out of control. Still was pummeled with jeers and shouts of "Go home!" Willis overhead a gallery member say, "So much for international goodwill."

Still's senseless quarrel with Gallacher made no difference. Hill rapped the winning birdie into the cup on the 8th green. He turned to the gallery and bowed in a mocking fashion. The Americans were again 2 up in the match. They would soon be 3 up at the turn after the Brits recorded a bogey at the 9th hole.

• • •

The afternoon matches crawled along on the incoming 9, precious daylight slipping away. The players were showing signs of mental and physical fatigue as the pressure of a closely contested Ryder Cup heightened.

Casper and Beard lost the 10th hole with a bogey to go 1 down, but the Yanks drew even at the 190-yard par-3 12th hole. Billy's putter came alive. He sank a 30-footer for a deuce and then dropped another birdie at 13 to put his side 1 up. The next two holes were halved with pars. At the par-4 16th, Butler struck back, rolling home a long birdie putt. The spectators cheered the bold effort that could pull their side even in the tight match, but Casper answered with a birdie from 10 feet to hang on to a slim lead. The four players reached the final hole with Great Britain still 1 down. Casper and Beard made a birdie to close out the match, a 2-up victory for the Americans, who had won three of the last eight holes en route to an 8-under 66.

"I was probably beginning to feel a little relief. I'd tied a match and lost one, and now had won something and was able to contribute," Beard later said.

Going to the Americans, the first point of the afternoon made the overall score Great Britain 7, United States 6.

• • •

Huggett, "every outline hard with determination," reported Ward-Thomas, birdied the par-4 11th to cut into Hill and Still's 3-up lead. The 12th, where Still talked to PGA Tour commissioner Joe Dey about baseball, was halved with pars. The Welsh Bulldog birdied again at the par-5 13th hole. The U.S. lead had shrunk to 1 up.

Despite the concerted efforts of British and U.S. officials, the second match was still being played under a cloud of ill will. The crowds had calmed down, but they still could not resist opportunities to boo and goad the two American villains. At the 13th, when Still's tee shot found a bunker, shouts of "Good" filled his ears.

As Trevillion later recalled about the galleries, there were many spectators who didn't approve of that kind of talk, but they also didn't drown out the fighting words. It might have been impossible. He remembered one man in particular, a veteran wearing five war ribbons on his chest.

"This is not 1969. It's 1939—war has been declared. It's the Battle of Britain and I know what I'm talking about. The lads are out of the trenches. It's hand-to-hand fighting and Still's asking for a smack in the mouth. If one of those Yanks' balls come anywhere near me, my boot's going straight on it. I'm burying it six feet under. Let's see him get out of that!"

•　　•　　•　　•

Tommy Aaron recalled the large crowds and rowdy atmosphere at Royal Birkdale more than forty years later. "I remember it being hostile, very much so. In fact, we were warned—maybe by Snead—don't be surprised . . . , if you hit a bad shot, they may applaud to get under your skin. They were very much for their team."

"I think there was a little bit of hostility there due to Eric's captaincy, really," Barnes later said. "I think Sam Snead also had something to do with it because he was just as abrasive, and I think it automatically went into the spectators."

"In those days," Casper later said, "a lot of times when you missed a putt there would be clapping. Many of the times this happened, it would be irritating to Dave Hill, but yet maybe it wasn't they were clapping because the U.S. missed, but they were clapping because their side either won or saved the hole. It was hard to interpret just what it meant. Of course, him being so volatile, he expressed himself very strongly."

"I'd played places where there were favorites," Beard later said, "but I'd never played anywhere where they were rooting against you and clapped when you missed a putt." Uncomfortable with conflict, Beard detested much of the scene at Royal Birkdale that week. "It was almost nauseating. Here we are all men out here, and it was just a very unpleasant feeling, but it was part of what was going on."

When asked decades later if 1969 was a particularly hostile Ryder Cup, eight-time veteran Alliss replied, "No more than usual. When we went to the United States, the home team is supported by the home supporters. Nothing wrong in that."

•   •   •

After knocking his tee shot into the fairway bunker at the par-5 13th hole, Still disappeared into the dunes for five minutes. Hill and seemingly everyone else wondered where his beleaguered partner had gone. Willis momentarily considered the possibility that Still had abandoned the match, but the golfer reappeared. Walking along the 13th fairway, Still shouted at the crowd, "In America we treat you like kings, but here you treat us like tramps."

Both sides carded 3s at the long par-3 14th hole. At 15, Nicklaus, Sikes, Littler, and Douglass arrived to root on their embattled teammates as they clung to a 1-up lead. Two policemen also arrived, which had a calming effect on the spectators. The match moved to the par-5 17th with no change in the score. Great Britain was 1 down with 2 to play.

Hill lashed two prodigious wood shots on the 510-yard hole and made the green. Huggett and Gallacher recorded a birdie they hoped was good enough to send the match to the last hole. Perhaps they could salvage a tie and earn a half point for Great Britain. Still was on the putting surface in 3 shots, 6 feet from the hole, closer than Hill.

"[Hill] says, 'Knock your putt in,'" Still said decades later.

If Still could secure the birdie, then Hill could make a bold attempt for eagle, which, if successful, would win both the hole and the match. Still stroked in his putt. According to Still, his partner called what happened next.

"He says, 'See those people on the hill? Tell them this match is over.' "

Hill took measure of the medium-range eagle putt and gave it a decisive rap. There was never any doubt. "Right in the heart," Still said. The Americans prevailed 2 and 1. The overall score was tied: Great Britain 7, United States 7.

The match—arguably the most acrimonious in Ryder Cup history—was over. The four combatants shook hands with each other and referee Melville, except for Hill, who refused to shake Melville's hand. Mrs. Hill tried to persuade her husband to make peace. He refused, saying it was a matter of principle.

"Be a sport, Dave," came a shout from the crowd.

*   *   *

Aaron and Floyd could keep the U.S. momentum going—if they could hang on to their 1-hole lead against Bembridge and Hunt. The slight edge was not the result of outstanding play, as Aaron recalled. "Neither one of us played very well."

They halved the first six holes of the incoming 9 with the Englishmen: pars at 10, 11, 12, and 14; birdies at 13 and 15. When the match reached the 16th hole, the two sides had matched scores on twelve consecutive holes. The home team clawed back with a Bembridge birdie from 9 feet to square the match with 2 holes to play. After pars at 17—Floyd missed a 5-foot birdie putt to win the hole for the U.S. side—the four men came to the last hole tied, the precious point still at stake.

They reached the final green in four hours and fifty-five minutes, another long Ryder Cup round. It was nearly dark, the lights of the white clubhouse shining in the near distance. With Aaron and Floyd in with a par, it was up to Bembridge. The match and a slim lead for Great Britain rode on his 5-foot birdie putt. Bembridge missed. The crowd groaned. The match was halved. The overall score was Great Britain 7½, United States 7½.

In the day's final match, Jacklin, Coles, Trevino, and Barber were dueling in the increasing darkness. Neither side could take command. They started the back 9 deadlocked, and only two holes changed hands coming to the 18th. The United States fumbled away the par-4 11th hole with a bogey and then squared the match with a birdie by Barber from 24 feet at the par-3 14th. Both sides birdied the par 5s——13, 15, and 17—arriving at the last hole tied.

However, Trevino's caddie, Aitchison, didn't make it to the 18th. In an odd accident, the Scottish bag toter broke his left ankle after departing the 17th green. Jacklin recalled the incident, and how Birkdale's rutted paths through the heather apparently upended the caddie. Aitchison's instinct to help someone along the uneven ground ultimately caused the injury. The caddie reached out to catch a falling child, and someone following close behind bumped the heavy golf bag he was lugging. He lost his balance and tumbled to the ground, landing on his back, as Jacklin remembered. "I heard a crack and knew the worst," Aitchison said.

"Hell, the British should have given Willie a team blazer," Trevino later quipped in his autobiography.

Minus his fallen caddie, Trevino and company soldiered on as the sky darkened. Reaching the final green, where 5,000 fans awaited the outcome, a half moon overhead, all four men had birdie putts that could conceivably win the hole and the match. As Jacklin recalled, it was so dark that automobiles were maneuvered into position so their headlights could shine toward the green and help the players see.

Coles putted first and missed. Jacklin was next, only 4 feet from the hole after a fine pitch shot. The Open champion also missed. Then it was Trevino, who had skillfully blasted out of a greenside bunker and was fractionally closer to the hole than Jacklin. Trevino missed.

The gallery couldn't see much, if anything, but as Mark Wilson reported in *Golf World*, "They got the gist of what was going on by listening. The language of golf is international—especially missed putts."

It was up to Barber, who, inexplicably, still wore his dark glasses even though it was nightfall. If he could sink his 40-inch birdie putt, the Americans would win the match and take the overall lead for the first time. The two captains watched the man wearing aviator sunglasses prepare to putt, although it was nearly impossible to see the golf ball and the cup. Perhaps that was also the case for Barber, because he, too, missed his short putt.

"I just couldn't see," he offered afterward, as if someone needed an explanation from a man wearing sunglasses in the dark.

The four men shook hands and headed to the clubhouse. It was nearly eight o'clock. The Americans had rallied. It was now a dead heat.

AFTERNOON FOURBALL RESULTS

Casper-Beard (USA) defeated Butler-Townsend (GB) 2 up
Hill-Still (USA) defeated Huggett-Gallacher (GB) 2 and 1
Bembridge-Hunt (GB) halved with Aaron-Floyd (USA)
Jacklin-Coles (GB) halved with Trevino-Barber (USA)
Session total: United States 3, Great Britain 1
Overall score: Great Britain 8, United States 8

At the end of two days, the Ryder Cup was tied. As on the day before, the Americans had won the afternoon session, and by the same score, 3 to 1. Seven of Friday's eight matches had reached the final hole. Of the sixteen matches played the first two days, only two hadn't gone the distance.

"Brown's decision not to rest Townsend and Jacklin was understandable," reported Ward-Thomas. "He had to follow the winning vein and strive for a lead. Ultimately it did not quite bear fruit."

The two days and 72 holes had taken a toll on the players, some of whom voiced concerns about a three-day Ryder Cup format that included two rounds each day. Singles were ahead, 36 more holes of pressure-packed golf. The Ryder Cup trophy and national pride were at stake.

•   •   •

Reporters sought comments from the players in the afternoon's second match, called "a thoroughly bad-tempered affair" by Crawley. A shaken Still talked about his humble beginnings, thanking God that he was gifted with the ability to play golf. Then he expressed his regrets for what transpired in fourballs. "I got shook up and I'm real sorry."

"It all happened in the heat of the moment," Gallacher explained. "Many things were said which are best forgotten."

Hill refused to comment on the volatile match, skipping the press conference attended by his partner and opponents.

Huggett had seen enough of Hill to decide he was an outstanding competitor. "He is tough and uncompromising," Huggett told reporters, "and if you ask me about his sportsmanship I have no comment. I simply repeat he is a great player."

Not all was put to rest, though. Huggett and Hill were said to have renewed hostilities later that night at the Prince of Wales Hotel.

Asked about the highly contentious fourball match more than forty years later, Huggett said, "What do you expect from four feisty people?"

Reminded in 2013 of the four players in the ill-fated match, Nicklaus said, "They'd fight to the end of anything."

"We weren't the villain. We were the victim," Still said in recent years.

There was, as Willis reported, at least one light-hearted moment on Friday. At the end of the long day of fourball matches, forty-five men gathered around a man telling jokes in the Royal Birkdale clubhouse—Lee Trevino.

• • •

Captain Brown expressed satisfaction with the tie score, pointing out that it was rare for Great Britain to go into singles play not trailing the Americans. Brown was confident that his boys would give it their best in singles the next day.

Also looking ahead to the sixteeen singles matches, Captain Snead said, "It's been a hell of a match." He complimented British play, singling out Huggett and Townsend. The U.S. skipper also voiced regret that his players hadn't made several crucial putts.

"The Americans," wrote Tupper, "... with a dozen men who have won 19 tournaments and over a million dollars among them this year, are still favored, if barely."

The British players had reason to be confident after matching shots with the Americans on Thursday and Friday. Alliss, who two years earlier suffered his side's worst defeat in Ryder Cup history, saw opportunity. "I felt we had a great chance of winning the match," he later said.

In Alliss's estimation, the United States had a weaker team in 1969. Granted, players such as Aaron, Barber, Douglass, and Hill had proven themselves in the professional ranks, but they were playing a long way from home on unfamiliar turf, and Alliss felt they might crack under the suffocating pressure.

The final day of the Ryder Cup would not be a mere formality as it had been so many times since 1927. Great Britain was energized by the rare prospect of victory. The United States faced the real possibility of only its second defeat in more than three decades. This was a highly discomforting thought for the "we'll-never-be-able-to-go-home-again Americans," as *Sports Illustrated*'s Brown said they would be if the unthinkable happened.

Either buoyed by opportunity or burdened by expectations, the twenty-four players and their captains retreated to the Prince of Wales Hotel on Friday night to await the dawn and the sixteen singles matches that would decide the outcome of the 1969 Ryder Cup.

—13—

SATURDAY: MORNING SINGLES

It was September 20, nearly the autumnal equinox, and the final day of the 1969 Ryder Cup. The 10,000 spectators that would line the fairways and surround the greens at Royal Birkdale began arriving early in the morning. To accommodate sixteen singles matches—eight in the morning and eight in the afternoon—as well as a trophy presentation, the opening tee shot would be in the air at 8:30 A.M.

Many spectators dug into their pockets or handbags for a shilling to buy the Daily Draw Sheet. The transaction complete, here were the morning matches they studied with interest:

MATCH	TIME	GREAT BRITAIN	UNITED STATES
1	8:30	Peter Alliss	Lee Trevino
2	8:40	Peter Townsend	Dave Hill
3	8:50	Neil Coles	Tommy Aaron
4	9:00	Brian Barnes	Billy Casper

(continued)

192

MATCH	TIME	GREAT BRITAIN	UNITED STATES
5	9:10	Christy O'Connor	Frank Beard
6	9:20	Maurice Bembridge	Ken Still
7	9:30	Peter Butler	Raymond Floyd
8	9:40	Tony Jacklin	Jack Nicklaus

Mr. Bill McIntosh was the official starter for the morning session. Printed in a box near the middle of the draw sheet was "PRESENTATION: The Presentation will take place in the area of the 18th green, 15 minutes after the last match has finished. The Earl Marshal, the Duke of Norfolk, will present the Ryder Cup Trophy." His actual name was Bernard Fitzalan-Howard, the 16th Duke of Norfolk, who, among his many official duties, had organized the coronations of King George VI and the current queen, Elizabeth II.

On the bottom half of the draw sheet, the spaces for player names for matches 9 through 16 were blank because the lineups would not be announced by the two captains until lunchtime. The afternoon session would begin at 1:15 P.M.

Captain Eric Brown's morning lineup revealed an unmistakable pattern. Beginning with veteran Alliss, who would be playing in his final Ryder Cup match, the order alternated between experienced players and rookies. Townsend followed Alliss, steady-hand Coles was next, then first-timer Barnes, and so on. The mixture of veterans and youth was a sensible approach. Jacklin would anchor the British side. He would face the Golden Bear—Nicklaus.

"I always wanted to play against the best," Jacklin later said, "and even though I was the Open champion, I regarded Jack as the man to beat under any circumstances."

Not playing for the Brits were Alex Caygill, Bernard Gallacher, Brian Huggett, and Bernard Hunt. Caygill had only played in one match alongside Huggett. Hunt had seen action twice. It was no surprise that these men were sitting out. On the other hand, Huggett and Gallacher were forces. Brown was saving them for the afternoon singles—and he told Gallacher (and perhaps Huggett) as much. The captain felt the acrimonious match with Hill and Still had taken a toll on Gallacher and Huggett, so he sat them down that morning, their competitive juices burning inside.

"He did the right thing in leaving me out," Gallacher later said, "because by the afternoon I was anxious to get playing."

Captain Sam Snead might have had a knockout combination in mind. Trevino and Hill, the top U.S. players that week, would go out one-two for the Americans, a proverbial left jab and right cross. It wouldn't get much easier for the British boys. After the third Yank, Aaron, came Casper and Beard. Still, Floyd, and Nicklaus completed the U.S. lineup. The four idle players were Miller Barber, Dale Douglass, Gene Littler, and Dan Sikes.

After watching his team lose morning sessions on Thursday and Friday, Snead wanted a fast start that would propel the United States into the lead. Forget American domination. The U.S. grip on the Ryder Cup was in serious jeopardy. The morning matches would set the tone. Snead could write the player names in the blank spaces on the sheet, but the nonplaying captain could not hit the shots that could win holes, matches, and points. After turning in the draw sheet, he could only hope that his team would finally nose ahead in the matches. Otherwise it was going to be a long flight home.

•   •   •

The BBC was set to provide expanded radio and TV coverage of the final day of the Ryder Cup. Beginning at 10:31 A.M., following *Melody Time*, BBC Radio 2 would broadcast the morning singles action until noon, when *Meet Margaret* aired. After *Sports Parade: The Fighting Life of Henry Cooper*, coverage of the afternoon singles could be heard on BBC Radio 3 beginning at 1:00 P.M. Television coverage of the matches would begin on BBC-1 at 11:35 A.M.

Peter Alliss would be a part of the BBC broadcast team as he had been the first two days, but now he stood on Birkdale's 1st tee peering at the familiar opening hole, a par 5 of just under 500 yards with out-of-bounds down the right-hand side and a sandbank to the left. The weather conditions were benign, still mostly windless, the course playing slower and softer than usual. The British had hoped for harsher elements—a strong southwest wind off the Irish Sea, for example—but little in the way of weather had materialized since the matches began on Thursday. Nonetheless, the home team had still managed to stay with the Americans.

A few minutes before 8:30 A.M., Alliss, the first man out for his team, awaited the start of his final Ryder Cup match. His opponent was the jovial but dangerous Lee Trevino. Alliss cut a handsome figure in the team uniform: a powder blue sweater, with a white long-sleeved polo shirt underneath, and black pants. Always hard to miss, Trevino looked especially bright in the Saturday colors for the U.S. of A.: a cardinal red sweater, a white shirt, and dark blue slacks. Trevino wore a billed golf cap. Alliss was hatless.

No player on either team had more Ryder Cup experience than Alliss. The Ryder Cup "mattered like hell," he later said, partly because of family pride. There was more to it than the Alliss name, though. Country, captain, and teammates motivated the Englishman to always bring his best.

"I think it was having the experience of making a mess of it in 1953." Alliss said more than forty years later. "I was in a way so terrified of letting the side down again that my concentration levels went up."

Alliss's tactics against Trevino would be no different than any other time he teed off in match play. It was mano a mano.

"Many people," Alliss said, "including Bobby Jones, said you play the course. I never did that—I played the man. If he went out-of-bounds, I made sure that I didn't go out-of-bounds. I always felt that all you had to do in match play was to be one shot less than the other fellow on each hole. It didn't matter if you were around in 76 if you won."

Alliss was a splendid ball striker who could expect to play well from tee to green, but how would he and his George Low—model putter get along?

At 8:30 A.M., "with the dew still heavy on the ground and the mist barely off it," reported Donald Steel, official starter McIntosh announced the two players, and the crowd applauded. Trevino and Alliss teed their golf balls and rifled their opening drives toward the distant green. The morning singles had begun.

•   •   •

Neville Greenhalgh had reason to be concerned on Saturday morning. Greenhalgh's official title was "chief crowd controller," a post he had held at Royal Birkdale since 1964 when members of the club's council asked Greenhalgh to assume stewarding duties for the Dunlop Masters Tournament. First of all, it was the final day of the Ryder Cup, the climax of an international sporting event at which TV cameras would be trained on players, Royal Birkdale, and the thousands of spectators who had flocked there to watch the action. Secondly, after Friday afternoon's bitter four-ball match that resulted in unruly crowd behavior, Greenhalgh realized how quickly order could break down.

Paul Trevillion had seen it from Day 1. "[The stewards] could tell if the crowd were running, Great Britain were ahead," he later said. "Walking—they were struggling. But there were one or two games which saw more than one steward knocked off their feet. One steward complained to me it was like trying to control an armed mob. At times we only kept one or two spectators off the greens, thanks to the police."

Greenhalgh hoped sportsmanship and proper gallery decorum would prevail on Saturday. If problems arose, it wouldn't be due to lack of planning. Greenhalgh had overseen stewarding and crowd control for every major event at Royal Birkdale since his introduction in 1964. His home course had set a standard that was emulated by other championship events. Greenhalgh's methods were accepted practice at the British Open. They had been well tested at the 1965 Ryder Cup played at Royal Birkdale, which saw Great Britain's largest golf crowds to that point. One important feature was to erect temporary fencing on the final five holes to keep the swelling galleries a safe distance away from the players while still allowing them to see virtually every shot.

With the help of his wife, Joan, Greenhalgh had been perfecting plans for the 1969 Ryder Cup since the end of May. They recruited about forty senior stewards, as well as hundreds of other volunteers. The senior stewards were assigned to specific sections of the golf course, with at least two supervising each section at all times. Mrs. Greenhalgh mailed invitations to prospective volunteers, coordinated the recruits, and managed a mountain of paperwork. By Thursday's start of the Ryder Cup, the Greenhalghs had moved operations from their home to a tent that was located a short distance from the Royal Birkdale clubhouse.

It seemed nothing had been left to chance, and yet, as witnessed on Friday, the Ryder Cup could bring out the worst in some spectators.

"We will get the odd stupid watcher," Greenhalgh told Nicholas Tremayne, "who simply must climb inside the ropes, but nowadays few people are prepared to make fools of themselves in front of a large crowd."

What Greenhalgh and others probably didn't know was that someone else was influencing crowd behavior at Royal Birkdale—Trevillion.

"The crowd," Trevillion later said, "was infiltrated by the very small Great Britain army formed on the practice ground orchestrated by the baton I held. During the practice rounds, I recruited with a few laughs and fighting talk at least fifty mad keen teenage golfing fans to mingle with the crowd around the green, to be the Great Britain team's cheerleaders."

Forty-three years later Trevillion called his "army" one of his best memories of the 1969 Ryder Cup. He also remembered the mood swings at Birkdale: "surprised, buoyant, and vocal" on Thursday; "an armed mob" and "police who made their presence felt" on Friday.

"The Americans had walked into a Birkdale storm," Peter Willis later said, "and the man who blew up the storm was none other than Paul Trevillion."

What would the mood be on the final day? How would the large crowd behave with the Ryder Cup hanging in the balance for the first time since 1957?

•   •   •

Townsend and Hill, the slender, dark-haired men who looked like brothers, were the next match out. Hill still had a bitter taste in his mouth from Friday afternoon fourballs. "Oh, we won," he would later say about the match against Huggett and Gallacher, "but it ruined the whole damn thing."

Townsend had the unenviable task of going up against the red-hot American, who often played surprisingly well when he was mad, which seemed to be his normal mood. Townsend had already faced Hill twice, in Thursday morning foursomes and Friday morning fourballs, coming away with 2 points for his team. Townsend anticipated that he was in for a tough match.

"[Hill] was a very good player," Townsend acknowledged years later.

Despite his exceptional play, Hill battled mental demons on the golf course. "I had a lot of negative thoughts, but I'd defy them," he later said.

Not well known outside of Great Britain, Townsend was also showcasing considerable golf skills in 1969. "I was a good iron player, particularly a good long iron player, and I had a good short game. I probably wasn't the best driver of the ball."

His short-game prowess made him a good match-play competitor. "Sometimes I didn't play that well but I managed to put a score on the board, and that can be quite hard to play against in match play."

Hill and Townsend departed. Coles and Aaron were on deck. At the 1st green, Alliss sank a birdie putt to take a 1-up lead on Trevino.

Coles, who would turn thirty-five in less than a week, was playing his fifth consecutive match. He liked match play, and it showed in his game. Coles won the *News of the World* Match Play in 1964 and 1965 and was a solid Ryder Cup performer. "I had a pretty good record in the Ryder Cup for singles match play. I enjoyed the challenge," Coles later said.

Partnering twice with Huggett and twice with Jacklin that week, Coles had posted a 2-1-1 record, but the physical and mental pressure had taken a toll. By Saturday morning, Coles's competitive fuel was running low.

"I always was playing every game, which in those days was thirty-six holes a day. I'd said to Eric, the captain, I have one game left in me for the singles. He said, 'Okay, Neil. I'll rest you this afternoon.' "

Coles's Saturday morning opponent would quietly go about his business, ignoring the Englishman as much as possible. Aaron's match-play philosophy was to play his own game and accept the results.

"I tried not to approach match play like I was playing an individual," Aaron later said. "I just tried to approach it like I was playing the golf course. Of course, if he did something unusual like hit it out-of-bounds off the tee, I might take a different approach to how I played the hole. Or if I was 2 up with 2 to play, I might take a little different approach, but I didn't try to get too involved with what he was doing, my opponent. I tried to focus on playing the best round I could play."

At 9:00 A.M., Barnes and Casper, both hatless, followed Coles and Aaron. Ten minutes later, Beard and O'Connor teed off. O'Connor, who had faced Beard in foursomes, made an enduring impression on the American. His right shoulder still tender, the oldest player on either team hit his first shot of the match into the rough. Beard walked over, inspected the lie, and determined that his opponent was in "deep trouble." Most players would have been, but not O'Connor—at least not on this occasion.

"He went in there with some kind of wood, had a very abrupt pickup on the backswing, and the ball flew straight up out and right onto the green," Beard later said about the shot that was one of his most distinct memories of his first Ryder Cup. "I couldn't have gotten a 7-iron in on it, but he did it with the wrist, the abruptness of the angle of attack, and obviously had some experience."

It would not have surprised Beard's foursomes and fourballs partner. "Christy could do more with a 4-wood out of the rough than any man I've ever seen," Casper later said.

O'Connor carded a birdie at the par-5 opening hole, Beard made a bogey, and Great Britain was 1 up in the fifth match. Alliss made his second consecutive birdie to go 2 up on Trevino after 2 holes. Matching birdies and pars at holes 1 and 2, Hill and Townsend were all square. Coles was 1 up after Aaron bogeyed the par-4 2nd hole. Barnes and Casper both birdied the 1st hole.

Barnes faced a stern challenge in Casper, but at least he was comfortable at Royal Birkdale. "I was brought up on links courses, so I was very much at home playing that type of golf. I was always a very good driver of the golf ball, which, of course, is vitally important on most links golf courses because if you finish up in the rough it can be pretty thick and wiry."

If, however, the large, powerful man from Surrey faced a chip or a pitch, he was a mess. "My putting wasn't bad, but my short game was horrendous, and it didn't matter how much practice I did. It was more luck than judgment if I managed to get the ball up and down from 20, 30 yards off the green. If I had a delicate little wedge shot over a bunker, oh, God, that was an absolute nightmare."

Bembridge and Still were the next two opponents to leave Birkdale's 1st tee. Bembridge jumped ahead with birdies on the first two holes. Still wanted to win a point for the United States, but he also hoped to avoid the controversy that had overshadowed Friday's fourball match. He would try to ignore what Bembridge was doing.

"The biggest thing with match play is play your game," Still later said. "Only play your opponent if he's got two more shots than you, then you play your opponent. But other than that, you play the golf course."

At 9:30 A.M., in the morning's seventh match, Raymond Floyd teed off against Peter Butler. Wearing a billed cap and two-tone golf shoes, Butler was looking for his first point, having lost in his two matches with teammates Hunt and Townsend. In his three matches, Floyd had won, lost, and halved, but Butler had at least one advantage on the talented U.S. player with three victories that season. Alf Fyles was on Butler's bag.

•   •   •

Alf Fyles had roamed the fairways and sand dunes of Royal Birkdale since he was eight, the tender age at which he began his long career as a caddie. Regarded as Great Britain's No. 1 caddie, Fyles carried for a range of top professionals, whether British, American, or South African. Fyles had caddied for Masters champion Gay Brewer in a victory at the lucrative 1967 Alcan Golfer of the Year Championship at St. Andrews. He also worked for Gary Player when the South African played in the British Open and other tournaments in the British Isles.

Fyles—"a man with the golden touch, the confidant of champions, and psychologist supreme," Tremayne wrote—knew the fundamentals and subtleties of the caddie trade as well as any man. Hard work was at the core of the job, Fyles explained. Early on, he learned his trade from "Little Mac," the caddie for Ryder Cup hero Dai Rees. Little Mac taught Fyles "the most important lesson of all"—silence. Speak sparingly, and, as a general rule, only when spoken to. If Fyles was asked by a player for a yardage, he knew the number. Fyles had paced off nearly every championship golf course in Great Britain and had notebooks filled with course details and distances to prove it. During tournaments he was in the habit of walking the course each morning, which included recording the distance from the front of each green to that day's hole position.

Fyles also knew the importance of a clean-cut appearance. The same went for the player's equipment: Never fail to keep his golf clubs, golf balls, and other effects spotless and in perfect order. On-course conduct and position (where to stand, for instance) were also a crucial aspect of the trade. So was being stone-cold sober.

"If I haven't got a clear head in the morning," said the caddie, who enjoyed a drink but never had more than two during a tournament, "I'm no use to my man—and it's my living that's at stake as well as his."

Alf wasn't the only Fyles at Royal Birkdale that week. His father was also there, working as a locker-room attendant in the distinctive white clubhouse. Players on both Ryder Cup teams would become acquainted with father and son, whose hard work was in dedicated service to their home club, the players, and the ancient game.

•   •   •

The morning's last match, featuring golf titans Tony Jacklin and Jack Nicklaus, attracted the largest crowd at Royal Birkdale. Jacklin had played in every match and was undefeated, winning three and halving one. Nicklaus, competing in two matches with partner Dan Sikes that produced a win and a loss, was well rested for singles, apparently part of Captain Snead's strategy. Now the Golden Bear faced Britain's new golf hero on enemy turf.

Although Jacko was in the midst of a terrific run of golf, he would later assess the match-play format and decide it wasn't his strong suit.

"It's a bit hit and miss," Jacklin said in 2012. "It's a very different game to stroke play. It's more of a gambler's game. You can go at the flag. You can win a hole with an 8. It was never my forte, let's put it that way. I didn't excel at it over the years, when I look back. I had moments, but I wasn't that good a match player."

Nicklaus later said he liked all the Ryder Cup formats, including singles. He played his own game, to a point, not unlike Alliss. "You play the course, but you play the guy, too. You watch what your opponent does, and when your opponent gets himself in trouble, you might alter how you play the course. If your opponent stuffs it on a tough hole and you know he's going to make 3, you don't play a safe shot."

Hundreds of men, women, and children strained to get a look at the marquee matchup. The spectators were boisterous; they also maintained decorum. By and large, they were knowledgeable golf fans with an abiding affection for the game. They applauded and cheered Nicklaus at times, but they roared with abandon for countryman Jacklin. After both carding birdies at the par-5 opening hole, the two star players matched pars on the next four holes. Through the 5th hole, the morning's anchor match was deadlocked.

Trevino had fought back with birdies at 7 and 9 to tie Alliss at the turn, each man posting a 34. The Merry Mex struck a tee shot at the short par-3 7th that barely cleared a front bunker and stopped 18 feet from the hole. He sank the putt for a winning deuce. Two holes later, at the 9th, the flat-swinging Texan dropped a 27-foot birdie putt.

After staying even with Hill through the first four holes, Townsend ran into trouble. His American "brother" reeled off three birdies in four holes to build a 3-up lead. More than forty years later, Townsend vividly recalled the beginning of Hill's front-9 spurt.

"We got on the short par-4 5th hole," Townsend said, "and I hit quite a nice second shot into about probably not more than 3 or 4 meters. He hit his second shot into the greenside bunker. I thought, 'Oh, I might get one back. He might take 5 or I might make a birdie. That might get me back in the match.' The next thing, he holed the bunker shot and I didn't hole the putt."

Making a bogey at the par-4 9th hole, Townsend sank deeper into the hole, 4 down after carding a 36 that trailed Hill's 32. "He played wonderful golf against me in the first nine holes," Townsend said.

In the third match, Coles had gone 2 up with a birdie at the par-4 3rd, but Aaron narrowed Coles's margin to 1 up with his birdie at the par-3 7th hole. Coles hung on to his slim lead as he and Aaron made the turn in 34 and 35, respectively. Meanwhile, Barnes was 1 up on Casper at the halfway point after twice building a 2-up lead on the American.

O'Connor followed his brilliant recovery shot at the 1st with a 3-putt bogey at the 2nd hole, a gift to Beard that evened the fifth match. The Louisville man was solid around the greens, a chief reason why he made a comfortable living on the PGA Tour.

"My short game was always, mechanically, the best part of my game. I hit the ball pretty straight. I was a pretty good iron player," Beard later said.

From that point on, with the exception of a sloppy bogey at the par-5

6th hole, it was all O'Connor. He hit fine approach shots at 4, 5, 7, and 8, while his opponent struggled through the opening 9. The Irishman recorded three birdies against two bogeys for a 35. Beard made no birdies and carded four bogeys for an un-Beard-like 40. O'Connor would begin the incoming nine with a comfortable 3-up lead.

After dropping the first two holes to Bembridge, Still hung on all the way to the clubhouse, not losing more ground to the 24-year-old Englishman. Still's nine consecutive pars gave him a 36, putting him 2 down to Bembridge, author of a 34. In the seventh match, Butler slipped ahead of Floyd with a birdie at the par-5 6th hole and then made another birdie at the following hole to take a 2-up lead on the American. Butler bogeyed the 9th, but so did Floyd, preserving Britain's 2-hole advantage in the second-to-last game.

U.S. anchorman Nicklaus fell behind Jacklin at the par-5 6th, often a birdie hole, on which the Golden Bear made a ragged bogey. Jacko collected his second birdie of the day at 9 to increase his lead to 2 up. He was out in 34, Nicklaus in 36, an unenviable spot for the American considering Jacklin's stellar play that week. It certainly didn't help that Nicklaus was struggling to hole short putts.

"From tee to green he was Jacklin's master, but his putting was abysmal," reported *The New York Times*'s Fred Tupper.

Nicklaus missed from 7 feet for eagle at the 1st and from 3 feet for birdie at the 5th. Both putts, if made, would have won the holes for the blond American. At the 6th hole, the seven-time major champion missed an 18-inch par putt that gave Jacklin the lead. The extra rest had not seemed to help Nicklaus, but there was still a lot of golf to be played.

The eight morning singles matches favored the hosts at the halfway point: Great Britain was ahead in six of the games. The United States led one—Hill vs. Townsend. The Trevino-Alliss match was all square.

It was looking like another dismal morning for the American boys.

•　　•　　•

If nothing else, the Yanks had two things going for them on Saturday morning. Their names were Lee Buck Trevino and James David Hill.

Trevino birdied the par-4 10th hole for his first lead of the match. He maintained his slim lead as he and Alliss halved the next five holes with pars. Hill saw Townsend momentarily cut into his 4-up margin when the Englishman chipped in for a birdie at the 412-yard 11th hole. "Townsend earns first big roar of the day," Willis reported. Maybe Townsend's splendid short game provided some much-needed hope in what had been a one-sided match. If so, it all but vanished on the next hole. Hill won the par-3 12th with a bogey, and the lead was again 4.

"I was gone in the match," Townsend later said. "He had played very well. You get that in Ryder Cups. People do play very good golf sometimes."

Another birdie and a par by Hill and it was over on the 14th green, a 5 and 4 victory for the American.

Not long after Hill and Townsend shook hands, Trevino earned the second U.S. point of the day, claiming a 2-and-1 win over Alliss. Great Britain's first man out had fought hard, but the putter ultimately failed him. "I had missed eight putts of under 10 feet, and that, I thought, was enough of that."

It was an unsatisfying end to his long and largely successful Ryder Cup career. Alliss put aside his golf clubs and retired to the BBC broadcast booth to commentate on the remaining matches during the climactic final day.

• • •

The completion of the first two matches by late morning signaled a new development. For the first time in nearly two and a half days, the United States had taken the overall lead, 10–8. Two matches, 2 U.S. points, finally an encouraging start for Captain Snead and his men, but there were still six matches on the golf course. At that moment, most of them favored Great Britain.

Beard, for one, was on the ropes in the fifth match. O'Connor was playing well, even putting well, not his normal strength. With bogeys at 1, 4, 5, and 8—and no birdies—on the front 9, Beard was off his game. He was proud to be on the team, but he had not found any kind of comfort zone at the Ryder Cup.

"As an amateur, I never did do well in match play," Beard said decades later. "I still don't like any resemblance of match play today."

Beard parred the 10th to halve with O'Connor and went 4 down at the 11th hole after O'Connor made his fourth birdie of the round. Both men carded 3s at the 190-yard par-3 12th, and then, with another birdie, the old man of the Great Britain team closed out the uneasy American on the 13th green. O'Connor's 5-and-4 win pulled the British to within a point of the United States.

Up ahead, Beard's University of Florida teammate was in a tense battle with Coles. Four decades later, Tommy Aaron was unable to recount many details about his 1969 singles match at Royal Birkdale, but he did recall his opponent. "I just remember that Neil Coles was a very odd player," Aaron said. "He addressed the ball with his clubface very shut, and he didn't hook the ball, hit[ting] the ball pretty straight. He was a good player."

Making his fifth consecutive Ryder Cup appearance, Coles had been a formidable opponent in singles during a period of American domination. "Particularly driving was a major part of my game," he later said. "I didn't hit many crooked tee shots. I had a pretty good short game. Putting was probably the weakest part of my game at that stage, but I was a pretty consistent player through the green."

Coles's lead increased to 2 up when Aaron bogeyed 10. Then Coles stumbled, conceding the 11th hole, bogeying the 12th, and making a par to Aaron's birdie at the 13th. Winning three consecutive holes, including a birdie from 40 feet, Aaron had erased the deficit and gone 1 up, troubling news for Captain Brown, who must have expected a Coles victory against the U.S. rookie.

"I was very consistent and probably drove it a little bit straighter during those years," Aaron later said. "I was playing pretty good. I could hit the ball pretty close to the hole with my approach shot."

Both players parred the next two holes, and the match reached the 16th with Aaron hanging on to a 1-up advantage.

Following in the fourth match, young Barnes did not look over-matched against the great Casper. They traded pars at 10 and 11. Barnes then birdied the par-3 12th hole to go 2 up. Casper bounced back to win the 13th. The 14th hole belonged to Barnes after a Casper bogey. An upset was in the making. The son-in-law of Open champion Max Faulkner was 2 up on Casper with 4 holes to play.

Still had two problems on Saturday morning: Maurice Bembridge and the unfriendly crowd that had cast him as a villain on Friday after-noon. Bembridge was 2 up as his match with Still moved to the par-4 11th hole. "Still was taking a hammering from the gallery," reported Willis. When the American missed a 3-foot par putt on the 11th green, "one fan nearly collapsed with laughter." It got worse. Still made a second consecutive bogey at the par-3 12th to go 4 down to Bembridge with 6 holes to play. Except for his caddie, Still was all alone, surrounded by too many hostile fans. The relentless pressure may have exposed a few cracks in his golf game. Firebrand Dave Hill was not there to pick up his teammate. This was singles. It seemed the sixth match was all but over.

Butler, 2 up on Floyd at the turn, bogeyed to lose the 11th hole and held on to his 1-up lead after halving the 12th with a par. In the morn-ing's final match, Nicklaus parred 10 and 11 but went 3 down to Jacklin at the 12th hole when he missed a 2-footer for par. Short misses were be-coming a habit for the Golden Bear on Saturday. Great Britain was ahead in every match on the incoming 9, except for Coles and Aaron, but even that game was about to turn their way.

It began on the par-4 16th hole, where Coles sank a 15-foot birdie putt to level his match with Aaron. When his golf ball dropped into the cup for a 3, Coles displayed rare emotion, punching the air with an uppercut. An Aaron birdie at the par-5 17th was unable to hold off the charging

Englishman. The London native cracked his 4-wood onto the green 2 inches from the flagstick for a kick-in 3, an eagle. "Never has a shot been so needed or so welcome," reported Donald Steel. The stroke of pure genius put Coles 1 up with 1 hole to play. Aaron made another birdie at the last hole, but it was no use because Coles also got his 4.

Beginning the final three holes with a 1-up lead, Aaron finished admirably—par, birdie, birdie—and lost. Coles heroically closed out the third match with a birdie-eagle-birdie spurt to claim a point for Great Britain.

The two golf nations were again tied: Great Britain 10, United States 10.

Brian Barnes stood on the 15th tee with a 2-up lead on Billy Casper. Could Barnes hang on? Maybe, but he would have to beat a man who had only lost four of twenty-three Ryder Cup matches.

．　　．　　．

"When I was growing up, I caddied," Casper said in 2012, "and then later on, I could play at a club. In my high school years, I played for quarters, a quarter Nassau. If I won four ways, well, then I could buy a new Spalding Dot to play with the next day."

Casper chuckled at the memory.

"I was learning competition very early in my life," he continued. "You played match play that way, and that's what you played when you played on the Ryder Cup team. I had enjoyed playing match play all my life because of that. I always liked it when I had one person that I had to worry about. I really felt that I had the advantage."

．　　．　　．

Casper drove left on the 536-yard par-5 15th and caught a break when his ball landed in a left-hand bunker but hopped out onto the turf. He positioned his second wood shot 100 yards short of the green. Then he struck a wedge that stopped inches from the hole, a conceded birdie. Barnes left his putt for a tying 4 short. The rookie's lead was 1 up with 3 holes to play.

At 16, a par 4 with a wide fairway, Barnes drove into the deep rough down the left-hand side. His only play was to slash the ball out of the thick grass toward the green. Casper landed his second shot on the putting surface and sank a long putt for birdie. The match was tied.

Barnes again drove into the rough at the 17th—this time down the right-hand side. Casper was sitting nicely in the fairway. Barnes recovered for his par, but Casper's third birdie in as many holes gave him his first lead in the match with 1 hole to go.

Barnes boomed one of his best drives of the match on the par-5 18th hole. This time, Casper's tee shot was astray, flying into the right-hand rough. The American caught a break, though. His golf ball came to rest on a lone bare patch surrounded by thick grass. Tom Barnes, Brian's father and a part of the walking gallery, lamented Casper's good fortune after an errant drive. "The luck in golf can be cruel," the elder Barnes said to Trevillion.

At the green, his son's eagle putt to win the hole and halve the match stopped inches shy of the cup. Casper coaxed home a curling 8-footer for a 4 to halve the hole and win the match, 1 up. Billy had birdied the last four holes to squeeze out a victory and earn a vital point for his team. The United States was back in the lead by a single point, 11 to 10.

Nicklaus showed signs of life at the par-5 13th hole. His eagle from 75 feet—a "tramliner," as Steel called it—cut Jacklin's margin to 2. The galleries, raucous at times, showed their appreciation for America's star player. One photograph of morning singles shows Nicklaus kicking up his left leg when his putt from the green's fringe rolled into the cup. A large group of spectators are applauding in the background, many with broad smiles on their faces. The eagle at 13, his first winning hole against Jacklin that morning, was only a momentary boost. He stumbled at the next hole, the long par-3 14th, where he again failed to sink a 2-foot putt. With four misses within 3 feet in fourteen holes, Nicklaus had apparently lost his ability to hole short putts. Surely no one rooting for Great Britain would want Jacklin to concede any putt over a foot to his U.S. opponent.

The end came soon after. The Open champion birdied the par-5 15th hole to close out Nicklaus, who finished with a lackluster bogey 6. The large crowd, noisy from the start, "went delirious," noted Trevillion, when Jacklin sank the birdie putt that earned another point for the home country. The Ryder Cup was tied once again: Great Britain 11, United States 11.

Decades later Trevillion recalled Eric Brown's reaction to the Nicklaus-Jacklin singles match that morning. "This is Nicklaus's first Ryder," Trevillion remembered the captain saying, "and I don't believe Jack realizes what it all means, how important it is for both teams to win the Ryder Cup. Can you tell me how Tony hammered the world's greatest golfer 4 and 3 this morning? Jack's playing like he would much rather be back home fishing."

Whatever Nicklaus's mindset, he later said he expected to win. "Jacklin was the type of player I never thought could beat me. Yet he did. I was totally surprised when he beat me in the morning."

Two matches were still to be decided. One of them looked hopeless for Snead's men—Still had fallen into a 4-down chasm against Bembridge. "I had a chance to really grow," Still later said. "I'm [4] down with 6 holes to play to Maurice Bembridge."

Still won the par-5 13th with a birdie to cut Bembridge's lead to 3. At the par-3 14th hole, Still missed the green with his tee shot. "Much of the crowd were delighted," reported Willis. Yet Still salvaged his par, while Bembridge made a bogey. The American had cut his opponent's lead in half.

According to Willis, Bembridge proceeded to play the following par-5 hole like a 15 handicapper. He eventually conceded the 15th to Still. The Englishman's lead was down to 1. Captain Brown offered encouragement as Bembridge walked off the 15th green. The slim margin held for a hole, as both players made par at the 401-yard par-4 16th. With what must have seemed like all of Great Britain against him, the hard-charging Still summoned another birdie to level the match at the 17th, the first of the two finishing par-5 holes.

It was anyone's match. Another prized point, perhaps already banked in Captain Brown's mind an hour earlier, was up for grabs. The side that won it would claim the overall lead.

• • •

With Jacklin's victory over Nicklaus on the 15th green, Butler and Floyd, playing in the seventh match, which trailed Bembridge and Still, were the last players on Royal Birkdale. It was a tense match with few birdies, neither man at his best. After closing the deficit to 1 down at 12, Floyd lost the 13th to a Butler birdie but bounced back with a winning par at the 14th. The two men halved the next three holes as Butler grimly hung onto his 1-up lead. Floyd was bunkered twice, saving his par at 16 and failing to make a birdie at 17 that would have evened the match.

They came to the 18th tee with Floyd needing a win on the last green to halve the match. If Butler could tie his opponent's score on the 18th, he would win the match 1 up and earn another point for Great Britain. They stared in the distance at the only two other players still battling. Bembridge and Still were striding toward the final green, the large clubhouse in the background.

• • •

Ken Still remembered the final hole of his first and only Ryder Cup singles match forty-three years later. "So now, the 18th hole, they changed the tees. They put the tee down to the left." The new tee placement altered both the angle and the distance to landing areas. Still did a mental calculation and figured it was 275 yards to the right-hand fairway bunker. You can't reach it, his caddie advised.

"I guess the adrenaline was flowing," Still said, "because . . . one bounce and right in the trap."

The charge fell short. "[Bembridge] hit the fairway. He birdied it. He beat me 1 up."

Still made a bogey 6, a disappointing finish to a tumultuous two days. He tossed his golf cap in the air when it was over, a sardonic gesture according to one member of the British press. Bembridge smiled broadly, a relieved and ecstatic rookie who had won his first Ryder Cup singles match for his teammates, his captain, and his country.

"All I've got to do is tie him on the last hole, and I didn't do it, but at least I didn't quit," Still later said.

Soon after, arriving at the final green, Floyd made his first birdie in his singles match against Butler. It came too late, because Butler also carded a tying 4 on the 18th hole to hang on for a 1-up victory. "Never can Butler have played his faithfully steady game so well under pressure," reported Ward-Thomas.

The morning's last two matches and points had gone to Great Britain. With twenty-four matches completed, Great Britain led the Ryder Cup, 13–11. After losing the first two matches courtesy of U.S. standouts Trevino and Hill, Great Britain had won five of the other six morning matches.

MORNING SINGLES RESULTS

Trevino (USA) defeated Alliss (GB) 2 and 1

Hill (USA) defeated Townsend (GB) 5 and 4

Coles (GB) defeated Aaron (USA) 1 up

Casper (USA) defeated Barnes (GB) 1 up

O'Connor (GB) defeated Beard (USA) 5 and 4

Bembridge (GB) defeated Still (USA) 1 up

Butler (GB) defeated Floyd (USA) 1 up

Jacklin (GB) defeated Nicklaus (USA) 4 and 3

Session total: Great Britain 5, United States 3

Overall score: Great Britain 13, United States 11

Captain Brown's men had won the morning—again. It was only the fifth time in eighteen Ryder Cups that Great Britain had outpointed the United States in a singles session. To say the captain was excited to have a

2-point lead on the Americans going into the final singles session would not adequately describe his euphoric mood. Brown was "beside himself with joy," reported Mark Wilson, one of several press members who took note of the buoyant Scot at lunchtime.

Gallacher long after remembered a positive sense of anticipation. "We did have a feeling that we could do something. We were at home, and I think the crowd sensed that as well."

Captain Brown's final decisions on the eight men he would send out that afternoon against the U.S. team were, in all likelihood, already made. The draw for the final singles session—based on his and Captain Snead's lineups—would soon be revealed.

The math was simple: Great Britain needed $3\frac{1}{2}$ points in the eight afternoon matches to capture the Ryder Cup for the first time in a dozen years and only the second time since the Great Depression. In other words, the eight selected British lions, whatever their mixture of youth and experience, needed to win three matches and to halve another to take back the Cup. It's no wonder Eric Brown, a Ryder Cup player and captain who inhaled oxygen and exhaled fire, was "beside himself." Brown and his twelve men stood on the precipice of Ryder Cup history.

—14—

SATURDAY: AFTERNOON SINGLES

Reporters assembled for a lunchtime press conference, at which Great Britain Ryder Cup Captain Eric Brown "was so excited and happy he could hardly talk," Peter Willis reported. A wide grin on his face, Brown did manage to say at least a few coherent words during the break between singles sessions. "Before play began I would have settled for four-all in the morning." Instead, the British side had come away with 5 of a possible 8 points in the opening singles. As bullish as Brown had been about his team's chances against the Americans, the performance of his twelve men had exceeded his expectations as the Ryder Cup reached its final stage.

U.S. Captain Sam Snead also could hardly talk, but for an entirely different reason. Continuing a disturbing trend, Snead's team had fallen into another hole on Saturday morning. (They had been outscored 11–5 in the three morning sessions.) The Americans had only one afternoon left to salvage the Ryder Cup and return to U.S. soil with national pride intact. While Brown radiated pure joy, Snead, as Mark Wilson reported, said little in public, saving his words for his twelve players in the confines of the locker room. It was do or die, and Captain Sam Snead, like Captain Ben Hogan before him in 1967, wanted no part of a Ryder Cup defeat.

The eight afternoon singles matches that would determine the verdict were as follows:

MATCH	TIME	GREAT BRITAIN	UNITED STATES
9	1:15	Brian Barnes	Dave Hill
10	1:25	Bernard Gallacher	Lee Trevino
11	1:35	Maurice Bembridge	Miller Barber
12	1:45	Peter Butler	Dale Douglass
13	1:55	Christy O'Connor	Gene Littler
14	2:05	Brian Huggett	Billy Casper
15	2:15	Neil Coles	Dan Sikes
16	2:25	Tony Jacklin	Jack Nicklaus

Captain Snead would again lead off with his two stars that week—Hill and Trevino, both winners in the morning. This time, however, they were in reverse order: Hill off first against Barnes, Trevino in the second spot facing Gallacher. In the next three matches, Snead brought fresh players out of the locker room: Barber, Douglass, and Littler. Douglass had played once, a losing effort on Friday with Hill. Littler would be playing his third match, Barber his fourth.

Snead placed Casper, Sikes, and Nicklaus, who struggled against Jacklin that morning, at the bottom of the lineup. Sikes was making his first singles appearance. It was also the nonpracticing lawyer's first match since Friday morning. If the outcome depended on the last three matches, the captain must have felt these three men could handle the pressure as well as, or better than, anyone on his team. The strategy could also backfire on the American skipper. It was certainly possible for Great Britain to collect the 3½ points it needed to win the Ryder Cup in the first five or six matches, thus negating the impact of Sikes and Nicklaus, and perhaps

Casper. However, by frontloading Hill and Trevino with their combined 6-3-1 record that week, perhaps Captain Snead wasn't overplaying his hand. In any event, his first five men would need to play well enough for Casper, Sikes, and Nicklaus to have the chance to clinch the Ryder Cup at the end of a long, tense afternoon.

Sitting out the final session were Tommy Aaron, Frank Beard, Raymond Floyd, and Ken Still. All four men had lost in the morning, all at the last hole—except for Beard, who was routed by O'Connor. The four U.S. rookies would be on the course rooting for their teammates. Playing or not playing, all twelve American backs were to the wall.

Captain Brown employed a similar strategy, bracing his lineup with veterans in the fourth through eighth spots, a bulwark against a U.S. rally he'd be a fool not to anticipate. Just as Great Britain had dominated the mornings, the Americans had owned the afternoons by a margin of 6–2. Despite an American squad with only two Ryder Cup veterans, it would be a grievous mistake to underestimate the resolve of Snead's men. Brown would send out three of his young lions—Barnes, Gallacher, and Bembridge. Then the captain would unleash his strongest wave of men—Butler, O'Connor, Huggett, Coles, and Jacklin, all experienced in Ryder Cup battles.

Huggett was ready to face Casper in the sixth match, or any other man on a golf course. "I loved head-to-head games," he said four decades later. "They suited my attitude. Never say die."

Jacklin, the only Great Britain player besides Neil Coles to play in all six matches, also embraced his role as last man out against Nicklaus. "In those days, it was more or less a given that the two best players would be the anchormen, and that's what seemed to happen."

Coles, however, was physically and mentally spent. The Englishman was surprised to be going out at 2:15 P.M. for his second singles match that day and sixth match since Thursday morning. "I was told by the captain that I would play one game [on Saturday]," Coles later said, "because I really shot my bolt. I played every round up to that point. I told him I only had one good game left in me."

It was a good game indeed, a stirring three-hole rally that stole a point from Aaron. Coles had done his job—or so he thought. "As soon as I came in, Eric said, 'I'm sorry. I've got to send you out again. You're playing well.' But I know that Bernard Hunt was in fresh. He hadn't played. I don't think Alex Caygill had gone out. In those days, not everybody played."

Captain Brown ignored any signs or possibilities of physical and mental strain and instead saw a courageous thirty-four-year-old veteran who could win another point for Great Britain that afternoon. "He was working basically on form," Coles said. "You just won. You must be feeling good, but I wasn't."

Neither Hunt nor Caygill played in either singles session. The absence of Caygill was not shocking, but no Hunt on Saturday might have raised more than a few eyebrows. In nine Ryder Cup singles matches since 1953, Hunt had won three, lost three, and halved three, an admirable record against the Americans. Had Brown erred by not including the veteran in his final lineup?

Peter Alliss would be describing shots rather than hitting them at Royal Birkdale on Saturday afternoon. Percy's son had taken his seat behind the BBC microphone, a chair he would warm for decades to come. Peter Townsend was also finished. He had played every match to that point. Now, accompanied by his wife, Lorna, he would watch his teammates fight for those cherished 3½ points.

"I remember the last day. The crowds were unbelievably excited because they thought we might win," Townsend later said.

As Willis reported, Townsend was "completely engulfed by autograph hunters" before the final singles session got under way, along with his valiant teammate Jacklin.

·　　·　　·

They called them "buggies" and "golf cars." The forerunner of the modern golf cart, the electric Harbilt was a fixture at Royal Birkdale during

217

Ryder Cup week. About two dozen Harbilts were in use by rules officials, the BBC, the Ryder Cup captains, PGA officials, scorers, and others.

A few years earlier a managing director of a British engineering company used an electric buggy for a golf round "and immediately lost interest in the game for the rest of the afternoon." Mike Warrington convinced his company to build a prototype of a new golf buggy. The Harbilt was initially manufactured as a three-wheeler. A four-wheel model came later. Fully charged by being plugged into an electrical source, the buggies could run for thirty-six holes. The Harbilts were British made with British materials, except for the Goodyear tires imported from the United States. Due to their wide weight displacement, they did no damage to fairways or other parts of golf courses.

Harbilts began to sell on both sides of the Atlantic. In England, one customer arrived at the Harborough factory in his Rolls-Royce driven by his chauffeur. His Harbilt was loaded on a trailer, and he and his chauffeur commenced a tour of golf courses.

At Birkdale, BBC camera crews wheeled around the course in Harbilts to capture and transmit the Ryder Cup action to hundreds of thousands of television viewers. In addition, Captains Brown and Snead were everywhere, driving an estimated 150 miles in their buggies during the matches.

•   •   •

At 1:15 P.M., Mr. Donald Ross announced the day's ninth match and the first game of the afternoon: Brian Barnes of Great Britain versus Dave Hill of the United States. The two men were physical opposites. Hill was 5'11" and skinny, weighing less than 150 pounds. Barnes was burly, 6'2" and tipping the scales at about 200 pounds. Because this was golf rather than football or boxing, size offered no particular advantage or disadvantage. The lean American and the brawny Brit were both solid ball strikers. With an upright golf swing that featured a wide turn and well-coordinated leg action, Hill cracked his opening drive on the 493-yard par 5. Then Barnes put his weight into one, and they were off.

However, as Barnes recalled decades later, he felt rushed. "I came off the 18th green after playing with Billy in the morning ready to have a little bit of time for lunch. Eric came straight up and said, 'Right, you're out in ten minutes,' or whatever. I had about a quarter of an hour change around, where I managed to get a sandwich and a cup of tea or a beer . . . and straight out to the bloody golf course again, which I didn't really enjoy too much," Barnes said, chuckling.

Two by two, ten minutes apart, the other seven afternoon singles matches departed the 1st tee. Early in the session, Willis heard a comment from the gallery after a loud roar. "That's the Americans missing another putt."

After matching birdies at the 1st hole, Barnes found trouble and conceded the 2nd hole to go 1 down, then fought back with a birdie at the 212-yard par-3 4th hole. The feisty Hill birdied the 5th to retake the lead and extended it to 2 up at the par-5 6th hole when Barnes took a bogey in a match that, like others that afternoon, would be a battle of wills as the men fought fatigue and the unfamiliar pressure of an extremely tight Ryder Cup.

Barnes's wife and father were following along. (The elder Barnes eventually removed his identification tag because people were constantly asking him if he was Brian's father.) Brian and Hilary Barnes had gone to the cinema the night before the final singles matches. The couple saw the popular new film *Battle of Britain*, starring Laurence Olivier, Michael Caine, and Trevor Howard. "It was nowhere near as exciting as the battle going on here today," Hilary told Paul Trevillion.

Having his wife in the gallery was one thing; teammates watching was another.

"I hated people, the rest of my teammates, coming and watching," Barnes later said. "As far as I was concerned, that put far too much pressure on. I'd far prefer them to go back into the clubhouse and rest and leave me

219

to it. Whereas a lot of other people liked the idea of their teammates coming to gee them on, I felt it was completely unnecessary to do so."

While Barnes was unsettled about being out on the golf course so soon after his heartbreaking morning match with Casper, Gallacher was like a Thoroughbred in the starting gate. "I was really wanting to play. Eric came up and said, 'You're playing this afternoon and you're playing Trevino.'"

Gallacher relished the matchup with the Merry Mex, but despite making an opening birdie, the spirited young Scot was 1 down as he walked off the 1st green because Trevino made an eagle. Gallacher evened the match with a birdie at the par-4 3rd hole; Trevino reclaimed a 1-up lead with a birdie at the short par-4 5th hole.

Trevino was a tough opponent. After losing his Thursday foursomes match with Still as his partner, Lee had reeled off three wins and halved one match Nonetheless, as Gallacher's caddie, Stewart Logan, remembered, his player did not fear the 1968 U.S. Open champion. "Gallacher looks over at me and says, 'I'm gonna beat this guy!'"

Gallacher's match-play philosophy was to focus on his own game and try not to get caught up in what Trevino or any other opponent was doing.

"I just played the course," Gallacher later said. "It's just simple as that. It's like the Bobby Locke approach to life. The same as Ben Hogan. I used to read their books. You're playing the course . . . just trying to get 'old man par.' And if you get par and the other guy gets a birdie, good luck to him. Your job is to go out there and play par. That's been my mantra my whole life, really."

Bembridge, who had desperately hung on in the morning to defeat Still, "looked desperately tired in his clash with Miller Barber," reported Trevillion. Without a single birdie on the scorecard, Barber was on his way to an outward 9 of 1-over-par 37. Astonishingly, it would result in a 4-up lead. Bembridge would bogey his way through most of the opening 9, destined for an ugly 42.

With Great Britain down in three of three matches, Butler provided some much-needed hope to the home nation. The Birmingham native charged to a 3-up lead after 4 holes against Douglass, off to a poor start, conceding the 1st hole and picking up bogeys at the 2nd and 4th.

In the day's thirteenth match, Littler jumped on O'Connor with birdies at the first two holes to go 2 up, but the Irishman held steady with pars, and when Littler stumbled with bogeys at 3 and 6, the match was all square. It was early, but the matches were not shaping up well for Great Britain—ahead in one, down in three, and tied in the other.

Behind them were the final three matches: Huggett versus Casper, Coles versus Sikes, and Jacklin versus Nicklaus. "Jack wasn't on his game, really," Jacklin later said. "I beat him comfortably in the morning. We went out again."

Casper, like his teammate Trevino, started fast with an eagle but relinquished the lead with consecutive bogeys at the 4th and 5th holes. Huggett had nosed ahead, but he knew to be wary of the dangerous Casper, a player known for his comebacks. Their match was marked by emotional outbursts, even from the composed Casper. At the 3rd hole, Billy reflexively threw his arms and mallet putter overhead when his birdie putt from the edge of the green rolled into the cup. Then it was Huggett's turn. The Welsh Bulldog punched the air when he followed Casper into the hole for a tying birdie. The crowd was delirious. Even Casper, seated on the ground beside the green to conserve his energy, appeared to grin when his opponent's golf ball rolled into the cup.

In his first singles appearance, Sikes was not sharp in the afternoon's second-to-last match, but it was no handicap as his opponent, Coles, was struggling to regain his morning form. When Coles walked off the 18th green with a hard-earned point against Aaron, he thought his Ryder Cup was over.

"That was the problem," he later said about being sent out against Sikes. "I'd sort of come in thinking, that's me done for the day. You totally relax and switch off, and then you've got to switch back on again."

Neither player managed a birdie in the first six holes. Sikes might have silently reveled in his good fortune, because five pars and a bogey had netted him a 2-up lead on Coles as they arrived on the 7th tee.

Anchormen Jacklin and Nicklaus halved the first three holes with par, bogey, and par, not exactly inspired golf. However, Captain Brown noticed a different Nicklaus that afternoon.

"Did you see Jack's face on the 1st tee? He's packed his fishing rod away," Trevillion recalled Brown saying. "This morning Tony was playing the name. Tony's now up against the man. Tony will have to play out of his skin to get even a half."

The Golden Bear broke ahead with a birdie at the long par-3 4th hole. The lead was short-lived. Jacklin birdied the par-5 6th hole, Nicklaus made bogey, and the afternoon's final match was all square.

Starting an hour and ten minutes earlier in the afternoon opener, Hill had stretched his lead on Barnes to 3 up through 9 holes. Following his high-strung teammate, Trevino was 1 up, and then 1 down after Gallacher finished with birdies at holes 8 and 9, shooting a 33 on the outward 9. Bembridge was in a deep and dark hole against Barber. Douglass birdied 5 and 6 to close the gap against Butler. O'Connor and Littler were even after 7 holes. Huggett clung to his 1-up edge on Casper.

The eight singles matches were evenly split as the afternoon progressed.

GREAT BRITAIN 13, UNITED STATES 11

MATCH	HOLE	PLAYERS	STATUS
9	9	Barnes vs. Hill	US 3 up
10	9	Gallacher vs. Trevino	GB 1 up
11	8	Bembridge vs. Barber	US 3 up
12	8	Butler vs. Douglass	GB 1 up
13	7	O'Connor vs. Littler	All square
14	7	Huggett vs. Casper	GB 1 up
15	6	Coles vs. Sikes	US 2 up
16	6	Jacklin vs. Nicklaus	All square

The afternoon's third match, pitting Bembridge against Barber, was the first contest to finish. Going birdie-par-birdie, Barber closed out one of Britain's young lions on the 12th green by the score of 7 and 6. It was the most lopsided margin in a Ryder Cup characterized by tight matches. Despite the lackluster performance, Bembridge had performed admirably in his Ryder Cup debut, netting $2\frac{1}{2}$ points for his side in five matches. The thirty-eight-year-old U.S. rookie had accounted for 2 points in four matches.

The Yanks had pulled within 1—Great Britain 13, United States 12.

In the afternoon's lead match, Hill, a persistent thorn in Great Britain's side, was anything but sharp on the incoming 9. He bogeyed 10, 11, and 14, but Barnes, having troubles of his own with bogeys at 11, 12, and 14, was still 2 down as the match reached the par-5 15th hole. Whether due to fatigue, pressure, or both, this and other matches had surely reached a stage where pars were more cherished than normal. Hill proceeded to par the 15th and 16th holes to finish off Barnes, who could do no better than bogeys. It was a 4-and-2 win for Team USA, mounting another of its afternoon comebacks. The Ryder Cup was tied at 13 apiece.

British prospects were looking more desperate as the remaining matches crept along the fairways between the sand dunes. Of the six matches, Great Britain led in two, trailed in three, and was deadlocked in one—the final game, Jacklin and Nicklaus. Tension was escalating on and off the fairways. Willis spotted Tommy Aaron and Frank and Patty Beard at the 11th green cheering hard for the U.S. team. Leading off with three of his young lions, Brown had only one left—Gallacher, the fellow Scot from Bathgate. Could he get his captain 1 of the $3\frac{1}{2}$ points?

Gallacher had a reason not to fear Trevino, even though Trevino was a fearsome competitor against Great Britain that week. Gallacher was having the best season of his young life, but that wasn't the reason he felt comfortable going head-to-head against Trevino. Rather, it had everything to do with what happened in Scotland shortly before the Ryder Cup.

•   •   •

"About a week beforehand," Gallacher said in 2013, "I'd played Lee Trevino and Orville Moody in an exhibition match in Edinburgh. A big crowd turned out."

Gallacher won that exhibition match against the 1968 and 1969 U.S. Open champions. In afternoon singles at the Ryder Cup, it was the luck of the draw for Gallacher. He and Trevino were in the No. 2 position for their respective teams.

"Eric came up and said, 'I don't think you can get a better draw than this. You know what type of player Lee is, and I think you can beat him.' That's what made me at the time not scared of playing Lee, because I'd met him, had played with him and against him.

"I know he's a great player, but Lee could make you relax. Yes, he's very competitive, but, still, you're having a nice game. You do feel like you're playing with somebody you can speak to. I enjoyed his rapport with the galleries and I enjoyed his jokes and everything. It actually made me relax. I was ready to play Lee Trevino. In fact, I would have felt uncomfortable playing anyone else. I didn't know anyone else. He was the one guy I felt, whether I win it or not, I was going to enjoy my game."

Gallacher also recalled something else about the Merry Mex—his huge popularity with the British spectators. "The galleries didn't know whether to root for Lee or to root for me," Gallacher said. "He walks up the fairway, joking to people. He can't stop himself. He likes people."

•   •   •

Down a hole to the young Scot at the turn, Trevino lost the par-4 10th with a double bogey to go 2 down. There were no wisecracks. Trevillion wrote, "For the first time in the series, Trevino was not smiling. He knew he had a fight on his hands."

Willie Aitchison, Trevino's fallen caddie, couldn't work with a broken ankle, but that didn't keep him away from Royal Birkdale on Saturday. Wearing a sport coat and necktie, Aitchison was spotted watching the action next to British PGA officials Geoffrey Cotton and Lord Derby. He wore a cast on his broken left ankle and hopped about using crutches. At one point, as Aitchison showed Trevillion his new cast, a woman overheard the two men talking and held out her forearm. She also had on a cast decorated with several signatures. One of them was Sam Snead's.

Trevino caught a break at the 11th hole—Gallacher made a bogey—and the U.S. player was again within 1. Hitting after Trevino at the 190-yard par-3 12th hole, Gallacher struck a sublime 2-iron and sank his birdie putt. The lead was back to 2, and, after tying pars at 13, Gallacher went 3 up at the 14th hole when the not-so-merry Mex took a bogey. There was no Casper-like comeback for Trevino. The end came on the next green. The Scot sank a 6-footer for par to put away the American by the impressive margin of 4 and 3.

"I was so determined to win I could have beaten anybody," Gallacher said at the time. More than four decades later he fondly remembered praise from his captain. "I went out there and just played inspired golf, got up early on, had a good front 9, and never let Lee get back in the game. And then when Eric puts his arm around you when I finished on the 15th green, it made me feel as if it's the greatest moment of your life."

The skid stopped. A point went up on the scoreboard for Great Britain. With three matches complete, the tally was Great Britain 14, United States 13. Two and a half more points and the Ryder Cup trophy would not make the return trip to America.

"[Gallacher] inspired the recovery," reported Donald Steel, "and in all future matches in which he undoubtedly play will never win a greater victory. It laid the foundation of hope."

After being 3 down early in the afternoon's fourth match, Douglass had clawed back. The tall Oklahoman squared his contest against Butler on the par-4 10th hole—with a bogey. The two players halved 11 and 12 with pars. Then the Englishman spurted. A birdie at 13. A par at 14, where Douglass carded a bogey. Another birdie at 15. Butler was 3 up with 3 holes to play, another British point within tantalizing reach. Behind them, it was almost all USA. The Yanks led in three matches. The Jacklin-Nicklaus duel was knotted. Great Britain badly needed Butler's point.

It went on the board at the 16th hole, where Butler and Douglass halved with bogeys. The Englishman won 3 and 2 on what turned out to be one of the finest days of his career. Butler had entered the day winless in seven Ryder Cup matches, including two defeats in singles to Tony Lema and Arnold Palmer. By late Saturday afternoon, Butler had won both of his singles matches, edging Floyd and defeating Douglass. The British were another point closer to their goal.

Four points were still up for grabs. Great Britain needed 1½ points to reach the winning total of 16½ points, but the United States led in three of the remaining four matches.

GREAT BRITAIN 15, UNITED STATES 13

MATCH	HOLE	PLAYERS	STATUS
13	14	O'Connor vs. Littler	US 1 up
14	13	Huggett vs. Casper	US 1 up
15	13	Coles vs. Sikes	US 4 up
16	12	Jacklin vs. Nicklaus	All square

Not on his game, O'Connor had fallen to 3 down when Littler birdied the par-3 12th hole. The Irishman, at times struggling to find the fairway, battled back against the smooth-swinging American. At the par-5 13th, O'Connor reached the green with a drive and a 6-iron for a winning birdie. At the par-3 14th hole, both men found the sand with their tee shots. O'Connor played the better bunker shot, and when he sank the 6-footer for par, he was only 1 down to Littler.

Directly behind them, Huggett, with consecutive bogeys at 9 and 10—where the Welshman missed an 18-inch par putt—relinquished his lead. Casper maintained his 1-up edge as the two players halved the next three holes with pars. Despite a 38 on the first 9, Sikes was in command of his match against Coles. Birdies at 10 and 14 gave the nonpracticing lawyer what appeared to be an insurmountable 4-up lead.

"Sikes was a good competitor," Nicklaus later said about his teammate and partner. "He was sort of a gruff guy, but he was a nice guy."

"He had a great desire to win everything," Casper recalled.

Jacko and the Golden Bear, shooting 37 and 38, respectively, on the outward 9, were locked in a seesaw battle. Jacklin had taken the lead with a birdie at the long 8th but lost it after a double bogey at 9 and a bogey at 10. A Nicklaus bogey at the 12th hole evened the anchor match, neither man able to find many birdies on the links course. They had one each—Nicklaus at 4, Jacklin at 8—but there were four par 5s ahead.

O'Connor missed a golden opportunity to pull even at the 15th hole. Littler 3-putted for a bogey 6. Unfortunately, so did O'Connor. The Irishman was bunkered at the par-4 16th and conceded the hole, putting him 2 down with 2 holes to play. At the 17th, hitting his second shot through the green, O'Connor managed to get up and down for his birdie, but Littler matched his 4, and it was over, a 2-and-1 victory for the American. The Ryder Cup was again tied because Sikes, as expected, had closed out Coles on 15, a comfortable 4 and 3 win.

Both sides now needed 1½ points—to pry the Cup out of U.S. hands in Great Britain's case, or to complete a rally that would salvage national pride for the United States. With thirty of thirty-two matches complete, the Ryder Cup would be decided by the four remaining players on Royal Birkdale: Huggett, Casper, Jacklin, and Nicklaus.

•　　•　　•

After a conspicuous absence on Thursday and Friday, clouds rolled across the sky above Royal Birkdale, and a fierce wind arrived from the southwest off the Irish Sea. "It came in raging," Tupper reported, "with rain squalls." "The skies had darkened," noted Ward-Thomas, "and, as if in tribute to the moment, a fresh wind bore down over the dunes."

Casper held a 1-up lead on Huggett when he stepped onto the 16th tee and surveyed the 401-yard par 4. The stiff breeze made the 16th a "fearsome hole," said Ward-Thomas, and Casper, hoping to position his tee shot in one of Birkdale's widest fairways, instead visited a bunker. Billy was bunkered again with his approach shot. From the fairway, Huggett lofted a nifty pitch toward the flagstick. Casper, seeing the cause was lost, conceded the hole. They were tied with 2 holes to play—the finishing par 5s, both playing downwind.

A full hole behind them, neither Jacklin nor Nicklaus could gain an edge. The star players of their respective teams halved 13 with birdies, 14 with pars, and 15, where Jacklin bravely holed an 8-footer, also with pars. With 3 holes to go, the new Open champion and the seven-time major winner were deadlocked, as was the other remaining match and the overall score late on Saturday.

GREAT BRITAIN 15, UNITED STATES 15

MATCH	HOLE	PLAYERS	STATUS
14	16	Huggett vs. Casper	All square
16	15	Jacklin vs. Nicklaus	All square

Huggett and Casper negotiated the 510-yard 17th hole as the rain blowing in from the sea began to dampen the ground. Women tightened the scarves on their heads, and men, some wearing sport coats or long jackets, secured their caps and hats in the windy conditions. Laying two off the back of the 17th green, Casper deftly chipped his third shot to within gimme distance, a birdie. The pressure shifted to Huggett, who also was long with his second but had not chipped as close as his opponent. He had a 6-foot putt to secure a tying birdie. "He crouched over the ball for an eternity," reported Gwilym Brown, "and then punched it into the cup." Still knotted, the match moved to the final hole. "That has to be the greatest putt of the whole deal," said Sikes, one of several players turned spectators.

At 16, hitting first, Jacklin deposited his tee shot into a fairway bunker. Nicklaus followed with a huge drive into the wind. The Golden Bear made a routine par to win the hole after his determined opponent was unable to recover. "Well holed, well holed," Willis heard the PGA Tour's Joe Dey say to Nicklaus as he walked off the 16th green.

The Yanks held a slight edge: 1 up in the anchor match with 2 holes to play and dead even in the other contest as Huggett and Casper started down the 18th. If it held, the United States would pick up the 1½ points needed to take home the gold chalice for the fifteenth time in eighteen Ryder Cups.

Both Casper and Huggett reached the last green in two swings. Both players sized up eagle putts that could win the match and score a critical point for their teams. Casper went first from a distance in excess of 30 feet. He missed but had his 4. Huggett, from 30 feet for victory, charged the hole with his eagle try. His golf ball rolled across the rain-dampened green and stopped nearly 5 feet beyond the cup. The small man had to sink it to halve his match with Casper.

The crowd fell silent as Huggett studied the putt for captain and country. Then a tremendous roar rushed in like a sudden blast of wind. It came from the direction of the 17th green.

．　　　．　　　．

The par-5 17th hole measured 510 yards, but it would play considerably shorter with a fresh wind at the backs of Nicklaus and Jacklin. The drive needed to negotiate a narrow opening between two large sand hills. Nicklaus hit first, then Jacklin, both men smacking long drives down the fairway. Slightly behind Jacklin, Nicklaus surveyed his second shot to the heavily bunkered green, two traps to the right and three hugging the left and front-left of the putting surface. He chose a 7-iron and launched a shot that Ward-Thomas called "perfectly flighted" toward the flag. The golf ball landed and rolled to a stop 12 feet short of the hole, a splendid shot under any circumstances, but especially at that moment.

It was Jacklin's turn. He reached for his 5-iron. The British Open champion slashed his second toward the green, but he had come off the shot ever so slightly and it drifted right—"headed for the willow scrub," reported Gwilym Brown. Jacklin's golf ball landed to the right of the green, fortuitously caromed left off a sand bank, and rolled onto the putting surface, some 50 feet from the cup. He was away and would putt first. Nicklaus was within relatively close range of an eagle that could close out the match.

Jacklin took measure of the long eagle putt and then settled over the ball, gripping his Ping putter. With the Golden Bear hovering near the hole, he knew he needed to take a good run at this one.

"All I was trying to do was make the putt, but it was . . . a bloody long way," Jacklin later said.

Thousands of spectators surrounded the green. In addition, since it was the final match, a thick line of fans crowded into the fairway about 30 yards from where Jacklin hunched over his putt. Jacklin's caddie, Willie Hilton, tended the flagstick and anticipated the stroke, his player's white leather golf bag slung over his left shoulder.

Australian Peter Thomson, a five-time Open champion, had the call for the BBC telecast. "Tony Jacklin putting for 3 on the 17th," Thomson said, "and if ever he needed a putt to go in the hole, it's this one." Before Thomson finished, the ball came off Jacklin's putter and covered half the distance to the cup. As it rolled closer, within 5 feet of its destination, a low sound increasing in volume and pitch rushed out of the large gallery. When the ball dove into the hole, the crowd exhaled a delirious roar that seemed to lift caddie Hilton right off his feet. Jacklin's man gave a little hop and made a quick thrust of the flagstick with his right arm.

"It's in! It's in!" exclaimed Thomson. Jacklin smiled and nodded to the exuberant fans. "Well, what a thing to do at a time like this," added the astonished announcer.

· · ·

On the 18th green, the silence momentarily shattered, Huggett determined that the eruption one hole away conveyed a singular meaning—Jacklin had defeated Nicklaus in the anchor match.

"The last I knew about the last game, Tony versus Jack," Huggett said four decades later, "Tony was 1 up with a few holes to go. When a victory roar came from the [17th] green, I thought Tony had won, leaving me a 5-footer to win the Ryder Cup for Great Britain and Ireland."

It wasn't just Huggett who thought so.

"Along with everyone else around the 18th green," Trevillion later said, "I believed Brian Huggett's putt, if it went in for a half with Billy Casper, would win the Ryder Cup. The tension was unbearable."

Huggett took his stance, his feet close together, slightly pigeon-toed. He struck the putt firmly with his mallet-headed putter, and the golf ball dropped into the right half of the cup. The Welshman, in a burst of emotion, unleashed a right uppercut because his decisive stroke had sealed a Ryder Cup win for Great Britain—or so he thought.

"Well, he's every right to do that," commented the BBC's Henry Longhurst as the exultant cheers washed over the emotional Huggett. "Isn't that wonderful?"

"He was a tenacious little [player], Huggett, real competitor," Jacklin later said.

Their match halved, each man netting a half point for his team, Huggett and Casper shook hands. Billy remembered it well more than forty years later.

"Huggett started crying," Casper explained. "He thought they had won the Ryder Cup, and I'm hugging Huggett on the 18th green while he's crying."

"Huggett's crying on the green," Coles affirmed. "He thought he'd won it."

"So that's all square, and Huggett overcome," said Longhurst from his BBC broadcast position as the Welshman fell into the arms of British PGA officials, including his captain. As Huggett would soon find out, Jacklin's brilliant eagle at 17 hadn't beaten Nicklaus. The Ryder Cup wasn't over.

.   .   .

When Jacklin's long eagle putt tumbled into the cup on the 17th green, "he raised his eyes to the heavens in relief and wonder," reported Ward-Thomas, "as Nicklaus gave him a cooly old-fashioned look."

"Tony was miles away," Nicklaus later said about the monster putt. "The hole gobbled it up."

"There's an element of luck involved in that," Jacklin said. "Of course, I was trying to make it. All you can do is try."

"[Tony was] able to make something happen when you didn't expect it to happen," Nicklaus added, "and that was one of those things. I did not expect someone to knock in a [long] putt, but he did those kind of things."

All eyes were on Nicklaus. Could he answer?

In his familiar crouch, gripping his putter, a George Low Sportsman Wizard 600, the Golden Bear settled over his 12-foot eagle putt. Not far behind him at the edge of the green, also in a crouch, his blue-suited caddie watched and waited. If Nicklaus sank it, he'd halve the hole with Jacklin and maintain his 1-up lead heading to 18.

"What a lot rests on the outcome of this putt," said Thomson on BBC Television. "Jack Nicklaus—" Before the announcer could finish, the twenty-nine-year-old pro stroked the golf ball. A little more than halfway to the hole and Nicklaus knew he'd missed, coming out of his crouch and moving toward the ball, which drifted right and stopped less than a foot from the cup.

"No, it's gone astray," Thomson said, "and Tony Jacklin has won this hole with a 3, and the match now is all square."

Nicklaus recalled the reversal of fortunes at 17. "It looks like I can actually close the match out right there. Instead of going to the last hole [1 up]—or not even have to play the last hole—I have to go to the last hole even."

Following the last match, a part of the armbanded press contingent, Ward-Thomas summed up the moment. "After 31 matches, and as many hours of golf, the Ryder Cup depended on one hole."

Townsend recalled the nervous excitement during that final quarter hour. "The atmosphere around the place was electric. Nobody knew what was going to happen."

It was about 6:00 P.M. when the final two players stepped onto the final tee in fading light. With the breeze at their backs, the 513-yard par-5 18th hole was easily reachable in two shots. The tee was set to the right, and drives that favored the right side could avoid bunker trouble to the left. Jacklin had the honors. Using a 3-wood, he struck a solid tee shot that rolled to a stop far down the fairway.

"That's a very fine aggressive drive by Jacklin," said the BBC's Longhurst.

Nicklaus followed with a 3-wood that also found the fairway, a little short and left of Jacklin's drive.

"He stood on his toes and gave that a bit extra for luck," Longhurst commented.

The two men walked off the 18th tee and headed toward their golf balls. Nicklaus called out to Jacklin, walking ahead.

"I waited, and he caught me up. We walked together then," Jacklin later said.

"Are you nervous?" Nicklaus asked.

"I'm petrified," Jacklin replied.

The Golden Bear smiled. "If it's any consolation, I feel exactly the same way you do."

• • •

At the 18th green, Huggett had finally grasped the situation after moments earlier sinking a putt that teammate Alliss later called "one of the bravest putts I have ever seen in my life."

Trevillion also recalled Huggett's opponent at that moment. "I looked straight at Casper to see his reaction and was amazed to see a smile on his face, but it quickly turned to a look of concern. Huggett had shed his last drop of blood. He was painfully unsteady on his feet as he walked over to shake the outstretched hand of Casper. Casper then put his hand on Huggett's shoulder and guided him towards Eric Brown."

Trevillion later asked the American what he thought when Huggett's putt dropped. "You have to admire that sort of courage," Casper told Trevillion. "They could have filled the hole in and Huggett would still have putted out."

Reality set in for Huggett. "[I] learnt leaving the green from our captain that Tony had holed for an eagle at 17 to get level. That meant we could still lose."

By this time, players from both teams had assembled at the final green. The Americans gathered at the back of the green included Aaron, Beard, Casper, Floyd, and Still—men who decades later would recall details of the tense conclusion.

"My wife and I had sat down to have lunch in a hospitality tent or a tent they had set up for the U.S. team," Aaron said in recent years. "I walked around to the 18th green. I watched them play out."

Nearby was Beard. Next to him was Still, one of Beard's best friends on tour.

Members of the Great Britain team had also congregated at Birkdale's 18th green—Barnes, Coles, Huggett, Gallacher, and Townsend among them, players who long after clearly remembered that Saturday afternoon.

Along with the large gallery, the U.S. and Great Britain teammates looked out on the fairway and spotted the player wearing the red sweater, blue pants, and white golf shoes. Jack Nicklaus was preparing to hit his approach shot to the green where they were waiting.

·   ·   ·

Three bunkers bordered the 18th green, one to the right and toward the front of the putting surface, and two on the left-hand side, one of which fronted a portion of the green. The pin was set in the left-center portion of the green. With relatively short second shots on the finishing par 5, the trio of bunkers, save a mishit or misjudged shot, were unlikely to come into play.

Captain Brown had hustled up the fairway to inform his last player on the course how things stood. "I thought Jacklin might think that Brian had won his match, so I said to him, 'We still need you, kid, to win.'"

Jacklin felt the weight of the moment. He also knew Nicklaus felt the strain after their brief exchange. "Did I feel better that he said that? Maybe," Jacklin later said. "We were in an unenviable situation. Whatever anyone tells you, you don't want to be there. All that pressure, all your teammates around the 18th green, and the result on your shoulders."

At that time and throughout his career, Nicklaus, unlike others, relished pressure situations. "I actually liked those kind of moments," he later said. "I always thought it was fun."

From the left-hand side of the fairway, Nicklaus, with a short iron in his hands, made a controlled, three-quarter swing. His golf ball landed on the green, hopped, and rolled to a stop about 20 feet to the right of the flagstick.

Jacklin followed, using an 8-iron. His rhythmic swing sent the golf ball on a more aggressive line. It was heading toward the hole.

"By then, I was leading with the lower body, the legs, and my tempo was absolutely perfect," he later said. "That's why I could go at the pin and not be afraid."

His ball cleared the corner of the front-left bunker, bounced hard past the flagstick, and rolled to the back of the green, 30 feet from the cup. Both players were on in 2 but would have long eagle putts.

"Considering how nervous they were, and the situation, they both played fantastic." Townsend later said. "I think that's because they were two players who were on top of their game at that time, and so their games stood up."

It was more proof that Jacklin's golf swing would deliver when it was needed most. Long after, Tony mentioned the film showing "Nicklaus and I both hitting our second shots to the 18th green in the '69 match, under all the extreme pressure. Our swings and leg movement were virtually identical. There was no rush there at all. That's when I had it all together."

Before Jacklin's approach shot had landed, the large crowd rushed into the 18th fairway a short distance from the front of the green to watch the conclusion of the Ryder Cup. Wearing armbands and clutching small flags, course stewards hurried forward to establish a boundary to restrain the mass of spectators. Behind them Nicklaus and Jacklin and their caddies would have to wade through the excited throng to reach the 18th green, where the match-deciding putts awaited them.

Moments later the two players and their two caddies stepped out of the small sea of people. Longhurst announced the arrival of Nicklaus and Jacklin at the green. "So just the two of them. They've got a putt each to come. And these putts will decide the entire Ryder Cup match of 1969."

Beard was perched on the edge of the green. "I'm in the fringe with Kenny Still and we're sitting there elbow to elbow. Everybody knows what's going on."

"Everybody was right there behind the 18th hole," Floyd remembered.

The two men surveyed their respective lines to the hole, including the area around the cup, at one point standing next to each other. "The slight drizzle had made the green both dark and damp," Trevillion reported.

After taking measure of his 30-footer, Jacklin would go first. He had just made a long putt to square the match. Now he had a putt to potentially beat Jack Nicklaus for the second time in one day and to win the Ryder Cup. As Jacklin stilled himself over his golf ball, Nicklaus watched from the edge of the green, legs crossed and leaning against his putter. The Englishman firmly rapped the eagle putt and watched it track toward the hole dead on line, but the ball didn't have enough pace and stopped 2 feet shy of the cup.

"No," said Longhurst.

Jacklin tilted his head back, looked skyward, and closed his eyes. His uncooperative putter momentarily rested on his left shoulder.

"Anguished Jacklin," added the BBC announcer.

The gallery groaned and shrieked. One or two distraught female spectators began to cry.

"I was trying to make the putt. It was slower than I anticipated maybe," Jacklin said decades later. "You're going through all the positive right things, and I came up short."

Jacklin marked his Dunlop golf ball and steeled himself for what was to come. "I knew I was going to have to make that putt. I was very tough minded at the time."

All attention shifted to Nicklaus, a last chance for a player on either team to clinch a hard-fought victory. The Golden Bear stalked his 20-foot eagle putt. He never played a shot before he was ready. It often took him considerable time to play, longer than others, a Nicklaus trademark that in this instance only heightened the nearly unbearable tension. He finally took his stance and froze over the golf ball in his trancelike fashion.

"Nicklaus has this long one to win the Ryder Cup for his side," Longhurst told the viewers in the British Isles glued to their television sets. One of them was a fourteen-year-old named Gordon Simpson watching the telecast at his home in Stonehaven near Aberdeen. The boy was mesmerized.

The ball was away from Jack's putter and charging toward the cup before Longhurst completed his sentence. Unlike Jacklin's effort, Nicklaus's putt had ample speed—too much. The golf ball, racing by, missed an inch or two to the right of the cup and kept going.

"Oh," Longhurst said, "and he's gone a long way past."

Nicklaus faced a putt that was nearly 5 feet in length.

"I wouldn't have been surprised if Jack had made his putt, because that's the kind of thing he did all the time," Jacklin later said. "He made more damn putts on the 18th green than anybody I ever saw. Then he rams it 4½ feet past. I couldn't believe it."

Jacklin had come up short on the rain-dampened green. Did Nicklaus overcompensate on his 20-footer?

"I tried to make the putt," Nicklaus said in recent years, "but I wasn't trying to ram it in the hole." It was a mistake, "probably just stupidity," he added, chuckling. "You don't put yourself in a position to lose a match on the 18th hole. Why would I put the whole Ryder Cup on knocking it that far by the hole?"

The hope of winning was replaced with the fear of losing. He had missed a handful of shorter putts during his loss to Jacklin that morning.

"It was about 4½ feet, downhill slider to the right," Nicklaus said, "and that to me is about as tough a putt as there is in golf."

"It was a difficult putt," Aaron later said. "That was not an easy green to putt."

"The greens were anything but carpets. They weren't bad greens, but they were not like today," Beard said.

"I'm glad it wasn't me that had to make the damn thing," Jacklin said.

Nicklaus went to work, studying the 60 inches between his golf ball and the cup, "counting the blades of grass," as Wilson reported. The British golf writer overheard one of many tormented spectators say, "Oh, God. I'll die before he hits the bloody thing." One nervous woman expressed a sincere desire to faint. A man next to her actually did.

The players gathered around the green waited nervously.

"Jack took a long time on his putt. His was a good 5-foot putt," Gallacher said.

"He took his time looking over every putt," Floyd said. "Jack was a very methodical player. He had a routine."

"We know if he misses we're in deep trouble," Beard said.

"I know if I would have been in his position that would have probably been the most difficult putt I'd ever had in my life, at that time," Floyd said. "Under the circumstances, knowing if he misses that putt, we lose the Ryder Cup."

Not far away, just south of the clubhouse, telephones were off the hook in the press room so the lines would be open to quickly relay the outcome of the final match, which would also decide the Ryder Cup. "I felt more relaxed covering wars," joked one reporter.

Gwilym Brown, like Wilson, Trevillion, Ward-Thomas, and others in the press corps, was at the 18th green when Nicklaus, at last, took his stance and set the putter head behind his golf ball. "The silence," Brown later wrote, "was so complete the unvoiced prayer for a miss was like a wave of heat."

The blond American hovered over the 5-foot birdie putt. "I was terrified," Nicklaus would confess afterward. "I wasn't just putting for me. I was putting for my country."

Longhurst summed up what was at stake to television viewers throughout Great Britain: "The awful thought of that by missing this one he might go into history as losing the Ryder Cup."

Then Nicklaus stroked it. This time there was no doubt. The ball plopped into the middle of the hole. "He stood over it for an inordinate amount of time," Gallacher remembered, "and just knocked it straight in."

"Well done, indeed," Longhurst said. "There won't be a single man here who wanted him to miss that."

Jacklin knew what was required of him. "I stood there thinking, 'Right, now back on the job,' knowing that I had to make that putt."

Nicklaus bent over, but instead of retrieving his ball from the cup, he picked up Jacklin's ball mark. Jacklin would not finish out. Nicklaus had conceded the short putt. He smiled, extended his right hand, and said, "I don't believe you'd have missed that putt, but I would never give you the opportunity in these circumstances."

"I was shocked," Jacklin later said.

The players shook hands. Jacklin threw his left arm around Nicklaus's shoulder. Nicklaus wrapped his right arm around Jacklin. They smiled and patted each other because they were friends—and also because they were relieved. "It had been a draining experience for both of us," Nicklaus later said.

"And it's a half," Longhurst announced.

The large gallery saluted the two players and the ending to the eighteenth Ryder Cup with sustained applause.

"They halve the hole, they halve their match, and the two countries halve the Ryder Cup," said Longhurst while thousands of spectators at Royal Birkdale and television viewers across Great Britain watched Tony Jacklin and Jack Nicklaus walk off the 18th green arm in arm.

• • •

The United States had once again rallied in the afternoon to achieve the odd and unsatisfying equilibrium offered by a tie. They had nearly won. They also had narrowly escaped defeat.

The British suffered the disappointment of not getting the 3½ points needed to win the Ryder Cup for the first time in a dozen years. There was also a mixture of joy and pride in not losing to the Americans.

AFTERNOON SINGLES RESULTS

Hill (USA) defeated Barnes (GB) 4 and 2
Gallacher (GB) defeated Trevino (USA) 4 and 3
Barber (USA) defeated Bembridge (GB) 7 and 6
Butler (GB) defeated Douglass (USA) 3 and 2

Sikes (USA) defeated Coles (GB) 4 and 3
Littler (USA) defeated O'Connor (GB) 2 and 1
Huggett (GB) halved with Casper (USA)
Jacklin (GB) halved with Nicklaus (USA)
Session total: United States 5, Great Britain 3
Overall score: Great Britain 16, United States 16

The final score of Great Britain 16, United States 16 was the first tie in the forty-two-year history of the Ryder Cup. After three days and thirty-two matches, the eighteenth Ryder Cup ended without a winner and a loser, although members of both teams felt like one or the other as they began to reflect on the close matches and the conclusion they witnessed on the final green.

—15—

AFTERMATH

After the matches ended, Captain Eric Brown, that mastermind of morale, pairings, and the draw, was momentarily confused when it came to the simple matter of arithmetic, and his confusion made him a miserable man. Somehow during all the closing drama and tension Great Britain's fierce leader had miscalculated his sums. He thought his side had lost.

"I'm pleased we played so well," Brown said. "But to lose such an excitingly close match by only half a point was a very fine performance."

Snead, standing nearby, wore a puzzled expression. He was painfully aware of the 16–16 score. Brown was embarrassed when informed the matches had not ended in another British defeat. He was also ecstatic.

"The moment he realized his error, there was no wider grin to be seen in the whole of Lancashire," Trevillion reported.

Snead also addressed the press. "The British played better than we in the morning matches," he said. "I thought it might be close, but spare me that one again." The Great Britain squad had impressed the Slammer, and he called the just-concluded Ryder Cup "the greatest golf match you have seen in England."

"We are going to beat the Americans. A few more good youngsters and we will have a hell of a team," Brown promised.

A tie meant the holder of the Ryder Cup—the United States by virtue of its 1967 victory—would retain the Cup until the matches resumed in two years.

However, for Snead and several of his players, this was no consolation. They were not satisfied with a tie. In fact, they were upset that Nicklaus had given Jacklin the 2-foot putt on the final green.

•   •   •

At the time, and in the years that followed, the scene that played out with Tony Jacklin and Jack Nicklaus on Royal Birkdale's 18th hole would be seared into the memories of the American players who had watched from the green's edge. Of those who discussed it four decades later, only one— Ken Still—recalled a team meeting afterward during which Jack Nicklaus explained the concession. Regardless of what was said or unsaid that Saturday evening at Royal Birkdale, players harbored strong feelings about how the 1969 Ryder Cup ended.

All remembered that Nicklaus had a difficult 5-foot putt under the most trying circumstances. If he missed it, in all likelihood the United States would lose the Ryder Cup.

Still remembered the doubters. "And everybody's saying, gonna miss it, gonna miss it, gonna miss it—talking about Jack. I said, 'You guys are all negative. Jack Nicklaus will not miss that putt.'" Asked who the doubters were, Still added, "I'm not going to name names because I don't remember who it was."

"He had a very difficult putt on a difficult green that he holed," Tommy Aaron said.

As Raymond Floyd recalled, the circumstances, including Jacklin's proximity to the hole, turned up the pressure. "Maybe Tony's putt was 6 inches farther than a normal routine gimme," Floyd said. "So if Jack knows [Tony is] going to make it . . . Jack has to make it to halve the Ryder Cup. I think that was a helluva lot of pressure."

"He makes this putt," Frank Beard said, "and I remember very clearly, 'Man, we can't lose now. We've got a chance to win.' It never crossed my mind, 'Well, we got the Cup so we're going to keep it.' I wanted to win the match. So did everybody else."

Members of the Great Britain team were also processing the nerve-racking situation.

"The measure of the man is that he always holes those crucial putts at the time," Gallacher later said. "That was really a big putt. The admiration that you have for Jack is enduring."

What happened next surprised virtually everyone on both teams.

"We're all kind of patting each other on the back," Beard recalled, "rolling on the ground or something when he makes the putt. With that, he reaches down and picks up the coin. Kenny Still said to me, 'Is he doing what I think he's doing?' And I looked and kind of turned my head. 'He gave him that putt.' I don't remember what we said after that. We were shocked."

"Jacklin was surprised," Aaron said. "He was getting ready to put his ball back and putt."

"I don't remember someone saying, 'Well, we get to keep the Cup,' but it was not much of a consolation, to be very honest with you," Beard said.

"It was sort of devastating to all of our people that were rooting for us because we wanted to see Jacklin putt that putt," Billy Casper said. "At the time, we were very shaken up with what Nicklaus did."

"It was missable," Beard said about Jacklin's putt. "When Nicklaus makes, the pressure would have been on him."

"He picked up Jacklin's coin. We were all shocked," Aaron said. "We couldn't believe that he had done this. In retrospect, it was a very sporting gesture to do, but I was totally shocked. I would have liked to have seen Jacklin putt that putt because it was not an easy putt."

"We worked so hard to get to where we were at that particular moment," Casper said, "and then to have that be the finalization of the Ryder Cup—it was quite a sensation for everyone concerned there."

Floyd had a different perspective. "I felt that it was the absolute right thing to do without doubt. When he gave Tony that putt, I leaped up. We had beaten them so badly for so many years, and actually we were losing the Ryder Cup in that day."

Somehow in that dramatic moment, or perhaps beforehand, under near-crushing pressure Nicklaus had worked out in his mind the concession of Jacklin's 2-foot putt that would result in the first tie in Ryder Cup history.

"I can't imagine [Nicklaus] thinking beyond making [his] putt," Aaron said. "Maybe he was, and maybe when he made it, it just occurred to him that he'd concede Jacklin's putt for whatever reason he had."

"I don't think he ever planned it," Beard said. "It may have crossed his mind about how good it would be for everybody if we halved this match, but that would have happened on the tee. No, I know Jack. It never crossed his mind until he picked the coin up. Because he was so into his game, into golf, into doing it as a competitor, and not losing—we could have lost the Cup. His mind could not have wavered."

"I think that was the spur of the moment," Casper said. "And I think the reasoning for it was that we had won the Ryder Cup [two years] before, and so it meant that we kept the Ryder Cup."

"He reacted so quickly I got the impression it was just a spur-of-the-moment thing that he did without giving it a lot of thought," Aaron said.

"So we had a team meeting after the thing, and Jack explained it," Still said. "[Jack said] 'I would never have given it to him for a win. Only if it was a tie, and I didn't want to see him miss it in front of his countrymen.'"

"It wouldn't happen today," Aaron said.

•   •   •

Decades later Nicklaus offered an explanation of the concession that seemed to shock everyone except the man who made it.

"I respected what Tony had meant to British golf, the first hero they'd had in a long time," he said. "If he had missed that putt—which I don't think he ever would have—it would have killed him, killed his career. I'm thinking about that, but I'm not thinking about that. I don't really know why—I instinctively just did that. I just felt that that was the right thing to do."

There was more to it than Nicklaus's concern for Jacklin, another personal conviction that led to the surprise ending.

"I've always felt that the spirit of the matches was camaraderie and for bragging rights and for the good of the game and the whole bit. I always felt like that was what international competition was about. Obviously, you tried to win, but it was not about winning. It was about the sportsmanship and what it meant from the bragging rights from the guys."

·   ·   ·   ·

Whatever the players felt or thought, and whatever explanation was provided by Nicklaus behind team doors on that Saturday evening in September 1969, that was the end of it. Nothing much, if anything, was said.

Asked years later if any players approached Nicklaus about the concession, Casper said, "Not to my knowledge . . . but I know that a number of us were disappointed at that particular moment."

"Jack traveled in another world," Beard said. "He just traveled in a more elite-thinking world. It wasn't that he left us out. I just don't recall asking him. I was just in shock. I'm sure you'd like to hear two or three of us went up and got Jack in the locker room and demanded this and—that never happened."

Among those who were stunned and upset by the gesture of America's star player was Sam Snead.

"I thought a tie was a pretty good result," Nicklaus said. "My captain didn't necessarily think so."

"[Snead] didn't like any part of it," Floyd said. "He wasn't happy with the whole thing."

• • •

Word got around that the U.S. team wasn't exactly thrilled with the display of sportsmanship by Jack Nicklaus on the 18th green at Royal Birkdale.

"I must say it occurred to me at the time what Sam Snead . . . might have been thinking," Peter Alliss later commented, "and what he might have said to Nicklaus."

"I heard Sam Snead wasn't very happy about it," Bernard Gallacher later said. Nor, as he recalled, were some of the "hard-nosed Americans."

"Some of the bad feeling remained with the players afterward," Brian Huggett later said.

Snead would later be quoted as saying, "When it happened, all the boys thought it was ridiculous to give him that putt. We went over there to win, not to be good ol' boys. I never would have given a putt like that—except maybe to my brother."

Nicklaus, who had first played with the legend at the age of sixteen, understood his captain's competitive mentality. "Sam liked to win no matter what it was. That was just Sam's mode. Not that that was bad. Sam's mode was once you get somebody down, you keep them down. That's why he was a great competitor and a great player, but in that particular instance I didn't feel that after it was done that he was justified to be that upset."

No matter how much Captain Snead disliked the concession, and no matter how much he may have griped about it to others, he never brought it up in conversation with his star player, at the time or anytime later.

"He never said one word to me," Nicklaus said in 2013.

• • •

The Great Britain team viewed the concession differently.

"We were disappointed with a draw," Gallacher said in 2013, "but, at the end of the day, of course, Jack Nicklaus gave Tony Jacklin a 2-foot putt on the last green. It was a great match between their best player and our best player. A perfect finishing match."

Jacklin's teammates felt Jacklin would have made the putt had it not been conceded by Nicklaus.

"I thought Tony would have holed it anyway," Gallacher said. "It was probably longer than a gimme, that's for sure. It was probably creeping up to just outside 2 feet."

"Nicklaus picked Tony's ball up when it probably was about 2 to 2½ feet," Townsend said. "It wasn't a missable putt in most circumstances. In that circumstance, it was probably definitely missable."

"I'm sure Jacko would have holed it," Huggett said, "because he was a great putter, but you never know."

You never know. Few things are certain, especially in the fickle game of golf. It was the very reason several of the American players wanted to see Jacklin face the short knee-knocker with the Ryder Cup on the line—and why Nicklaus didn't.

"Jack realized that if Tony had missed that particular putt the only thing that would have happened was that everybody would have forgotten that Tony had actually won the Open championship," Brian Barnes later said. "All they would have remembered was him missing the putt to have tied the Ryder Cup."

"[Nicklaus] could also see what a devastating effect it could have on someone like Tony if he missed that short putt on the last green," Townsend said. "To be able to have that foresight at that stage in the proceedings—not many people are given to that."

Like their opponents, members of the Great Britain team wondered aloud how Nicklaus arrived at the concession. They also marveled at the act and the man behind it.

Barnes spoke of "the wonderful ability that Jack had under severe pressure to think as clearly as he did and giving Tony that putt on the 18th green."

More than forty years later, Jacklin had no regrets about how things played out in the final moments of his singles match with Nicklaus. There was no second-guessing. He had always appreciated the gesture. Asked if he ever felt there was any lost glory for him and the British side by not holing out on the final green, Jacklin said, "I don't go there. I've never gone there. I think I would have made the putt."

For obvious reasons, the 16–16 ending was as satisfying to the British as it was disappointing to the Americans. It was due, in part, to the odd nature of ties in sports, and not unlike a legendary tie in college football the year before, in 1968. Both teams entering the game with records of 8-0, heavy underdog Harvard rallied in the closing minutes to tie Yale, snapping its rival's sixteen-game win streak. The famous headline in the *Harvard Crimson* read, HARVARD BEATS YALE, 29–29.

"After the losses that we'd had, it was a big plus," Neil Coles later said about the 1969 tie. "We never thought we'd get near them."

"It was a very exciting week, no doubt about it. I don't know how the hell we did it, to be honest," Jacklin said in recent years.

The Great Britain team also attached a larger significance to the gesture and the Ryder Cup than was immediately evident to some members of the U.S. squad.

"They didn't look at the big picture," Townsend said. "They thought [they] could win, and Tony could miss this putt, and that's all they were interested in. Nicklaus could see the big picture. He could . . . see that it was great that the match would be halved."

"I felt it was just the right thing to do at the time," Gallacher said. "In the cold light of day, [the Americans] probably realize that it's good for the Ryder Cup."

"I thought it was a great sporting moment from not only the greatest golfer but also one of the world's greatest gentlemen," Huggett said. "It was very sad that some of the USA team did not have the same feeling as Jack. I suppose that's what made the difference between a great man and others."

Gallacher recalled the final moments that stirred such strong feelings and that created such indelible memories. "I was sitting by the green. I just thought to myself, 'Jack Nicklaus, you're great,' and I've been thinking 'Jack Nicklaus you're great' ever since that day."

•   •   •

A short while after Nicklaus and Jacklin exited the 18th green, the two teams, wearing sport coats adorned with Ryder Cup insignias, reassembled for a presentation ceremony. Bleachers and chairs had been set up a short distance from the front of the 18th green. Three standing microphones and a table on which rested the Ryder Cup trophy were positioned in front of the area where the players, captains, officials, and dignitaries were seated. Many spectators had stayed for the ceremony. Indeed, the matches had ended in a draw, but for the British faithful the taste of a tie after so many bitter losses was nearly as sweet as a victory.

A player from the opposing team said as much. "You have developed new blood and a new outlook," Miller Barber said after the matches ended. "I would feel we had won if I were British."

"It has now become an even contest," Casper said.

"This tie is one of the greatest things that has happened to golf in many years," Barber added.

At his home in Stonehaven, young Simpson had been captivated by the Ryder Cup.

"My golf knowledge was confined to watching the Open on BBC," Simpson later said, "but it was the sight of Jacklin versus Nicklaus and the famous concession allied to Brian Huggett's emotional outburst which resonated in my teenage head! I was hooked from that moment."

The boy would go on to a career in golf and later become the director of communications for the European Tour.

At one point, with Captain Eric Brown at the microphone, the Great Britain team was asked to stand. Basking from the applause, the players smiled and laughed, partly because Huggett had hopped onto his chair, appearing much taller than his 5'6" stature.

The two captains posed for press photographers, smiling and jointly holding the Ryder Cup trophy. Snead, wearing a dark-brimmed hat, held the base of the trophy while Brown took hold of a handle. The Scot looked forward to a day when he could wrap both hands around that Cup.

Peter Willis later recalled a celebratory scene that included the staunch captain and the relentless campaigner. "My final and most vivid memory," Willis said in 2013, "has to be of seeing Eric Brown and Paul Trevillion embrace each other behind the 18th green at the end of the match and give each other a massive handshake and hug just before Eric was to get one hand on the famous old trophy."

Trevillion, child of the Blitz, had rallied the troops.

"I still remember," he later said, "how embarrassed, even sheepish, the two or three Great Britain team members were who came up after the presentation and congratulated me on the *Golf Illustrated* campaign. My response? 'Where were you when we needed you?'"

Later, in the parking lot at Royal Birkdale, Trevillion unwrapped a large cigar, the kind Sir Winston Churchill puffed.

"I never knew you smoked," Captain Brown said.

"You are right. I don't," Trevillion replied as he climbed into his car.

As he rolled toward the exit, he flashed the two-finger "V for Victory" sign made famous by his hero, Churchill. Brown laughed and then shouted, "I've changed my mind. I will write the foreword. What's the title of your book?"

"Dead Heat," Trevillion shouted in reply before driving away.

Miss Rosalind Scarfe, the granddaughter of Samuel Ryder, attended the victory dinner that evening and posed for a photograph with her grandfather's famous trophy. Another sporting gesture was made at the dinner. Even though the 16–16 tie meant the United States had retained the Cup and was entitled to hold on to it for the next two years, U.S. PGA President Leo Fraser handed the trophy to British PGA President Lord Derby. Fraser felt, because of the tie, it was fitting to share the Cup, each side holding it for a year. The Ryder Cup would spend the next twelve months at British PGA headquarters at the Oval, the trophy's first extended stay in Great Britain in a dozen years.

"He thought it was good for the Ryder Cup," Gallacher said.

"The gesture by the Americans has sort of got lost in history," Jacklin said, "but I promise you faithfully that it happened."

The Great Britain team threw a party that night. One U.S. player attended—Billy Casper. "I was invited to it," Casper later said. "I was the only American that went, and attended and celebrated with them because that was my relationship with [them]."

At 1:00 A.M. on Sunday morning, Captain Brown, along with others, was dancing in the halls of the Prince of Wales Hotel. Brown stopped momentarily to catch his breath, long enough to assess his captaincy. "I made some good and some bad decisions, but most were good."

•   •   •

On Sunday morning and in the days and weeks that followed, newspapers and magazines on both sides of the Atlantic documented the historic Ryder Cup deadlock at Royal Birkdale.

BRITAIN'S CUP OF DRAMA OVERFLOWS IN TIE! read the headline in *The Sunday Telegraph*. "Bare facts alone can never relate the tenseness, the uncertainty and the thrill of the climax," Donald Steel wrote.

U.S. AND BRITAIN TIE IN RYDER CUP GOLF was the headline in *The New York Times*. "In the most stirring finish in the 42-year history of the Ryder Cup series," read Fred Tupper's lead, "Tony Jacklin, the British Open champion, sank a 50-foot putt at the 17th hole, enabling him to halve his match with Jack Nicklaus and give Britain a tie with the United States in this biennial golf series after three days of play."

"For years to come golfers will talk of the British performance in halving the Ryder Cup match at Birkdale," Pat Ward-Thomas wrote in a *Guardian* story titled UNFORGETTABLE FINISH TO THE RYDER CUP, "and of how it fell to Tony Jacklin and Jack Nicklaus to achieve the just conclusion to one of the most remarkable international contests in history."

On the Tuesday following the matches, the company that financed the Ryder Cup to the tune of about £30,000 placed a large advertisement in *The Guardian.* "Senior Service Limited, the first company to sponsor the Ryder Cup matches, congratulates both the British and American teams after the greatest international golf contest ever seen in Great Britain."

The 1969 Ryder Cup had been an unqualified success, attracting about 25,000 spectators to watch the thirty-two matches over the three days. Not long after, coverage in the weekly and monthly golf and sports periodicals landed on newsstands and arrived at homes and businesses.

WHAT A TRIUMPH FOR BRITISH GOLF! blared *Golf Illustrated.* Editor Tom Scott opened, "Those who were at Birkdale and saw the final stages of this year's Ryder Cup match will surely recall it again and again down through the years, for even if they live to be a hundred I doubt whether ever again they will see a finish charged with so much emotion or filled with such drama."

Golf World called the most recent Ryder Cup A MORAL VICTORY, INDEED, and *Professional Golfer* said BRITISH PROVE THERE'LL ALWAYS BE AN ENGLAND. In a special Ryder Cup supplement, *Golf Monthly* titled the cover story AMERICANS WERE LUCKY; it was penned by Dai Rees, the gallant captain of the last British victory.

Legendary golf writer Herbert Warren Wind would later highlight the 1969 Ryder Cup in the third edition of his classic book *The Story of American Golf.* "Many people felt this was the best Ryder Cup Match of all time," Wind wrote, "and no doubt it was. It was based on a tenacious effort by Britain and especially by Jacklin, the leader his country had been looking for, who went undefeated in his six matches."

The mood was different in some American sports pages. Three days after the 16–16 tie, *Los Angeles Times* columnist Jim Murray filed PAMPERED U.S. GOLFERS RETREAT FROM "GETTYSBURG." "I have a feeling they [the U.S. team] are on their way back from Gettysburg," Murray wrote. "Don't believe the communiqué that they 'tied' Britain, that the battle was indecisive. The 1969 Ryder Cup was a 'tie' only if you consider Caporetto to be one—or Waterloo."

Nine days after the final putt was conceded, *Sports Illustrated* might have best captured the American perspective with the title of its story on the Royal Birkdale drama: RYDER CUP 1969: A TIE MAY BE LIKE KISSING YOUR SISTER. Gwilym Brown prophesied in his conclusion, "Nicklaus sank the putt and saved the tie. His stroke saved the cup, too, but America's reputation as unbeatable was beyond repair. The Ryder Cup is a sports event again."

• • •

With seventeen of the thirty-two matches decided on the 18th hole, and five more finishing at the 17th, the 1969 Ryder Cup had been the closest contest in the long history of the competition.

"The script writer did a perfect job," television producer Don Sayer told *Golf Illustrated* editor Scott.

If awards had been handed out as they often are at sports banquets, Tony Jacklin was undoubtedly the Most Valuable Player for the Great Britain team. Jacko played in all six matches, logging 104 holes, more than any other player. He was undefeated, winning four matches and halving two others, for a total of 5 points.

Dave Hill, brilliant and irascible, was America's Most Valuable Player.

Hill also played in all six matches, winning four and losing two, for a total of 4 points.

Brian Huggett, who sank the gutsy 4½-foot putt at the last hole that he and so many others thought was to win the Ryder Cup and then tearfully embraced his captain, was Most Inspirational Player.

Jack Nicklaus, victorious in only one match, won the award for Outstanding Sportsman by virtue of his concession that guaranteed a halved final match with Jacklin and the first tie in Ryder Cup history.

The following individual totals in the 1969 Ryder Cup bear witness to standout performances, but, as is the case with many sporting events, the fuller drama is not evident in statistical recaps. (Points are allocated to each team member in foursomes and fourballs matches, which is why total points, 48, are greater than the 32 points available in the thirty-two matches).

GREAT BRITAIN

PLAYER	MATCHES	WINS	LOSSES	HALVES	POINTS
Jacklin	6	4	0	2	5
Coles	6	3	2	1	3½
Townsend	5	3	2	0	3
Bembridge	5	2	2	1	2½
O'Connor	4	2	1	1	2½
Butler	4	2	2	0	2
Gallacher	4	2	2	0	2
Huggett	5	1	2	2	2
Alliss	3	0	2	1	½
Caygill	1	0	0	1	½
Hunt	2	0	1	1	½
Barnes	3	0	3	0	0

UNITED STATES

PLAYER	MATCHES	WINS	LOSSES	HALVES	POINTS
Hill	6	4	2	0	4
Trevino	6	3	2	1	3½
Casper	5	2	1	2	3
Littler	3	3	0	0	3
Barber	4	1	1	2	2
Sikes	3	2	1	0	2
Aaron	4	1	2	1	1½
Beard	4	1	2	1	1½
Nicklaus	4	1	2	1	1½
Floyd	4	0	2	2	1
Still	3	1	2	0	1
Douglass	2	0	2	0	0

Jacklin did receive recognition for his team-leading contribution. The *Daily Express* awarded him £1,000 and an encased putter for being the best player on the British side. The newspaper also awarded Coles, Huggett, and Townsend for their outstanding play.

In the October 2, 1969, issue of *Golf Illustrated,* letter writers chimed in. Miss Anne H. of Staffordshire wrote, "It was not hard to see why Dave Hill has won three events on the U.S. tour this year. At Birkdale I thought he was by far the best of the U.S. team." Bill H. of Suffolk fancied the new British Open champion. "Tony Jacklin could be the next Arnold Palmer. His performance at Birkdale was out of this world."

After so many losses, including a 15-point shellacking in Houston two years earlier, how had the British team managed a tie?

Some reports, including the "Americans were lucky" postmortem by Dai Rees in *Golf Monthly,* credited the use of the large ball on the British circuit for two seasons leading up to the 1969 Ryder Cup. The British players had adapted well to the big ball. Their pitching and putting had rivaled the short-game skills of the Americans. Unlike in the past, the Great Britain team also got off to great starts each day, winning all three morning sessions.

There were still other explanations for the unexpected result.

"I felt the captain instilled in us this will to win," Coles later said. "I think Eric had a lot to do with it. I think Jacklin had a lot to do with it, his proving that one of us could win the Open Championship. Obviously, [he] was at the height of his game. He was probably the leader of that team, and it rubbed off on everybody else."

Whatever rubbed off apparently did wonders for his teammates, as Coles remembered. "Everybody seemed to be playing well that week. It was a strange thing. Even the guys that didn't play so well played well."

Jacklin thought playing links golf in front of supportive home crowds could not be underestimated.

Trevillion and Willis believed their defiant *Golf Illustrated* campaign supported by Captain Brown and others sparked a new attitude and created a winning atmosphere at Royal Birkdale.

"The 1969 Ryder Cup tie was no accident," Trevillion said in 2013. "It was a military planned assault on the unsuspecting enemy, the USA team. Only bad light and the rain-affected green kept the Jacklin putt short [on the final green] and saved them from defeat."

"This Trevillion-inspired campaign played a major role in the match ending in a tie," Willis asserted four decades later. The former deputy editor added that it "changed the atmosphere at Birkdale from negative to positive. The vibes reached the Great Britain and Irish team, followed by the golf fans, and the rest is history."

•　　•　　•

The press reported that Dave Hill and Ken Still had allegedly vowed to never again play golf in Great Britain. At least one of the two U.S. players extended an olive branch to an opponent from perhaps the most acrimonious and controversial match in Ryder Cup history.

"Hill invited Brian the following week at Oregon to have a practice round with him in the Alcan tournament," Gallacher later said. "Most of the players went on the same plane when we flew to the Alcan tournament in Oregon. Dave Hill asked him if he wanted to have a game with him."

"Dave Hill and I got together and the nastiness of our match was soon forgotten," Huggett later said. "We said we'd have a practice round in Portland, which we did."

In November *Dead Heat: The '69 Ryder Cup Classic* by Paul Trevillion was in bookstores. "Roddy Bloomfield believed what no other publishing house did—that we could win the Ryder Cup," Trevillion later said. Trevillion submitted copy and photographs during and immediately after the matches at Royal Birkdale. While others may have considered writing a book about the historic matches, *Dead Heat* would be the only one.

After the 1969 Ryder Cup, Tony Jacklin wrote a note to Jack Nicklaus. In it Tony said how impressed he was by Jack's gesture on the 18th green in the final match, adding that the larger meaning of the concession would be good for the game of golf. His heartfelt sentiment was prophetic, for that moment between him and Jack on the 18th green at Royal Birkdale would become an important part of Ryder Cup, golf, and sports lore. The unattempted 2-foot putt would become widely known as "the concession."

Jacklin later said his personal note to Nicklaus was the only time in his career that he wrote to another player about something that occurred on a golf course.

—16—

NEW ERA

On the flight home from the 1969 Ryder Cup, Jack Nicklaus thought about how physically draining the two singles matches against Tony Jacklin had been on the final day, a 36-hole march of pressure-packed golf. "That was the first time I ever got tired in my life," Nicklaus later said. Perhaps his soon-to-be thirty-year-old body was trying to tell him something.

On the heavy side throughout his first eight years on the PGA Tour, Nicklaus had always eaten pretty much as he pleased, weighing between 205 and 215 pounds. His doctor, O. F. "Rosie" Rosenow, told him not to worry about it—Jack was young, strong, and playing well—but that the day would come to shed some weight from his husky frame. In discussing it with his wife, Barbara, after the trip to Royal Birkdale, Jack realized that day had arrived.

When he got home to Florida, Nicklaus went on an eating regimen patterned after Weight Watchers and called his apparel company, Hart Schaffner & Marx, instructing them to send a tailor to North Palm Beach in two weeks because he would need new clothes for his slimmed-down body. His clothing sponsor chuckled, but the golfer was dead serious. He stuck to the new diet and routinely jogged around Lost Tree Club with five or six golf clubs, playing 18 holes in an hour or less. The tailor soon arrived from Chicago and took his measurements. Nicklaus shed 20 pounds in all, trimming seven inches from his hips. He slipped into a new wardrobe weighing 190 pounds, and not long after a new image was born.

Rejoining the tour that fall, Nicklaus won two tournaments in three weeks, the Sahara Invitational and the Kaiser International. "I lost distance," he later said about the weight loss. "I never hit the ball again as far as I hit it in the late sixties . . . but I hit it far enough."

.   .   .

After his stirring victory at the 1969 British Open and team-leading performance at the 1969 Ryder Cup, Tony Jacklin, with sports agent Mark McCormack and IMG urging him on, pursued opportunities on both sides of the Atlantic—to his detriment, he would later realize. "It was a disastrous thing to do, chasing every dollar," Jacklin said in his autobiography, "though I could hardly have understood the full effect of it at the time. My relationship with Mark and IMG in general soured as time went on, but I believed in that moment in time that Mark and all agents in general were actually there to better my and their clients' lives, not simply their own."

Another amazing triumph was in store for Jacko at Hazeltine National Golf Club in Chaska, Minnesota, site of the 1970 U.S. Open. The players liked Hazeltine about as much as they liked bogeys. Dave Hill verbalized what others were thinking, saying the only thing Hazeltine lacked was "eighty acres of corn and a few cows to be a good farm." He was fined, a routine occurrence for the outspoken pro.

Jacklin looked at the 7,151-yard layout, a long course for that era, and saw opportunity. It was a difficult track with many blind shots, and a strong wind was blowing. The tough playing conditions were similar to the championship links back home in Great Britain. Tony was hitting the ball well but putting rather poorly until he received a tip from the brother of tour friend Bert Yancey. The golf ball started rolling into the cup, and Jacklin opened with a 1-under 71 to take a 2-stroke lead over a trio of golfers. Meanwhile, Nicklaus, Gary Player, and Arnold Palmer carded 81, 80, and 79, respectively.

"It was carnage everywhere," Jacklin later said.

Firing a 70 on a calm Friday, the reigning British Open champion widened his lead to 3 strokes at the halfway point. On Saturday Jacklin teed off with Hill, who was greeted with moos from the gallery because of his Hazeltine comments. After another 70, Jacklin took a 4-shot lead over Hill into the final round. He did something uncharacteristic before teeing off on Sunday.

"I'm not a religious man, but I prayed that day," he later said. "Not to win, but I prayed for the strength to get through the day the best way I could."

Jacklin started well but hit a shaky patch on holes 4 through 8, where he missed short putts, hit a tree, and 3-putted. The pressure, he later admitted, was crushing him. "That was the most nervous I've ever been in my life."

Then Jacklin caught a break. He sank a 30-foot birdie putt at the par-4 9th hole that would have stopped well beyond the hole had it not dived into the cup. The pressure immediately lifted, and he coasted through the incoming 9 to shoot another 70 for a 7-shot victory, the largest winning margin in nearly a half century. No one else finished under par. Jacklin was the first Brit (who had not immigrated to the States) to capture the U.S. Open trophy since Ted Ray at the Inverness Club in 1920. He was also the first player to hold both the British and U.S. Open titles since Ben Hogan accomplished the feat in 1953.

In the space of eleven months, Jacklin had hoisted the Claret Jug, gone undefeated in a historic Ryder Cup, and won the U.S. Open. In search of the holy grail of golf greats and major champions—what made them different—he had discovered a simple answer.

"It brought me to the conclusion at the end of the day that it's courage that counts," Jacklin later said. "You have to have the ability for a start. Beyond that, it's just courage."

"[Jacklin] was a wonderful player," Frank Beard later said. "He and his wife and my wife and I . . . rented a house in New York during the Westchester Classic. We didn't hang out a lot, but I got to know him. He was a nice man."

"I believed then and I believe now that Jacklin did for British golf what Palmer achieved for golf in the USA," Paul Trevillion said in 2013.

·　　·　　·　　·

The high for Tony Jacklin was a low for Jack Nicklaus. The Golden Bear tied for forty-ninth at Hazeltine, his worst finish in a major. He recalled two emotions as he left Minnesota and soon after traveled to St. Andrews for the 1970 British Open: "embarrassment and anger." He had not won a major championship since his record-breaking U.S. Open victory three years earlier at Baltusrol.

Under blue skies on a windless Wednesday, Nicklaus hit every fairway and green en route to an opening 68 at the Old Course, putting him 3 strokes behind first-round leader Neil Coles, whose sterling 65 was a course record. The temperature plummeted and the wind came up, blowing harder and harder from the second round on. Nicklaus bundled himself in three sweaters to stay warm and carded a 69 to trail 36-hole leader Lee Trevino by 1. After a 73 in the third round, during which he hit the ball solidly in the strong winds but did not putt well, Nicklaus was still 2 off the pace set by Trevino.

The Golden Bear teed off in Saturday's final round in the second-to-last pairing with the defending champion, Jacklin, who, along with Doug Sanders, was tied with Nicklaus for second place. Given the tough conditions, Nicklaus determined that par golf would likely win the day and the tournament. He went out in 1-under 35. Trevino was faltering, and nei-

262

ther Jacklin nor Sanders was making a move. Three-putting a few times, Nicklaus came home in 38 strokes for a 73, 1 more than his target score. All he could do was wait for Sanders, who had miraculously got up and down from the greenside pot bunker on the famous Road Hole. A par at the short par-4 18th hole and Sanders, an eighteen-time winner, would capture his first major. The colorful Georgian reached the green in regulation and left his first putt 2½ feet short.

"Hey, Jack, you're still alive," Jacklin said.

The clinching putt was trickier than it looked. Sanders missed.

Nicklaus felt bad for Sanders but also recognized his opponent's misfortune was a tremendous opportunity. "I resolved that night to make the most of it," he later said. The next day, in an 18-hole playoff, Nicklaus sank an 8-foot birdie putt on the final hole to edge Sanders by a stroke, 72–73. In a spontaneous, un-Nicklaus-like display of emotion, he tossed his putter high in the air.

Jack had achieved his dream of winning at St. Andrews, the Home of Golf, in the process breaking a three-year majors slump. It was also his first major victory since his father, Charlie Nicklaus, had died from pancreatic and liver cancer at the age of fifty-six. This one was for his dad, but, in truth, so had been all the others.

•   •   •

Tony Jacklin never recaptured the magic of his 1969 and 1970 seasons. At Royal Birkdale in the 1971 British Open, Jacklin began the final round 1 shot behind leader Lee Trevino. He shot a 71 to finish third, 2 behind Trevino's winning total of 278. Defending champion Jack Nicklaus finished in a tie for fifth.

The next year, at Muirfield, an epic battle involving Trevino, Jacklin, and Nicklaus unfolded on the final day. As he had the year before, Jacklin trailed Trevino by 1 shot when the two players teed off in the last pairing. Nicklaus, who had won the Masters and U.S. Open that season in pursuit of the fabled Grand Slam, charged in front after trailing by 6 shots. The Golden Bear finished with a 66 and was the clubhouse leader.

Reaching the par-5 17th hole, Trevino and Jacklin co-led the British Open, 1 ahead of Nicklaus. Trevino bunkered his tee shot and then hacked his golf ball down the par 5 until his fourth shot took him to a grassy bank to the left rear of the green. Jacklin was on the putting surface in 3 shots, staring at an 18-foot putt for birdie.

Thinking he had thrown away the championship, Trevino then struck the improbable blow that smashed the major hopes of two men. His hurried chip shot rolled across the green and into the cup for a par. Jacko 3-putted for a bogey. Trevino parred the last to edge Nicklaus by a stroke, winning his second consecutive British Open.

"When his chip hit the bottom of the cup," Jacklin later said about Muirfield's fateful 17th, "and my par putt did not, nothing was going to be the same again."

Jacklin would never again challenge in a major championship. Nicklaus, gracious in defeat but terribly disappointed, would not stay down long and would go on to win a record eighteen professional majors.

•   •   •

British hopes were high heading into the 1971 Ryder Cup at Old Warson Country Club in St. Louis, Missouri. Great Britain had never won the Cup on American soil, but after the strong showing at Royal Birkdale and with a team that included Tony Jacklin and eight other returning players from 1969, victory seemed to be within reach. Returning captain Eric Brown certainly thought so.

Triple-digit heat assaulted the players during practice rounds, and then biblical rains forced a cancellation of the opening ceremony for the first time in the history of the Ryder Cup. After a good start in foursomes that resulted in a 1-point lead at the end of the first day, Great Britain's chances went awash in fourballs. The U.S. team captured 6½ of 8 points to take a 4-point lead into the sixteen singles matches on the final day. This time it wasn't close. The final score: United States 18½, Great Britain 13½. Playing in every match and posting a 5-1 record, Jack Nicklaus was the leading point-getter for the Americans.

The matches returned to Great Britain in 1973, and British hopes were again dashed, this time at Muirfield in Scotland. Another powerful U.S. team smothered their hosts by the score of 19–13. It got worse. In 1975, at Laurel Valley Golf Club in Pennsylvania and with Arnold Palmer at the helm, the United States beat Great Britain 21–11. In 1977, at Royal Lytham and St. Annes, where Jacklin had won the British Open eight years earlier, Great Britain suffered another lopsided loss despite a new 20-point format designed to make the matches more competitive.

"There's no pride in getting your ass kicked every year, and we had to endure that through the seventies. We weren't really going anywhere with it," Jacklin later said.

It was as if 1969 hadn't happened, or had merely been another blip during the Yanks' long run of Ryder Cup dominance.

·   ·   ·

Jack Nicklaus felt that something had to be done to strengthen Ryder Cup competition. How bad was it? Tom Weiskopf, a member of the 1973 and 1975 U.S. teams, qualified for the 1977 squad but chose not to travel overseas for the matches. Weiskopf later called it one of his biggest regrets. Nonetheless, while his teammates were playing for points in England, Weiskopf was hunting for bear in Alaska.

"You don't want that happening very often," Jacklin later said about Weiskopf's absence. "People are going to start saying it's nothing if the best players don't show up. Why bother?"

During the 1977 Ryder Cup, Nicklaus sat down with British PGA President Lord Derby one evening at the Clifton Arms Hotel to express his concerns and propose a solution. The U.S. players were honored to make the team, he explained, "but the matches just weren't competitive enough." Nicklaus also reasoned that Great Britain's players must be frustrated about the constant losses. When asked by Lord Derby how to fix the Ryder Cup, Nicklaus suggested the British team be expanded to include players from the entire European Tour, which had been in existence for five years and was growing in talent and depth. Lord Derby acknowledged the idea had merit and requested a formal letter from Nicklaus that he could present to other British PGA officials.

With no objection from Joan Scarfe, the daughter of Samuel Ryder, and with the support of the respective golf bodies, the change to a European team was implemented in advance of the 1979 Ryder Cup, to be played at the Greenbrier in West Virginia.

"It was the best thing that could happen to it," Neil Coles said in 2012. "I always felt that for us to keep losing kept pushing the European Tour back instead of going forward like we were. The Ryder Cup loss every two years was not doing us any good at all."

．　　．　　．

While Ken Still never played on another Ryder Cup team, his 1969 four-ball partner, Dave Hill, was on the U.S. squad in 1973 and 1977. Hill made his only appearance in the British Open in 1973, finishing in a tie for eighteenth. He had returned to Great Britain after all.

In 1989, Hill said he had played in Britain a few times and Royal Birkdale was probably the best golf course he ever played. "I enjoyed the Ryder Cup. It was the greatest thrill of my life." About the infamous match against Brian Huggett and Bernard Gallacher, Hill said, "Fortunately it was the one and only dark spot, because I loved the Ryder Cup."

．　　．　　．

After walking off the 18th green arm in arm at Royal Birkdale in September 1969, and despite both men playing on five more Ryder Cup teams over the next dozen years, Jack Nicklaus and Tony Jacklin never again faced each other in a Ryder Cup match. The two men were, however, destined to meet again in the Ryder Cup, even though Jacklin thought he was finished with it.

By the early 1980s, it was no secret that Jacklin was unhappy with the direction of European golf, both the tour he had helped start and the Ryder Cup team that had continued to struggle. Despite the expansion to a European team, the losing streak continued at the Greenbrier in 1979 and Walton Heath in 1981. It wasn't close either time. To add insult to injury, Jacklin, thirteenth in the points standings, wasn't picked for the 1981 team, and Seve Ballesteros, Europe's brightest golf star, was banned from the competition for playing too much in America, a decision Jacklin called "nonsense of the first degree."

"We played two European matches and we hadn't made a damn bit of difference because the approach was wrong," Jacklin later said.

Retired from tournament golf, doing commentary for the BBC, Jacklin was hitting balls on the practice range at Moortown Golf Club when European Tour Executive Director Ken Schofield and British PGA Secretary Colin Snape approached and offered him the Ryder Cup captaincy. He was dumbfounded.

With nothing to lose, the next day Jacklin agreed to be captain if all his conditions were met. He made it clear they were not negotiable. The veteran of seven teams, Jacklin knew full well that his side had not only played second fiddle to the U.S. team but looked the part. Jacklin insisted that the European team fly on the Concorde (like the Americans did), be allowed to bring along their own caddies, be outfitted with top-quality uniforms and golf bags, and meet in a dedicated team room. He also wanted three picks instead of two. Lastly, Jacklin wanted Ballesteros—if he could convince the Spaniard to play after the 1981 debacle. He needed assurances that the British PGA wouldn't stand in Seve's way.

"If they would have said no to any of the things, I would have just turned around and walked," Jacklin later said. "I didn't care about it. I cared too much about it. You can look at it whichever way you like."

The golf powers said yes to everything.

"The biggest thing was the team room. That Ryder Cup at Birkdale we were hunkering in a corner of a smelly locker room for team meetings. There was no team unity."

Captain Jacklin would face an old rival in the 1983 Ryder Cup at PGA National Golf Club in Palm Beach Gardens, Florida—Jack Nicklaus, also assuming his first captaincy.

Jacklin met with Ballesteros, who had just won his second Masters, at the Prince of Wales Hotel in Southport, England, the team hotel when Great Britain achieved the remarkable tie at Royal Birkdale in 1969. The new captain made his plea and then silently ate his breakfast while he patiently listened to the Spanish star vent about the mistreatment he had received from the European Ryder Cup committee. In the end, Jacklin's inspired and respectful appeal won over Ballesteros. "So okay," Seve said. "I come. I help you."

In addition to Ballesteros, Jacklin possessed emerging talent on his 1983 team that was beginning to shift the balance of power in professional golf away from U.S. shores. European team members Nick Faldo, Sandy Lyle, Bernard Langer, and Ian Woosnam would go on to win multiple majors. Nicklaus also fielded a strong U.S. team that included Tom Watson, Raymond Floyd, and Ben Crenshaw.

The Americans had won six straight Ryder Cups since the 1969 deadlock. There was still no national TV coverage for the matches, but change was coming. The Europeans invaded Florida, and at the end of the second day the Ryder Cup was knotted, 8–8. Captain Nicklaus, desperate not to lose—especially for the first time on U.S. soil—did his best Knute Rockne imitation, telling his players, "Show me some brass." The United States prevailed, barely, 14½–13½. "We hadn't won, but we'd turned a corner," Jacklin later said. Europe had good players. Now they also had belief.

Unlike the tie at Royal Birkdale in 1969 that stirred hopes, the narrow loss at PGA National in 1983 did mark a new beginning for the Ryder Cup. In 1985 at the Belfry in England, with Jacklin again leading Europe and Lee Trevino serving as U.S. captain, Europe won going away, 16½–11½. It was the first victory for a team on the eastern side of the pond in nearly three decades. The tide had turned.

At the epicenter of a resurgent Ryder Cup, Jacklin returned for his third straight turn as European captain in 1987. He again faced his friend and rival Jack Nicklaus on a course that Jack had built, Muirfield Village Golf Club in Dublin, Ohio, not far from where Jack took up the game. "We were quietly confident," Jacklin said.

Europe had another powerhouse team that included veterans Ballesteros, Faldo, Langer, Lyle, and Woosnam, plus a highly touted newcomer, José María Olazábal. Possessing a good team with no superstars and the home-country advantage, Nicklaus had the unenviable task of being the first U.S. captain in thirty years trying to win back the Cup. On the strength of a 4–0 fourball session during the afternoon of the first day, Europe took a commanding 10½–5½ lead into singles on the final day. The Yanks rallied in singles, but they were unable to close the gap, falling 15–13.

It was America's first home loss since the Ryder Cup began in 1927. Nicklaus lamented that his players couldn't finish close matches, so often the downfall of Jacklin's side in earlier years. A tough defeat for Jack was a euphoric victory for Tony. The 1987 matches in Ohio were the last time Jacklin and Nicklaus faced each other in Ryder Cup competition.

While the losing captain was done, the winning captain looked ahead to one more. Seventeen months after the sudden death of his wife, Vivien, because of an aneurysm—"My world was gone," Tony said—Jacklin and his dozen players arrived at the Belfry for the 1989 Ryder Cup. A big part of putting his life back together was marrying his new love, Astrid Waagen. Now Jacklin hoped to complete his long Ryder Cup career with one final flourish. Raymond Floyd, one of the ten American rookies in 1969, was the opposing captain.

Driven by Ballesteros and Olazábal, a tandem that became known as the "Spanish Armada," Europe enjoyed a 9–7 advantage heading into the singles matches on the last day, but the United States rallied on Sunday to forge a 14–14 tie. By virtue of its 1987 win, Europe retained the Cup, lengthening its new hold on Samuel Ryder's trophy to six years. The 1989 matches had ended in the second tie in Ryder Cup history. As a player and as a captain, Tony Jacklin had been in the middle of both of them.

EPILOGUE

Jack Nicklaus liked the idea that had awakened his friend Tony Jacklin in the middle of a Florida night. "It appealed to him," Jacklin said. It took time for certain pieces to fall into place, but sometime after their 2002 lunch meeting Jacklin and developer Kevin Daves approached Nicklaus and the manager of his golf course design company. The two Hall of Fame golfers decided to move forward on an exciting and unusual new project.

Nicklaus Design had designed hundreds of golf courses throughout the United States and around the world. Jacklin, by comparison, had only designed a few courses at that juncture. This one, however, would be different for both men, a golf course and community dedicated to a historic gesture and defining Ryder Cup moment that occurred more than three decades earlier on the other side of the Atlantic Ocean. It would be called the Concession Golf Club.

One potential snag—Nicklaus Design did Jack Nicklaus Signature Design golf courses, not typically relinquishing control or naming credit to others on the design aspect of golf-course development. Jack was very

271

hands-on and had a distinct design philosophy. Tony understood this, deferring to Jack when he and Daves met with the Golden Bear.

As Daves recalled in a 2009 interview, Tony told Jack, "I don't want to get in the way. I know you do these things."

"Tony," Jack replied, "if you are going to be involved you have to be involved completely." Then, with a wink, Jack added, "I'll make that concession again."

·   ·   ·

In 2000, in one of life's delicious ironies, Tony Jacklin served as a chaperone for Sam Snead. Meeting him at Dulles Airport in Washington, D.C., Jacklin accompanied the golf legend and 1969 U.S. Ryder Cup captain to St. Andrews in Scotland for a gathering of past British Open champions. The 1946 and 1969 champions enjoyed each other's company.

"We had a good time together," Jacklin recalled. "There were no hard feelings at all. Talk about coming full circle."

Snead, the Hall of Famer with eighty-two PGA Tour titles (seven of them majors) and eight appearances as a Ryder Cup player and captain, died two years later just short of his ninetieth birthday.

Scottish golf great Eric Brown, Snead's 1969 counterpart, died in 1986 at the age of sixty-one. People might have supposed that the fiercely competitive Ryder Cup captain, like Snead, was not a fan of how the 1969 matches ended, but in 2010 David Brown told the *West Lothian Courier* that his father was a close friend of Jack Nicklaus's and admired the concession on Birkdale's 18th green.

"Dad thought what Jack did was the biggest sporting gesture he'd ever seen. He approached Jack afterwards and told him it was a fantastic thing he had done."

The son also revealed that his father and mother had "spent some time living with Jack in America" in the latter years of his father's life.

• • •

It was decided. The Concession Golf Club would be designed by "Jack Nicklaus in association with Tony Jacklin." Located east of Interstate 75 in an undeveloped portion of the Sarasota-Bradenton area, the inland site included more than 1,200 acres of untouched land and wetlands populated with stately oaks and tall pines. Jack and Tony would lay out a challenging championship golf course on 520 acres of this wild Florida terrain, with no out-of-bounds, no parallel fairways, no crossing roads, and no bordering homes. Million-dollar residences would be constructed elsewhere on the vast property.

Nicklaus visited often during the design and construction phases. On one occasion in the summer of 2005, as Daves recalled, the sixty-five-year-old Golden Bear completed his British Open career on a Friday by sinking a birdie putt on the 18th green at St. Andrews in Scotland. The following Monday he arrived at the site of the Concession Golf Club. His design partner was also a constant presence. The goal, Jacklin said, was "to create a course worthy of world-class tournament play."

The Concession opened in early 2006. From the back tees, the par-72 championship course measured 7,474 yards and featured a slope rating of 155. The club entrance was situated on Lindrick Lane, named after the northern England course where thirteen-year-old Jacklin witnessed his first Ryder Cup in 1957. Jack and Tony teed it up for an inaugural round, perhaps wary of the demanding layout they had created. In a promotional video that preceded the opening, Nicklaus joked, "I just hope we can both break 80 on opening day."

Accolades followed. The Concession was named "Best New Private Course of 2006" by *Golf Digest* and has consistently appeared on other top course lists in major golf publications.

"It's a good golf course. It's tough," Nicklaus said in 2013.

In recent years, the Concession began to attract high-profile events such as the 2015 NCAA Men's and Women's Golf Championships. The hope, not surprisingly, is to someday host a Ryder Cup.

· · ·

Scattered throughout America and Europe, all but four of the twenty-four players who competed in the 1969 Ryder Cup were alive in 2013. U.S. players Dan Sikes (1987), Dave Hill (2011), and Miller Barber (2013) had passed away, as had Great Britain's Bernard Hunt (2013).

Many of the players were eager to share their memories of the historic matches and the surprising conclusion. The passage of time had allowed for a new or evolving perspective on what that long-ago tie and final-hole concession had meant to the Ryder Cup, and in some cases a hard-earned appreciation for the gesture.

Frank Beard, who played on one more Ryder Cup team in 1971 and finished his PGA Tour career with eleven wins, still played a regular game of golf in retirement in Palm Desert, California.

"There was not only no harm done, it was good on all fronts," Beard said about the concession. "None of it crossed my mind. Only later. I harbored some really bitter feelings for a long time. Not so much at Nicklaus. I liked Jack. It just took me a while to get over it."

Tommy Aaron, Beard's University of Florida and Ryder Cup teammate, won the 1973 Masters and earned a spot on his second U.S. Ryder Cup team that same year. Aaron sees three of his 1969 teammates— Nicklaus, Casper, and Floyd—every April in Augusta, Georgia, because all are Masters champions.

"It made Nicklaus a hero over there," Aaron said about the concession. "In retrospect, as the years have gone by, it was a great thing to do. I don't think I would have ever thought of it, though. I would have liked to [have] seen Jacklin hole the putt."

Billy Casper finished his Hall of Fame career with fifty-one PGA Tour victories, including three majors, and more Ryder Cup points than any other American player. He also served as captain of the victorious 1979 U.S. team.

"As time went by," Casper said, "we became much more appreciative of the sportsmanship which [Nicklaus] displayed when he did that. It really was one of the great things that happened in the Ryder Cup matches . . . I think that was one of the ingredients that started the turnaround in the Ryder Cup."

Tony Jacklin's foursomes partner, Peter Townsend, never got traction on the PGA Tour, but he did play on another British Ryder Cup team in 1971 and won tournaments in Europe, Africa, and South America.

"It was a fantastic thing," Townsend said about the Nicklaus-Jacklin ending from his home in Sweden. "They've been great friends ever since. I think it probably showed, more than anything, what a remarkable person Jack Nicklaus was."

Brian Huggett, the Welshman who sank the putt he thought had won the 1969 Ryder Cup, played on three more Ryder Cup teams and captained his side in 1977.

"A tie felt like a win in those days! Dave Hill played magnificent golf all week and saved the Americans," Huggett recalled.

"It [1969] was definitely a watershed year," Jacklin said. "There was no doubt about that."

Bernard Gallacher played on seven more Ryder Cup teams and followed Tony Jacklin as European captain, serving in that capacity for three consecutive Ryder Cups.

"Playing in the Ryder Cup was a big moment for me," said Gallacher, who has served as a Ryder Cup commentator for BBC Radio. "I do regret the incidents that I had with Ken Still and Dave Hill . . . but it was a great Ryder Cup, and I saw a great sporting gesture that endured to this time. And wherever the Ryder Cup is being played, they still talk about Jack's concession."

Ken Still, one of the U.S. players with whom Gallacher clashed, became a close friend and enthusiastic fan of Jack Nicklaus and his entire family. In 2013, Jack said he and "Kenny" talked on the phone a couple of times a week.

"Jack and I have talked about it numerous times," Still said about the concession. "Jack said, 'I would never ever give him that putt for a win. No chance,' he said. I have no problem with it." Moments later, Still added, "Jack Nicklaus is one of the classiest guys—he and his wife—I've ever met in my life, and I mean that from the bottom of my heart."

Raymond Floyd's Hall of Fame career included three more major victories after the 1969 PGA Championship and a total of nine Ryder Cup appearances.

"The Ryder Cup is about sportsmanship. That's why it was initiated, and goodwill, country to country," Floyd said from his Florida home, not far from where Nicklaus lives. "I felt immediately [the concession] was the right thing to do."

Beard offered perspective on the man who made it. "There were reasons that Nicklaus was the best there ever was, and only one of them was he was a great player. He was just way more mature and just had a better grasp of everything that went on in life."

For the man on the receiving end of the concession, it was much more personal.

"The fact was, he didn't have to do it," Jacklin said. "We were pals. We played a lot of practice rounds together. We fished together. There was a mutual respect there. I think all of these things contribute in the end. He knew I'd won the Open two months before. Britain had a new sort of hero, if you like. He didn't want anything to happen to spoil that."

Peter Alliss never left the broadcast booth after retiring as a player in 1969. He provided commentary for British Opens and other major golf events throughout the next four-plus decades. His memories of his final Ryder Cup as a player were bittersweet. "I thought we did well enough to have actually won the Ryder Cup outright that year, and I was not a great contributor as far as points were concerned, but it was my last and it was a very memorable occasion."

The British near-win created expectations that would go unfulfilled for another long decade.

"We thought that [1969] might start off a good run for us," Gallacher said. "It didn't really. We had to go through the seventies, then become a European side. Tony eventually became captain, and he was the most wonderful inspirational captain. He turned it around at West Palm Beach, where we had a really good performance. All went well after that."

Neil Coles played on a total of eight Ryder Cup teams and was the second golfer after Sam Snead to win a pro tournament in six different decades.

"It was Nicklaus who got in touch with Lord Derby to say the Ryder Cup is going to die unless you strengthen it," Coles said in the fall of 2012 at European Tour headquarters in Surrey. "He was responsible for bringing Europe into the Ryder Cup, to strengthen our team, and it's become the great event that it is today."

"The Ryder Cup is huge now worldwide, and in our country it's bigger than the Open to the man in the street," Huggett said. "Thank goodness for the support of the PGA of America back in the spring of 1978 when the decision was taken for the Great Britain and Ireland team to go European. Some people felt we should go rest-of-the-world like today's Presidents Cup. The correct decision was made at that time. With all due respect, the Presidents Cup is like a damp squib compared to the Ryder Cup."

"That year [1969] was very important along with changing the format to Europe," Floyd said. "Because we were an overwhelming winner in Ryder Cup all those years until Europe got into the mix. So I think that combination has made the Ryder Cup the golf event every two years now. Without question, that's the golf event."

· · ·

For Jack Nicklaus, little had changed as he considered the concession he made to Tony Jacklin forty-three years earlier. The biggest surprise for Nicklaus may have been all the attention it had received through the years.

"I don't think it was that big a deal," he said in his fifth-floor office at Golden Bear Plaza in North Palm Beach. "I still don't think it's that big a deal."

As Nicklaus pointed out, it was just a 2-foot putt, after all. "It was instinctively a thing I did because I thought it was the right thing to do."

That had always been a guiding principle for Nicklaus, which meant at least one thing hadn't changed since he and Jacklin halved their final singles match and thereby halved the 1969 Ryder Cup.

"Would I do it again? Absolutely."

The players who helped shape the modern Ryder Cup might wonder if a similar gesture could occur in today's hypercompetitive environment and highly partisan atmosphere. Bernard Gallacher, for one, would be eager to see another concession like the one he witnessed on Royal Birkdale's 18th green in September 1969.

"Even today I think that would be the right thing to do, even with all the pressure and TV cameras everywhere, and media and big partisan crowds everywhere," Gallacher said. "I think it would be the right thing to do today more than ever."

GLOSSARY

All square, square—a match is tied. (The match is all square.)

Birdie—one stroke under par on a hole. (See below for definition of "Par.")

Bogey—one more stroke than par on a hole. (See below for definition of "Par.")

Eagle—two fewer strokes than par on a hole. (See below for definition of "Par.")

Fourballs—a match-play format pitting two teams of two players, or four balls. Each golfer plays his or her own ball until the ball is holed or picked up. The lowest score on each team is recorded for each hole. Also known as better ball or best ball.

Foursomes—a match-play format pitting two teams of two players. Each team plays one ball and takes turns hitting the ball until it is holed. Also known as alternate shot.

Gamesmanship—using questionable methods and psychological ploys to win a match without violating the rules.

Halve, halved—a tie, whether a tied hole or a tied match. (They halved the hole. The match was halved.)

Match play—an individual or team format where the object is to win holes. An individual or team wins a match when ahead by more holes than the number of remaining holes. (They won 3 and 2. In other words, they were 3 holes up with 2 holes to play.)

Par—the number of strokes a top golfer would typically require for an individual golf hole, or for 9 holes or 18 holes.

Singles—a match-play format pitting player against player, each player from an opposing team.

Stroke play—a format where strokes are counted and recorded for each hole and added for a total score at the end of the round. The object is to shoot the lowest score possible. Also known as medal play.

APPENDIX A:
1969 RYDER CUP RESULTS

TEAMS

Great Britain—Eric Brown (captain), Peter Alliss, Brian Barnes, Maurice Bembridge, Peter Butler, Alex Caygill, Neil Coles, Bernard Gallacher, Brian Huggett, Bernard Hunt, Tony Jacklin, Christy O'Connor Sr., Peter Townsend

United States—Sam Snead (captain), Tommy Aaron, Miller Barber, Frank Beard, Billy Casper, Dale Douglass, Raymond Floyd, Dave Hill, Gene Littler, Jack Nicklaus, Dan Sikes, Ken Still, Lee Trevino

Scoring: A point was earned for winning a match. A half point was earned for a halved (or tied) match.

DAY 1 (THURSDAY, SEPTEMBER 18)

Morning Foursomes

Coles-Huggett (GB) defeated Barber-Floyd (USA) 3 and 2

Gallacher-Bembridge (GB) defeated Trevino-Still (USA) 2 and 1

Jacklin-Townsend (GB) defeated Hill-Aaron (USA) 3 and 1

O'Connor-Alliss (GB) halved with Casper-Beard (USA)

Session total: Great Britain 3½, United States ½

Overall score: Great Britain 3½, United States ½

Afternoon Foursomes

Hill-Aaron (USA) defeated Coles-Huggett (GB) 1 up

Trevino-Littler (USA) defeated Gallacher-Bembridge (GB) 1 up

Jacklin-Townsend (GB) defeated Casper-Beard (USA) 1 up

Nicklaus-Sikes (USA) defeated Butler-Hunt (GB) 1 up

Session total: United States 3, Great Britain 1

Overall score: Great Britain 4½, United States 3½

DAY 2 (FRIDAY, SEPTEMBER 19)

Morning Fourballs

O'Connor-Townsend (GB) defeated Hill-Douglass (USA) 1 up

Huggett-Caygill (GB) halved with Floyd-Barber (USA)

Trevino-Littler (USA) defeated Barnes-Alliss (GB) 1 up

Jacklin-Coles (GB) defeated Nicklaus-Sikes (USA) 1 up

Session total: Great Britain 2½, United States 1½

Overall score: Great Britain 7, United States 5

Afternoon Fourballs

Casper-Beard (USA) defeated Butler-Townsend (GB) 2 up

Hill-Still (USA) defeated Huggett-Gallacher (GB) 2 and 1

Bembridge-Hunt (GB) halved with Aaron-Floyd (USA)

Jacklin-Coles (GB) halved with Trevino-Barber (USA)

Session total: United States 3, Great Britain 1

Overall score: Great Britain 8, United States 8

DAY 3 (SATURDAY, SEPTEMBER 20)

Morning Singles

Trevino (USA) defeated Alliss (GB) 2 and 1

Hill (USA) defeated Townsend (GB) 5 and 4

Coles (GB) defeated Aaron (USA) 1 up

Casper (USA) defeated Barnes (GB) 1 up

O'Connor (GB) defeated Beard (USA) 5 and 4

Bembridge (GB) defeated Still (USA) 1 up

Butler (GB) defeated Floyd (USA) 1 up

Jacklin (GB) defeated Nicklaus (USA) 4 and 3

Session total: Great Britain 5, United States 3

Overall score: Great Britain 13, United States 11

Afternoon Singles

Hill (USA) defeated Barnes (GB) 4 and 2

Gallacher (GB) defeated Trevino (USA) 4 and 3

Barber (USA) defeated Bembridge (GB) 7 and 6

Butler (GB) defeated Douglass (USA) 3 and 2

Sikes (USA) defeated Coles (GB) 4 and 3

Littler (USA) defeated O'Connor (GB) 2 and 1

Huggett (GB) halved with Casper (USA)

Jacklin (GB) halved with Nicklaus (USA)

Session total: United States 5, Great Britain 3

FINAL SCORE: GREAT BRITAIN 16, UNITED STATES 16

APPENDIX B:
RYDER CUP RESULTS,
1927 TO 2012

(US = United States, GB = Great Britain and Ireland, EUR = Europe)

YEAR	SITE	SCORE
1927	Worcester Country Club Worcester, Massachusetts	US 9½, GB 2½
1929	Moortown Golf Club Leeds, England	GB 7, US 5
1931	Scioto Country Club Columbus, Ohio	US 9, GB 3
1933	Southport & Ainsdale Golf Club Southport, England	GB 6½, US 5½
1935	Ridgewood Country Club Ridgwood, New Jersey	US 9, GB 3

YEAR	SITE	SCORE
1937	Southport & Ainsdale Golf Club Southport, England	US 8, GB 4
1947	Portland Golf Club Portland, Oregon	US 11, GB 1
1949	Ganton Golf Club Scarborough, England	US 7, GB 5
1951	Pinehurst Country Club Pinehurst, North Carolina	US 9½, GB 2½
1953	Wentworth Golf Club Virginia Water, England	US 6½, GB 5½
1955	Thunderbird Ranch & Country Club Palm Springs, California	US 8, GB 4
1957	Lindrick Golf Club Yorkshire, England	GB 7½, US 4½
1959	Eldorado Country Club Palm Desert, California	US 8½, GB 3½
1961	Royal Lytham & St. Annes St. Annes, England	US 14½, GB 9½
1963	East Lake Country Club Atlanta, Georgia	US 23, GB 9
1965	Royal Birkdale Golf Club Southport, England	US 19½, GB 12½
1967	Champions Golf Club Houston, Texas	US 23½, GB 8½
1969	Royal Birkdale Golf Club Southport, England	GB 16, US 16

(continued)

YEAR	SITE	SCORE
1971	Old Warson Country Club St. Louis, Missouri	US 18½, GB 13½
1973	Muirfield Edinburgh, Scotland	US 19, GB 13
1975	Laurel Valley Golf Club Ligonier, Pennsylvania	US 21, GB 11
1977	Royal Lytham & St. Annes St. Annes, England	US 12½, GB 7½
1979	The Greenbrier White Sulphur Springs, West Virginia	US 17, EUR 11
1981	Walton Heath Golf Club Surrey, England	US 18½, EUR 9½
1983	PGA National Golf Club Palm Beach Gardens, Florida	US 14½, EUR 13½
1985	The Belfry Sutton Coldfield, England	EUR 16½, US 11½
1987	Muirfield Village Golf Club Dublin, Ohio	EUR 15, US 13
1989	The Belfry Sutton Coldfield, England	EUR 14, US 14
1991	The Ocean Course Kiawah Island, South Carolina	US 14½, EUR 13½
1993	The Belfry Sutton Coldfield, England	US 15, EUR 13
1995	Oak Hill Country Club Rochester, New York	EUR 14½, US 13½

YEAR	SITE	SCORE
1997	Valderrama Golf Club Sotogrande, Spain	EUR 14½, US 13½
1999	The Country Club Brookline, Massachusetts	US 14½, EUR 13½
2002	The Belfry Sutton Coldfield, England	EUR 15½, US 12½
2004	Oakland Hills Country Club Bloomfield Township, Michigan	EUR 18½, US 9½
2006	The K Club, Straffan Co. Kildare, Ireland	EUR 18½, US 9½
2008	Valhalla Golf Club Louisville, Kentucky	US 16½, EUR 11½
2010	Celtic Manor Resort City of Newport, Wales	EUR 14½, US 13½
2012	Medinah Country Club Medinah, Illinois	EUR 14½, US 13½

ACKNOWLEDGMENTS

Many people helped make this book possible. Rick Broadhead, my literary agent, guided me on the many aspects of tackling a second book. Rob Kirkpatrick, my editor, and the entire team at St. Martin's Press expertly shaped this book in numerous ways.

I owe special thanks to Tony Jacklin and Jack Nicklaus, both of whom were generous with their time and their recollections. Many thanks also to a pair of professionals who work for the two Hall of Famers: Karen Robinson (for Jacklin) and Scott Tolley (for Nicklaus). In addition to Jacklin and Nicklaus, other 1969 Ryder Cup players who contributed directly to this book are Tommy Aaron, Peter Alliss, Brian Barnes, Frank Beard, Billy Casper, Neil Coles, Raymond Floyd, Bernard Gallacher, Brian Huggett, Gene Littler, Ken Still, and Peter Townsend.

Both employed by *Golf Illustrated*, Paul Trevillion and Peter Willis were at Royal Birkdale in 1969, eyewitnesses of that historic Ryder Cup. It was my great fortune that Trevillion and Willis reappeared in early 2013 to share their many vivid memories and anecdotes. Their reporting and other contributions, past and present, added depth to the story.

Thank you to Graham Park for sharing memories of his father, Brian Park, the businessman who helped revive the Ryder Cup in Great Britain in the 1960s.

Thanks are due to the PGA of America, specifically Kelly Elbin, who helped me reach out to members of the 1969 U.S. Ryder Cup team. Phil Stambaugh of the Champions Tour was also a great help in contacting players and preparing the way for interviews. The European Tour's Gordon Simpson and Frances Jennings were my lifeline to members of the 1969 Great Britain Ryder Cup team. (Sitting down with Neil Coles at European Tour headquarters in Surrey, Simpson even conducted an interview for me and sent along the audio file.)

The United States Golf Association (USGA) in Far Hills, New Jersey, hosted me in its research center and sent me off with detailed and comprehensive materials on my subject. Special thanks to USGA librarian Nancy Stulack.

Friends, authors, and writers who helped and encouraged me along the way include John Boyette, Aly Colón, Sheila Colón, John Coyne, Roland Lazenby, and Don Van Natta Jr.

Thanks also to manuscript readers Jimmy Williams, a PGA club professional; Thomas Coyne, a retired university vice president; and Matthew Wurzburger, a University of Virginia student and *Cavalier Daily* sportswriter who generously devoted some of his summer break to this book and my golf blog.

Thank you to the readers of Armchair Golf Blog and my first book, *The Longest Shot*, both of which led to this second book.

Lastly, many thanks and much love to my wife, Sally, and daughters, Beth and Caroline, for their constant encouragement and support.

BIBLIOGRAPHY

BOOKS

Alliss, Peter. *Peter Alliss: An Autobiography.* Glasgow: Fontana, 1982.

———. *Peter Alliss: My Life.* London: Hodder & Stoughton, 2004.

Barkow, Al. *The History of the PGA Tour.* New York: Doubleday, 1989.

Beard, Frank. *Pro: Frank Beard on the Golf Tour.* New York: World Publishing, 1970.

Brown, Eric. *Knave of Clubs.* London: Stanley Paul, 1961.

Bubka, Bob, and Thomas Clavin. *The Ryder Cup: Golf's Greatest Event.* New York: Crown, 1999.

Coles, Neil. *Neil Coles on Golf.* London: Stanley Paul, 1965.

Concannon, Dale. *The Ryder Cup: Seven Decades of Golfing Glory, Drama and Controversy.* London: Aurum Press, 2001.

Hill, Dave. *Teed Off.* Englewood Cliffs, NJ: Prentice-Hall, 1977.

Jacklin, Tony. *Jacklin: My Autobiography.* London: Simon & Schuster UK, 2006.

———. *Jacklin: The Champion's Own Story.* New York: Simon & Schuster, 1970.

Kirkpatrick, Rob. *1969: The Year Everything Changed.* New York: Sky-horse Publishing, 2009.

McDonnell, Michael. *Golf: The Great Ones.* New York: Drake, 1973.

McMillan, Robin. *Us Against Them: An Oral History of the Ryder Cup.* New York: HarperCollins, 2004.

Nicklaus, Jack. *The Greatest Game of All: My Life in Golf.* New York: Simon & Schuster, 1969.

————. *Jack Nicklaus: My Story.* New York: Simon & Schuster, 1997.

Palmer, Arnold. *A Golfer's Life.* New York: Ballantine Books, 1999.

Simpson, Gordon. *Golfing Greats: Great Britain & Ireland.* Edinburgh: Sportsprint Publishing, 1989.

Smith, Seamus. *Himself: Christy O'Connor.* Dublin: Colorman, 1993.

Trevillion, Paul. *Dead Heat: The '69 Ryder Cup Classic.* London: Stanley Paul, 1969.

Trevino, Lee. *They Call Me Super Mex: The Autobiography of Lee Trevino.* New York: Random House, 1982.

Williams, Michael. *The Official History of the Ryder Cup, 1927–1989.* Somerset, UK: Butler & Tanner, 1989.

Wind, Herbert Warren. *The Story of American Golf.* New York: Alfred A. Knopf, 1975.

MAGAZINES

Golf Digest
Golf Illustrated
Golf Monthly
Golf World
Links Magazine
Professional Golfer
Sports Illustrated

NEWSPAPERS

Daily Telegraph (UK)

Deseret News (Salt Lake City, UT)

Glasgow Herald (UK)

Guardian (UK)

Morning Record (Meriden, CT)

New York Times

Observer (UK)

Pro Sports Weekly

Rome News-Tribune (Rome, GA)

Titusville Herald (Titusville, PA)

West Lothian Courier (UK)

PROGRAMS AND MATERIALS

18th Ryder Cup Golf Matches, Official Souvenir Programme

18th Ryder Cup Golf Matches Daily Draw Sheet

DVDS, VIDEO, AND PHOTOGRAPHY

1969 Ryder Cup footage, IMG

Colorsport, 1969 Ryder Cup gallery and images

The History of the Ryder Cup, European Tour Productions, 2004

YouTube

WEB SITES

ArmchairGolfBlog.blogspot.com

BBC.co.uk

CaddyBytes.com

ChampionsGolfClub.com

ESPN.com

Golf.About.com

GolfDigest.com

HistoryOrb.com

Independent.co.uk

Library.Thinkquest.org

Nicklaus.com

PGA.com

PGAMediaGuide.com

PGATour.com

RoyalBirkdale.com

RoyalLytham.org

RyderCup.com

RyderDiary.com

Scotsman.com

SeattlePI.com

SeattleTimes.com

StAlbans.gov.uk

Telegraph.co.uk

TexasGolfHof.org

TonyJacklin.com

VerulamGolf.co.uk

Wikipedia.org

WorldGolfHallofFame.org

INDEX

295